HEALTH AND SOCIAL CARE

Level 5

Diplo

leadership

for

health and social care

PJ Calpin
Eleanor Langridge
Belinda Morgan
Rebecca Platts
John Rowe
Terry Scragg

OXFORD

UNIVERSITY PRESS

Great Clarendon Street, Oxford, OX2 6DP, United Kingdom

Oxford University Press is a department of the University of Oxford.
It furthers the University's objective of excellence in research, scholarship,
and education by publishing worldwide. Oxford is a registered trade mark of
Oxford University Press in the UK and in certain other countries

First published by Nelson Thornes in 2012
This edition published by Oxford University Press in 2014

British Library Cataloguing in Publication Data
Data available

978-1-4085-1810-6

10 9 8 7 6 5

Printed in China by Leo Paper Products Ltd

Acknowledgements

Cover photograph: Daniel Laflor/iStockphoto
Page make-up: GreenGate Publishing Services, Tonbridge, Kent
Illustration: Angela Knowles

Although we have made every effort to trace and contact all
copyright holders before publication this has not been possible in all
cases. If notified, the publisher will rectify any errors or omissions at
the earliest opportunity.

Links to third party websites are provided by Oxford in good faith
and for information only. Oxford disclaims any responsibility for
the materials contained in any third party website referenced in
this work.

A. FORMELWGA.

Contents

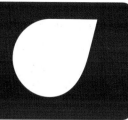

About this book

Welcome to your Diploma in Leadership for Health and Social Care Level 5 Course Book. The purpose of this book is to help you complete your Level 5 Diploma in Leadership for Health and Social Care and Children and Young People's Services qualification. This book provides complete coverage of the mandatory units of the three Adults' Social Care pathways – Adults' Residential Management, Adults' Management and Adults' Advanced Practice.

Qualification pathways

Chapters 1 to 5 cover the mandatory units for all three pathways. The other units mandatory for each pathway are covered by the chapters shown below. Refer to the **mapping grid** on the inside front cover for the different awarding body qualification unit codes for each unit.

If you are studying Adults' Residential Management you also need to work through the following chapters:

6   Lead and manage a team within a health and social care or children and young people's settings

7   Develop professional supervision practice in health and social care or children and young people's settings

8   Manage health and social care practice to ensure positive outcomes for individuals

9   Safeguarding and protection of vulnerable adults

10   Lead and manage group living for adults

11   Understand safeguarding of children and young people (for those working in the adult sector)

12   Lead person-centred practice

If you are studying Adults' Management you also need to work through the following chapters:

6   Lead and manage a team within a health and social care or children and young people's settings

7   Develop professional supervision practice in health and social care or children and young people's settings

8   Manage health and social care practice to ensure positive outcomes for individuals

9   Safeguarding and protection of vulnerable adults

11   Understand safeguarding of children and young people (for those working in the adult sector)

12   Lead person-centred practice

13   Assess the individual in a health and social care setting

If you are studying Adults' Advanced Practice you also need to work through the following chapters:

8   Manage health and social care practice to ensure positive outcomes for individuals

9   Safeguarding and protection of vulnerable adults

11   Understand safeguarding of children and young people (for those working in the adult sector)

12   Lead person-centred practice

13   Assess the individual in a health and social care setting

This colourful text contains the following features to help you learn the skills and knowledge required to lead and manage others.

Features of this book

Chapter opener – this page contains a brief introduction to each unit along with the learning outcomes you need to achieve.

Activity

Lots of activities to help you apply what you've learnt in the text to your day-to-day work. These include real life scenarios and encourage you to evaluate your own work environment and the best way to deal with problems. These activities include **Reflect, Analyse, Explain, Evaluate** and **Dealing with conflict**.

In Practice

'**In Practice**' boxes – a range of real life examples of different scenarios to provide context to the topics covered. They ask how you would approach the problem.

Remember

Remember features give you advice for things to keep in mind and ideas to help you with assessment.

Key Term

Key terms – during your course you'll come across new words that you may not have heard before. These words have been **emboldened** in the text and the definitions have been provided.

Are you ready for assessment?

Are you ready for assessment? – at the end of each unit you will find ten questions which recap the main points from the chapter.

Good luck!

Introduction

Assessment tips

Undertaking the Level 5 Diploma involves your being able to identify sufficient authentic, current, relevant and reliable evidence of what you know, understand and can do in relation to each of the qualification units.

Vocational, competence-based qualifications relate to work roles and responsibilities so evidence to demonstrate your competence will be drawn from your real work activities.

When thinking about evidence gathering for your qualification start with what is most familiar to you, i.e. your job role and responsibilities, and then match these to the diploma units. This is particularly important when you are choosing your optional units. Many of these units describe specialist areas of practice or delegated responsibilities. If, when you read through the assessment criteria for a unit, you cannot identify real work evidence to demonstrate your competence then this is not an appropriate unit for you to choose. The exception to this is the knowledge-only units as these do not require you to demonstrate workplace competence. These units could be considered as aspirational as you may choose them because they relate to your future career plans or service development.

Professional discussions

These are a good source of portfolio evidence. To get the most from a professional discussion however, you need to prepare beforehand. Your assessor should plan the discussion with you outlining the main areas to be covered and how they link to both your work and the diploma unit assessment criteria.

Professional discussions often follow an observation of practice and this can be an excellent opportunity to reflect on your practice, the reasoning behind the approach you took, what went well, how you might do things differently, and explorations of 'what if...' scenarios.

Professional discussions can also be used as a way for you to evidence your competence as well as your knowledge and understanding in situations that may be difficult or inappropriate for your assessor to observe. In these circumstances your assessor can ask you to talk through the situation and use relevant work products to substantiate your explanation.

Some examples of using work products as the basis for a professional discussion are:

- using your development plan to demonstrate your understanding of your development needs and how to meet these

- using recruitment and interview records etc. to evidence recruitment and selection competences

- using financial records to demonstrate managing budgets

- using quality assurance and auditing records to demonstrate how you manage quality within the service

- using minutes from meetings, reports, emails, letters, etc. relating to raising issues of concern and making recommendations for changes.

Remember that professional and reflective discussions can also be used as evidence for the unit related to professional development as well as the specific unit the discussion is based around.

Observations of practice

Your assessor will work with you to identify appropriate opportunities to observe you in practice. Direct observation remains a central part of vocational qualifications as well as the most efficient, effective and reliable method of evidence gathering. To ensure that direct observation of practice is effective, as a source of evidence, it relies on your preparing beforehand.

- Make sure you are clear about the assessment plan and what evidence you will be generating during the activity.

- Make sure you take time to read through the linked unit assessment criteria and understand these. Think about what questions the assessor may ask you following the observation and be prepared to answer these fully.

- Make sure other people who are involved in the activity being observed are aware of the assessor's role and be clear that they are there to assess you and not them.

- Ensure you have the necessary permissions, e.g. from the service user, family or other professionals.

- Plan time before the observation to prepare and remind yourself what you are going to be demonstrating.

- Plan time after the observation for feedback as this is an essential part of the process too.

Your assessor will use the assessment criteria to provide you with specific feedback following observations of work practice as part of your diploma, which will help you to recognise your knowledge and skills. Some of their feedback will relate to the way in which you relate to others, i.e. your values and attitudes, and this will help you to develop your self-awareness and improve your performance.

A good source of evidence, especially for the units relating to health and safety, is to show your assessor around your work place to demonstrate how health and safety is implemented and back this up with an observation of relevant health and safety work products, which could be records, audits, reports, etc. and a related professional discussion.

In the same way that much of the products and records generated through your day-to-day work can be used as evidence you may also identify, through undertaking the diploma, gaps in provision. These gaps may relate to policies and procedures or you may wish to improve these as a result of your learning. They can all be used as evidence for not only the specific unit but also for the unit related to professional development.

Witness and expert witness testimony

Working at a senior level in an organisation means that your work is predictably unpredictable and this can be difficult when planning observations of practice.

To capture your work performance effectively you and your assessor will need to look at ways to reliably evidence your competence. You may need to talk to other professionals to ask them to substantiate work undertaken with them.

Providing a witness testimony can be made easier for the potential witness/expert witness if you prepare questions for them to respond to, based on the assessment criteria you are trying to evidence. Your assessor may provide you with a specific form for this. Alternatively, your assessor may be able to voice record a witness/expert witness testimony.

Witness and expert witness testimony are both excellent sources of evidence and, as well as providing specific evidence, they are also an important means of substantiating the consistency of your performance and competence. If you have a manager, they are well placed to provide witness testimonies to confirm the consistency of your competence. See www.skillsforcare.org.uk/qualifications_ and_training/adultsocialcarequalifications for more information on assessment principles and expert witnesses.

Work products

There are numerous work products that you can use as evidence of your competence for all of the units within the Level 5 Diploma. These will vary from daily records to annual audits. You must ensure that when presenting work products you can clearly show your contribution and that this can be authenticated. Your assessor will not need to take any work products out of your workplace as long as they can record what was accessed and how it met the assessment criteria.

Be aware, however, of sensitive information and if you feel it necessary then anonymise records to avoid a breach in confidentiality.

Be prepared to answer questions relating to work products as your assessor will want to establish validity, reliability and authenticity.

If you familiarise yourself with the units within your diploma you will soon be identifying relevant work product evidence to present to your assessor for assessment so keep a note of what it is, where it is stored, and how it relates to your diploma. Keeping a diary is a good way of keeping track of potential evidence sources.

Chapter 1

Use and develop **systems** that promote **communication**

The aim of this chapter is to assess the level of knowledge, understanding and skills required to develop communication systems for meeting individual outcomes and promoting partnership working. The chapter explores the challenges and barriers to communication and the importance of effective management of information.

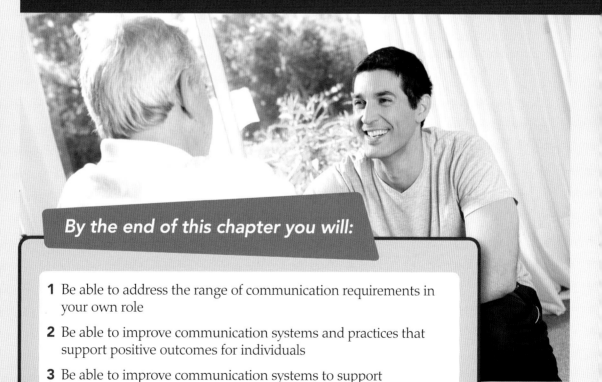

By the end of this chapter you will:

1 Be able to address the range of communication requirements in your own role

2 Be able to improve communication systems and practices that support positive outcomes for individuals

3 Be able to improve communication systems to support partnership working

4 Be able to use systems for effective information management

Be able to address the range of communication requirements in your own role

1.1

What you say, how you say it and how you behave communicates messages. Knowing how to encode and decode messages, and having a sound understanding of the appropriate communication channels available to you, is an essential skill for all professionals in the social care sector.

For example, a manager may pass on information about amendments to the organisation's policies, by providing their team with a verbal briefing of the main alterations that require implementation. However, if they were to send the same information to the people who receive support from the organisation, they may consider different channels such as a newsletter and different ways of encoding the information so that it will be understood by the intended audience. The newsletter could be produced in an easy-to-read format, using plain English (without jargon) and visualisation methods such as graphics and pictorial representation.

1.1.1 Review the range of groups and individuals whose communication needs must be addressed in their own job role

As a social care professional, you are required to communicate with both individuals and groups of people, whether they are the people you manage directly, senior managers, external agencies, the people your organisation supports or their families. You will do this through several methods including face-to-face meetings, training, consultation, undertaking assessments and planning, writing and delivering reports and networking. You will need a range of communication skills that enable you successfully to:

■ listen

■ disseminate information

■ deliver information

■ provide and receive feedback

■ use questioning to clarify

■ take written notes

■ formulate responses

■ negotiate, debate, compromise

■ make decisions.

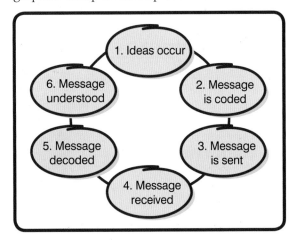

Figure 1.1 Argyle's communication cycle clarifies the six stages of information sharing

Activity

When working with groups, you should consider the dynamics of group communication. Being more aware of how groups respond in certain situations will enable you to manage any barriers that arise.

1. Research a group dynamic theory, for example the theory developed by R. F. Bales and Harvard University Social Relations Laboratory.

2. Consider the dynamics of your team. Observe the communication strategies put into practice during a team meeting.

standards and service-wide performance targets, then you will frequently gather data to communicate back to these external agencies.

■ If you are responsible for communicating a change in organisational policy to a large team, you will need to consider the most effective way to do this, for example via email or a team training session.

Activity

1. Think about the partnerships you work with. What are their different communication requirements?

1.1.2 Explain how to support effective communication within your own job role

The interactions you have with the people you support are highly dependent on your choice of communication method. People have a variety of support needs and communicate using a number of techniques, and their individuality and diverse backgrounds will also impact on how they choose to communicate. You must be aware of how you interact with the people you are supporting, and ensure that they have the necessary tools to interact with you.

■ Service users need to be able to provide feedback and reviews of the support and services that they purchase, they need to be involved in consultations about changes to services, and have the communication skills necessary to be able to report complaints and abuse.

■ If you are supporting someone within a holistic service delivery model then you need to be able to communicate effectively with a range of other external agencies. For example, if you are responsible for providing and monitoring information for national

You should ensure that your team has the skills to support people's communication needs. They will need to understand verbal and non-verbal communication skills and, where appropriate, receive specialist training in specific models of communication, such as Makaton. Each person you support should have an assessment and a communication plan in place that details how they choose to communicate and make decisions. Depending on the level of support somebody needs, the communication plan will be developed and monitored in partnership with other agencies and professionals, including psychologists, speech and language therapists and advocates.

Figure 1.2 You need to ensure that your team has the appropriate skills to support individuals' communication needs

1.1.3 and 1.1.4 Analyse the barriers and challenges to communication within your own job role and implement a strategy to overcome them

Some styles of communication may not be appropriate to some people because of their cultural differences. For example, they may have communication barriers that are related to their gender, their beliefs or their first language.

Table 1.1 lists a number of different barriers to effective communication and the potential causes.

Activity

1. For each of the communication barriers listed in Table 1.1, provide examples of how you would work to overcome them within your own job role.

Table 1.1 Barriers to communication

Barrier	Description
Behaviour	This may be the effect of symptoms people are feeling, or because they are unhappy or distressed, or unable to express in any other way that they need support.
Health issues	If people become unwell, lose or gain weight rapidly, appear anxious and have trouble sleeping then these may be signs that they need support.
Language	English will not be the first language of some service users and their families, and they may lack confidence using English, especially when speaking and writing.
Cultural	Cultural differences may include using words in different contexts, as well as speaking with different intonation and tones.
Values and belief systems	People's values and belief systems may impact on the methods they use to communicate. For example, how they receive and interpret a message may be different to its original purpose based on their own beliefs.
Disability	Communication may be impaired by sensory loss and physical disability.
Environmental	Noisy places mean it is difficult for people to be heard, and can be distracting. If the lighting is poor then it will be difficult for people to read or see signs.
Personality	Extroverts will be more confident communicators and may speak before they have digested the information. Introverts are more reserved and shy, preferring to listen and take time to consider a response.
Time	Hurried communication can mean context is lost and people do not have time to understand the information and formulate responses.
Use and abuse of power	People may feel that they are expected to communicate in certain ways due to the powerful influence of others.
Assumptions and stereotypes	If someone has a particular preconceived idea about another person then they may make assumptions about that person's communication abilities and skills.
Anxiety and depression	Personal and health issues can affect communication. For example, if someone is under stress, they may communicate in an aggressive and impatient manner rather than being calm and logical in their approach.
Self-esteem and self-image of others	People who have low self-esteem and poor self-image may find it hard to communicate, perhaps due to low confidence.

1.1.5 Use different means of communication to meet different needs

In your role, you will use verbal and non-verbal means of communication. Non-verbal means including the use of sign and pictorial methods as well as written forms of communication.

Table 1.2 lists some DOs and DON'Ts when communicating verbally.

Table 1.2 Think about the following when communicating verbally

DON'T	DO
cover your mouth when speaking, as some people will be lip-reading to support their understanding	speak clearly and slowly
use inappropriate language	be culturally sensitive and conscious of diversity
use offensive language	use intonation, tone and volume to add expression to your voice and communicate clear messages. Use **paralanguage**.
use overly complex language	ensure the words you use make sense and are meaningful to the person/ people you are giving the message to
use **jargon** and **slang**	be mindful of **abbreviations** and **acronyms**

If people don't understand what it is you are saying, they will feel left out of the conversation and not believe that they have anything of value to contribute. They may lose confidence in you and your ability to understand their support needs and aspirations. This kind of miscommunication could mean that you support people incorrectly, which could put you and them at risk of harm.

Activity

1. Consider how frequently you use slang, jargon and abbreviations in your work. Think of examples of when you have been communicating with your team members, the people you support and other professionals.

Grace is talking to Laura, to prepare for Laura's forthcoming review. They sit facing each other. Laura needs time to consider information and formulate a response. She sometimes needs encouragement to respond to a question.

Grace gives Laura eye contact when she is speaking and repeats back sections of the conversation to Laura, sometimes summarising what Laura has said, so that she is clear that she has understood.

Laura: 'I would like a job, but I'm not sure in what and I don't want to go on the bus on my own yet.'

Grace: 'OK, Laura, so you would like to think about different jobs that you could do, and then consider how you will get to and from work without using the bus on your own?'

Laura: 'Yes. I don't like the bus because it's full of noisy children and they push me.'

Grace: 'That doesn't sound very nice at all; I don't like noisy, packed buses either.'

1. The key points for **active listening** are: observing, repeating, summarising, reflecting feelings, and interpreting. Identify the key points of active listening in Laura's and Grace's conversation and consider how this supports effective communication.

Key Term

Active listening is a method of listening that involves understanding the content of a message as well as the intent of the sender and the circumstances under which the message is given.

Non-verbal skills include:

- body language such as facial expressions, posture, the positioning of your body, eye contact and the use of gesture

- signs and pictures, for example **blissymbol**, British sign language, Makaton and Braille

- assisted technology, such as speaking clocks, electronic sound boards and computer software

- use of proximity and touch.

Key Term

Blissymbol is a series of meaning-based symbols and pictures used by people who are unable to communicate verbally. Other sign and pictorial communication methods can be found on the internet.

Words are power; people have the right to communicate their needs and their preferences and to make decisions and choices to improve the quality of their life. Having the means to communicate empowers individuals. It also promotes their rights. Freedom of expression is in itself a human right, and it is essential that people are provided with the opportunities to express their views.

Working holistically ensures a person-centred approach. Person-centred services and self-determination are key principles of personalisation, along with human rights, citizenship and choice, and control. To empower people they will need the skills to speak up, and be involved in the design and delivery of their support.

Activity

1. Give examples of when you would use each of the following communication methods in your organisation:

   ■ personal

   ■ organisational

   ■ formal

   ■ informal

   ■ promotional

   ■ informative.

Figure 1.3 In good communication both parties are engaged

Be able to improve communication systems and practices that support positive outcomes for individuals

1.2.1 and 1.2.2 Monitor and evaluate the effectiveness of communication systems and practices

In social care, you keep records to make sure that you support people safely and consistently, and most importantly in ways that they have said they would like to be supported. You need to be aware of the communication needs of the people you support as well as your organisation. This includes:

■ different methods for sharing and storing information

■ personal files and communication plans

■ individual daily diaries

■ staff communication books.

This will enable you to ensure consistency of information and that everyone is aware of their responsibilities in working together to enhance the quality of experience for the people that you support.

Activity

describe

1. List the communication systems you have in your workplace. Who has the responsibility for maintaining and improving these systems?

To monitor the effectiveness of communication systems and practices, you need to consider the purpose of the system and what outcomes it aims to achieve from implementation. For instance, if you were to consider a communication plan devised to support an individual, this plan would be monitored to identify progress and success. For example: is the individual's ability to communicate progressing and are they successfully communicating their needs and wishes?

Figure 1.4 It is important to have clear criteria against which to assess the success of a communication plan

You will need to:

■ establish a baseline for monitoring

■ decide on a framework for recording agreed information

■ agree a review process whereby information can be tracked against the baseline to identify any progression in meeting the outcomes of the communication plan

■ consider whether the system successfully maintains confidentiality, complies with legal requirements, such as the Essential Standards for Safety and Quality, and meets with organisational requirements.

You would then use this information as a benchmark to evaluate the effectiveness of the system in achieving these outcomes.

1.2.3 Propose improvements to communication systems and practices to address any shortcomings

You can address any identified areas for improvement in communication systems and practices in a number of ways. You could present your proposals through written reports or discussion, clarifying the areas that you feel require improvement and, where possible, giving evidenced examples.

For example, you may wish to implement a revised format for team meetings, ensuring there is a clear agenda and that, as Chair, you ensure all actions are time-bound and team members are named as accountable against appropriate outcomes. You would need to consider who can access this information and when this is appropriate. It is therefore essential that records are current, complete and accurate.

1.2.4 Lead the implementation of revised communication systems and practices

As manager, your role is to lead revisions to communication systems and practices by:

■ communicating with staff on change through team meetings

■ involving others, for example by listening to ideas and problems

■ problem solving

■ being able to compromise

■ alleviating anxieties of others

■ designating new roles, responsibilities and practices

■ action planning that ensures timeframes for action, clarity on individual roles in achieving the outcome and then considering how this will be reviewed.

Be able to improve communication systems and practices that support positive outcomes for individuals

1.3

1.3.1 Use communication systems to promote partnership working

When working in partnership, clear lines of communication will identify lines of reporting, clarify accountability and enhance any decision-making processes. They include:

- electronic databases
- written records, such as emails and faxes
- face-to-face conversations
- handover records
- individual communication diaries
- personal files.

Shared records are utilised through partnership working. They:

- promote effective working practices between professionals, agencies and organisations
- facilitate the well-being of individuals and positive and improved outcomes
- promote partnership working by ensuring that relevant information is observed and monitored by appropriate people.

Shared information between support services, for example day service and home service, is used to record events, observations and incidents, etc., and to ensure consistency of support for the individual.

As manager, you will communicate with external agencies on a number of levels. Your organisation should have a policy for partnership working that considers the sharing of information, correct recording procedures and appropriate referral processes to different professional services.

1.3.2 Compare the effectiveness of different communication systems for partnership working

Computerised systems manage large amounts of data and can be effective if used across agencies, provided everyone records data in the same way. There are obvious issues regarding confidentiality, which may mean that some agencies can only have restricted access. In these situations, it is essential that all partners are clear on the reporting mechanisms to manage the information, and that there is an agreed standardisation for completing records across partnerships.

Another potential issue with shared records and limited access is ensuring that all views are equally represented. This raises power issues, for example who has access and who is excluded. Computerised systems do, however, provide faster responses and retrieval of information as well as offering an increased frequency by which information is collected and shared.

Data must be accurately maintained and updated or it will not be useful. Inaccurate information leads to mistakes that could be distressing, for instance sending letters to deceased people.

Activity

1. Reflect on your own experience of communication systems used for partnership working. Which of these worked well and which did not?

1.3.3 Propose improvements to communication systems for partnership working

Identifying and reporting issues with communication systems and proposing improvements can be undertaken via meetings or in reports. It is important to liaise with external partners through meetings. During meetings, you need to be able to demonstrate skills in:

- involving and listening to ideas and problems
- finding solutions
- being able to compromise
- alleviating the anxieties of others.

Activity   *In Practice*

Rob attends regional multi-disciplinary team meetings for practitioners supporting people with learning disabilities across the county. The meetings are an hour long and are set up to share information across agencies as well as update each other on any organisational changes.

The difficulty for Rob is that often an hour is not long enough to consider and manage all these issues. As a result, there are often no clear actions agreed. Rob feels like the meetings often go round in circles and nothing ever gets resolved.

1. What advice would you give to Rob so that he can propose improvements?

Activity

Identify a system of communication within your own organisation that requires improvement.

1. What are the specific issues and what are the improvements required?

2. How will you propose these improvements?

Be able to use systems for effective information management

1.4.1 Explain legal and ethical tensions between maintaining confidentiality and sharing information

Your duty of care, and your responsibility to safeguard individual privacy, could cause legal and ethical tension. Ethical dilemmas arise frequently throughout the social care sector, particularly when you work so closely and intimately with the people you support. There are a number of areas where, for one reason or another, you will find your own views may be different from those of others.

In certain circumstances you may have to break confidentiality and share information with someone else. You will need to do this when someone is at serious risk of:

- harm to themselves
- harm to others
- exploitation or abuse
- significant financial gain or loss.

All local authorities and providers of social care and support are required to have in place procedures for safeguarding. You will have a duty of care to ensure that the individuals you support and your staff are protected from harm.

Activity

1. Consider legal and ethical tensions in your own workplace between maintaining confidentiality and sharing information.

The law and standards that rule and guide your practice, and the handling of personal and confidential information, are summarised through a number of key documents:

- The Data Protection Act states the law on processing data on others.
- The Human Rights Act (1998, Article 8) covers the right to respect for privacy and family life.
- The Freedom of Information Act (2000) gives individuals the right to ask any public body for all the information they have, including any personal information they hold on you.
- Essential Standards for Quality and Safety – Compliance Criteria place a duty on care providers to constantly check the quality of their services. Complaints should be acted on properly and personal records kept accurate, safe and confidential.
- The Disability Discrimination Act (2005) places duties on providers to ensure disabled people are protected from discrimination, for example by ensuring equal access to the same quality and range of services.

- The Equality Act (2010) brings together various legislation on disability, race and gender and extends the focus to encompass age, gender reassignment, marriage and civil partnership, pregnancy and maternity, religion or beliefs, and sexual orientation.

- Public Interest Disclosure Act (1999) provides the means for people to raise genuine concerns about negligence, dangers to health and safety, crime and miscarriages of justice, regardless of the confidential nature of the information (often referred to as the 'Whistle Blowing Act').

1.4.2 Analyse the essential features of information sharing agreements within and between organisations

The area of confidential record sharing can be complex. It leads to questions such as:

- Who can access records and who is excluded?

- When is it appropriate to share?

- What are the boundaries to an agreement?

When considering information-sharing agreements, you will have to manage your duty of care and the best interest of the people you support. You will also need to respect the rights of the individual to privacy and dignity.

The Caldicott Principles provide the following framework for information sharing within and between organisations:

1. Justify the purpose for which the information is needed.

2. Only use personally identifiable information when absolutely necessary.

3. Use the minimum personal identifiable information possible; if feasible use an identifier number rather than a name.

4. Access to the information should be on a strict 'need-to-know' basis.

5. Everyone should be aware of his/her responsibilities to respect clients' confidentiality.

6. Understand and comply with the law. The most relevant legislation is the Data Protection Act 1998, the Police and Criminal Evidence Act (PACE) 1984 and the Human Rights Act 1998.

Activity

1. Consider information agreements and boundaries your organisation has with others. Identify the essential features of these and how having them impacts on the quality and consistency of information sharing.

1.4.3 Demonstrate use of information management systems that meet legal and ethical requirements

Information management systems must meet legal and ethical requirements, and you should ensure that confidentiality of all communications is maintained at all times. You should have policies and procedures in your workplace for secure record keeping, and it is your responsibility to ensure that your team is familiar with these.

Figure 1.5 You will need to make sure that confidentiality of all communications is maintained at all times

Activity

1. How do you ensure records are kept secure and confidential within your workplace? Which legal frameworks do you work within? When do you share information and how do you ensure you only share it on a 'need-to-know' basis?

Activity

1. What communication systems do you have in your workplace that are specifically designed to maximise opportunities for the individuals you support and to enable them to participate in the design and delivery of their support?

Positively promoting individuals' rights is essential. Where relevant, you need to involve advocacy services to enable individuals to express their views. Other person-centred approaches to your communication systems could include:

■ ensuring that all relevant information is available in accessible formats

■ ensuring that any decisions about support services which affect the lives of people who receive support from them do not happen without solid person-centred consultation processes.

It is vital that people are enabled by accessible communication systems to shape their future experiences of adult social care support and services.

Activity   In Practice

Beryl lives in a home with 24 other elderly residents. She has her own room but shares all other facilities with the other residents. Beryl wants to make a complaint about the cleaning lady who doesn't knock before coming in to clean her room. She asks you to help.

1. What would you do next and then how would you resolve this issue?

Are you ready for assessment?

✔ **Do you know the range of communication requirements and systems in your workplace?**

✔ **Do you know why it is essential to support communication in health and social care?**

✔ **Do you know the legal framework for maintaining confidentiality?**

✔ **Do you know the value of personalisation and the necessity to ensure that the people you support have 'a voice'?**

✔ **Do you know the barriers and challenges to communication systems and how to overcome these?**

- Do you know how to monitor the effectiveness of communication systems in your workplace?

- Do you know the impact on communication systems of multi-agency working and record sharing?

- Do you know how to maintain accurate records that are concise, complete and current?

- Do you know how to involve and listen to people, identify problems and create and implement solutions?

- Do you know the different communication systems for partnership working?

- Do you know the key points relevant to communication systems from the Data Protection Act (1998) and Care Quality Commission's 'Essential Standards for Safety and Quality'?

- Do you know the ethical features of information-sharing agreements within and between organisations?

- Do you know how to use information management systems that meet legal and ethical requirements?

- Do you know the circumstances when information can be shared and the boundaries of information-sharing agreements?

- Can you identify groups and individuals within your sphere of work and their different communication needs?

- Can you give examples used within your own workplace to explain the range of different communication methods?

- Can you analyse the importance of supporting communication in order to empower individuals, promote their rights and support personalisation?

- Can you identify how your organisation and you as a practitioner work to maintain confidentiality as part of your communication systems?

- Can you list the different types of barriers and challenges that could affect communication systems, identify three examples in your own workplace and suggest ways to overcome these?

- Can you lead the implementation of revised communication systems and practices within your own workplace?

- Can you use information management systems to meet legal and ethical requirements?

- Can you ensure the positive promotion of individual rights through the use of advocacy and person-centred approaches?

Key Term

Personalisation is the process by which state-provided services are adapted to suit the needs and preferences of the service user; in social care this means everyone having choice and control over the services they receive along with greater emphasis on prevention and early intervention.

References

Argyle, M., Furnham, A., and Graham, J. A. (1981) *Social Situations*. Cambridge: The Press Syndicate of the University of Cambridge.

Bales, R. F. (2001) *Social Interaction Systems: Theory and Measurement*. New Jersey: Transaction Publishers.

Charlton, J. I. (1998) *Nothing About Us Without Us: Disability, Oppression and Empowerment*. London: University of California Press.

Hirokawa, R. and Poole, M. S. (1996) *Communication and Group Decision Making*. London: SAGE Publishing.

Lefevre, R. (2011) *Rude Hand Gestures of the World: A Guide to Offending Without Words*. San Francisco: Chronicle Books.

Acts and Regulations

Data Protection Act (1984) and (1998).

Police and Criminal Evidence Act (PACE) (1984).

Public Interest Disclosure Act ('Whistle Blowing Act') (1999).

Disability Discrimination Act (2005).

Equality Act (2010).

Freedom of Information Act (2000).

Human Rights Act (1998).

Websites

Community Care (Online magazine), www.communitycare.com, accessed 21 June 2012.

Care Quality Commission, www.cqc.org.uk, accessed 28 June 2012.

Mental Health.net (Communication tips for dementia workers), www.mentalhelp.net, accessed 21 June 2012.

Social Care Institute for Excellence, www.scie.org.uk, accessed 21 June 2012.

Chapter 2

Promote
Professional
development

This chapter will help you to develop greater self-awareness in relation to your professional role and responsibilities. It will help you to understand the principles and importance of professional development and reflective practice in identifying and prioritising development goals and how to plan to meet these in order to improve your performance.

As a leader and manager, you are responsible for ensuring that workplace practices are up to date and meet current regulations, standards and frameworks for best practice. Using processes to manage both your own development and those of others is an effective means of promoting professional practice and leading by example.

By the end of this chapter you will:

1 Understand the principles of professional development
2 Be able to prioritise goals and targets for your own professional development
3 Be able to prepare a professional development plan
4 Be able to improve performance through reflective practice

Understand the principles of professional development 2.1

2.1.1 Explain the importance of continually improving knowledge and practice

In the past thirty years globalisation, innovation and technology have all been major influences on the pace of change in society. The health and social care sector has experienced significant changes during this time to the extent that change is now regarded as a part of everyday life. Significant social change has also taken place. For health and social care the impact of this change has meant that individuals have higher expectations of the quality of care and support. They also expect a greater level of involvement with a shift towards personalisation and partnership working. New models of care service delivery are also emerging to compete in the increasingly diverse social care market, e.g. personal assistants supporting individuals with personal budgets. These changes have resulted in a cultural shift with the professionalisation of the workforce and the requirement for continuing professional development.

Practitioners can no longer hope to set aside learning once they have achieved their professional qualifications. The Skills for Care workforce development strategy *Capable, Confident, Skilled* (2011) not only confirms the need for the workforce to become 'even more capable, responsive, skilled, well-trained and empowered' (p2) but clearly defines the implications in terms of skill development for the workforce to deliver each of the seven principles outlined in the government's *A Vision for Adult Social Care: Capable Communities and Active Citizens* (2010).

Professional development therefore must be viewed as a continuous process where knowledge, understanding and skills are being updated and improved to meet the ever-changing demands of the sector and service users.

Leitch (2006) identified the imperative for the UK workforce to develop world-class skills in order to compete in the world market. This would be best achieved by the government, employers and individuals working together and sharing responsibility to ensure that those entering the workforce gain appropriate skills, as well as those already in the workforce updating their skills. With a demographic of an ageing population, Skills for Health recognises that the majority of the future workforce is already employed and the way to meet the challenges ahead and develop a highly skilled and flexible workforce is through continuing professional development (2009:30). The Kings Fund report *NHS Workforce Planning – Limitations and Possibilities* identified that if the NHS was to 'thrive and survive' within the considerable financial constraints of current and future provision 'productivity will need to make a step-change, and much of the scope for improvement lies in the workforce' (2009:vii).

Legislation, research and inquiry findings, government policies, initiatives and guidance all impact on how care is delivered. As a manager you are responsible for ensuring you are up to date with all changes that affect service delivery. You need to be able to interpret any changes and understand how they will impact on service delivery. You are responsible for implementing changes to workplace policies and practice in order to remain compliant with legislation or to implement best practice initiatives to improve outcomes for service users. You are also responsible for ensuring that those you manage understand the reasons for, and effectively implement, any changes that are required.

Figure 2.1 A manager should update their team with professional developments in the sector

Activity

reflect *analyse*

1. Complete a table like the one below by identifying **at least one** change that has occurred in the past six months in each area where there has been a direct impact on service delivery.

2. Identify how you found out about the change(s); what action you took to respond to the change(s) and how the change(s) impacted on the quality of service delivery and/or practitioner knowledge and/or skills. The first area contains an example.

Change related to: (please provide specific detail, e.g. which law changed?)	How did you find out about the change(s)?	What action did you take to implement any resultant change(s)?	How did the change(s) impact on the quality of service delivery and/or practitioner knowledge and/or skills?
Legislation *Employment law*	*ACAS website*	*Reviewed and changed recruitment policy and procedure* *Discussed changes with others involved in recruitment*	*Ensured organisation remained compliant and kept team up to date*
Government policy			
Regulations			
Best practice (e.g. research findings or recommendations from an inquiry report)			

Activity

1. Think about the recruitment process. If your employment legislation knowledge and recruitment practices were not current, what would be the potential consequences for:

- you?

- your organisation or employer?

- job applicants?

2.1.2 Analyse potential barriers to professional development

Continuing professional development is a requirement in health and social care work and there are a number of factors that can act as barriers to this happening in practice. If the workforce is to rise to the challenge presented by the changes outlined earlier this will require a considerable cultural shift and a greater engagement and commitment to learning and development. Making that cultural shift may be a barrier to some individuals and organisations engaging in learning and development opportunities. The first step to overcoming any barrier is to recognise what it is. Once identified you can then put strategies in place to eliminate or reduce them. Barriers can be internal, e.g.

your own beliefs and feelings about learning, as well as external, e.g. access to learning opportunities.

One of the barriers to professional development can be a lack of understanding of which development opportunities suit your individual needs and preferences. Poor past educational experiences may have led you to believe that you found learning difficult and therefore something to be avoided. However, research has shown that adults learn differently from children, and that we all have preferences when it comes to how we learn. Understanding how you learn best will help you to choose development opportunities that you will enjoy and learn from (Rogers 2001). Theories about learning relate to how people:

- perceive information

- process information

- organise and present information.

Activity

1. Complete a table like the one below by identifying at least **six** potential barriers to your professional development and the action you can take to overcome them. An example has been given, to start you off.

Potential barriers to professional development	Internal or external factor?	The action I can take to overcome this
Lack of information regarding opportunities	External	Undertake internet research – use networks to find out what is available

Activity

1. Use an internet search engine to research learning styles and the range of questionnaires that can help you identify your learning preferences.

2. Undertake questionnaires for these two approaches: **VARK** (**V**isual, **A**ural, **R**ead/Write, **K**inesthetic) and **Honey and Mumford Learning Styles Inventory**. Briefly explain the key features of each approach and your findings from undertaking the associated questionnaire. Finally, evaluate the results in terms of their accuracy in identifying and describing your learning style preferences.

2.1.3 Compare the use of different sources and systems of support for professional development

Although some professional development may be undertaken alone, such as reading research documents, there are a number of other ways to provide support and enrich your development. Some sources of support may be internal to your organisation, for example supervision and appraisal, while others may be external, such as mentoring and training courses.

A popular method of professional development is action learning. First developed by Revans in the 1980s, action learning is an approach to both individual and organisational development. It is a process that involves working on real workplace issues and challenges using the experience, knowledge and skills of a small group of people coupled with skilled questioning. The aim is to reinterpret old and familiar concepts and produce fresh ideas and solutions. 'There is no learning without action and no (sober and deliberate) action without learning' (Pedler 2008:5). Action learning is particularly useful for leadership and management development as in these roles individuals are faced with practice dilemmas where there is often no prescribed solution. It is not simply learning by doing but learning through sharing insights with others as well as transferring learning into action back in the workplace. You can find out more about action learning by visiting http://www.actionlearningassociates.co.uk/actionlearning.html.

When planning your development, it is important to understand not only what sources and systems are available to you but also how each may meet your individual needs.

Not all sources and systems of support will be available or appropriate for you to make use of. To help you decide which would be the most effective for you to use, you will need to compare the similarities and differences between the different sources and also consider their value in relation to your identified needs, preferences and timeframe for change.

Activity

1. Use an example of a recent professional development activity and explain to your assessor how you reached the decision that the activity was appropriate for you to undertake. You will need to explain your rationale and the criteria you used to make a decision.

Activity

1. Complete the following diagram by identifying other sources and systems of formal and informal professional development support available to you.

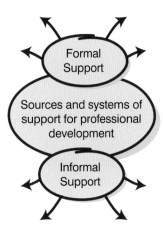

Formal Support

Sources and systems of support for professional development

Informal Support

2. Identify the key features of the following sources and systems in relation to supporting professional development. The first one has been started for you.

Sources and systems of support:	Key features are:
Formal support	*Pre-arranged with identified learning outcomes and expectations*
Informal support	
Supervision	
Appraisal	
Mentoring	

2.1.4 Explain factors to consider when selecting opportunities and activities for keeping knowledge and practice up to date

There are a number of factors you will need to consider when making decisions and planning your professional development. For example:

- Does the opportunity provide you with the outcome you desire/require?

- What funding is available to support your development or is it self-funding?

- What is the time commitment? Do you need to attend a course? Is there a self-study requirement?

- Does it fit with your career aspirations?

- Does it fit with your learning style preferences?

Not all factors or criteria will carry the same level of importance and so you may find it useful to weight the criteria you use to reach a decision or you could rank your criteria for decision making with ten points for the most important and one for the least important.

Activity In Practice

Cait has recently taken up the post of assistant manager at a small residential care home for older people with dementia. Previously she worked with physically frail older people. She achieved her Level 3 Diploma in Health and Social Care a year ago. She is keen to progress her career as her long-term plan is to become a manager.

1. Explain how each of the following factors will impact on Cait's decisions when planning her professional development:

   - her job role and organisational requirements, such as qualifications to meet regulations

   - the gaps in her current knowledge and skills, e.g. dementia care.

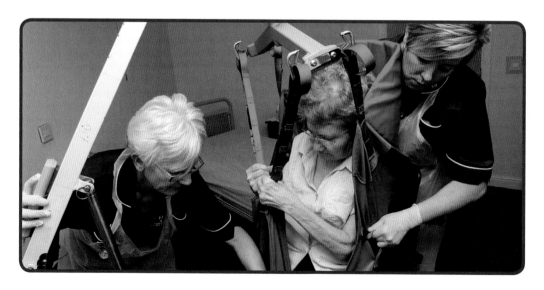

Figure 2.3 Teaching others is a good way to develop your practice

2.2.1 Evaluate your own knowledge and performance against standards and benchmarks

Your job description is a primary source of information regarding the expectations of your role and responsibilities. However, there are a number of other sources you will need to be familiar with to be effective in your role. These will also help you to identify any gaps in your knowledge and skills, and guide you in prioritising your professional development.

There are a number of standards and **benchmarks** used in health and social care. These include:

- codes of practice, e.g. General Social Care Council (GSCC) Code of Practice
- regulations, such as the Data Protection Act (1998)
- essential standards, e.g. the Care Quality Commission Essential Standards of Quality and Safety
- National Occupational Standards (NOS), e.g. the Leadership and Management for Care Services.

Evaluation requires you to take an honest and objective standpoint so you can weigh up the evidence presented and reach a considered and logical conclusion. Evaluating your current knowledge and skills will require you to reflect, gather evidence and then be honest and objective so that you are able to identify your strengths and weaknesses. When you use standards or benchmarks

in your evaluation, you will find it easier if you can identify real work examples that demonstrate what you know and can do. If you struggle to identify examples then this is likely to indicate an area for development.

Note: as of 1st August 2012 the GSCC function has been moved to the Health and Care Professions Council (HCPC), but the legacy codes and documentation still stand until newer implementations arise.

Key Terms

Benchmark is a standard used as a basis against which something can be assessed or measured.

Evaluation is examining something in order to reach a conclusion about its value, quality or worth.

Activity

Think about other standards or benchmarks that are used in your workplace. These may relate to performance targets agreed at supervision and appraisal or core competences developed and used within your organisation.

1. How do you evaluate your performance against these?

2. What evidence do you gather to substantiate your evaluation?

3. How do you present this to your manager (if appropriate)?

Activity

The following table includes some examples of the standards and benchmarks that apply to your area of work. Complete the table by evaluating your performance against each standard. The first one has been done as an example.

Standard or benchmark	How I evidence this is my practice
GSCC Code of Practice: 1.4 Respecting and maintaining the dignity and privacy of service users	*I address each individual using their preferred name. I discuss any sensitive or confidential matters in private, sharing only with those who have a need and right to know and where consent has been given. I treat individuals fairly and do not make value judgements or assumptions. I ensure that I speak to each individual at least daily to monitor their well-being and deal with any potential problems quickly. I stress the importance of privacy and dignity at induction, training and team meetings.*
GSCC Code of Practice: 6.6 Recognising that you remain responsible for the work that you have delegated to other workers	
Data Protection Act (1998): Principle 3 Personal data shall be adequate, relevant and not excessive in relation to the purpose or purposes for which they are processed	
CQC Essential Standards: Regulation 10 Assessing and monitoring the quality of service provision; **Outcome 16**: Lead effectively to manage risk. People benefit from safe, quality care because effective decisions are made and because of the management of risks to people's health, welfare and safety	
CQC Essential Standards : Regulation 23: Supporting workers; Outcome 14: Lead effectively to support staff. People who use the service are kept safe and their health and welfare needs are met because staff are competent to carry out their work and are appropriately trained , supervised and appraised	
NOS for Leadership and Management: M2c 2.4 Deal constructively with any conflict that may arise with colleagues	
NOS for Leadership and Management: LM1c 2.2 Demonstrate how own practice supports a positive culture in the team	

2.2.2 Prioritise development goals and targets to meet expected standards

When considering your professional development, you may identify a number of different goals and targets. However, it would be unrealistic to believe that you have sufficient time and resources to meet all of these at once. Some goals and targets may be long term or desirable rather than essential for your current role. To make effective use of time and resources, you will therefore need to prioritise these goals.

Prioritising will require you to identify criteria that can be applied to help you reach a decision about the importance and urgency of each goal and target. For example, this may include asking yourself questions such as:

- Is it a requirement for my current job role?

- Do I need to achieve this to comply with regulations or legislation?

- Do I need to achieve this immediately, in the next 2 months, 6 months or 12 months?

- Does it meet organisational goals and outcomes?

- How will it improve my knowledge, skills and/or practice?

- How will it improve service delivery and outcomes?

Remember

A good source of portfolio evidence would be a professional discussion following an observation of practice where you evaluate how your performance met the National Occupational Standards you were being assessed against.

Activity

1. Think about four of your own professional development goals and targets. For each one, identify which standard will be met when you achieve it, its priority for achievement and the criteria used to prioritise.

Professional development goal/target (1)

Standard to be met:

Priority for achievement:

Criteria used to prioritise:

Professional development goal/target (2)

Standard to be met:

Priority for achievement:

Criteria used to prioritise:

Professional development goal/target (3)

Standard to be met:

Priority for achievement:

Criteria used to prioritise:

Professional development goal/target (4)

Standard to be met:

Priority for achievement:

Criteria used to prioritise:

Be able to prepare a professional development plan

2.3.1 Select learning opportunities to meet development objectives and reflect personal learning style

Understanding how you prefer to learn is essential if you are to be effective in selecting the right opportunities to meet your development needs within the limitations of time and funding resources.

The work of David Kolb has probably had the most significant influence on how we think about adult learning and teaching. According to Kolb (1984), 'learning is the process whereby knowledge is created through the transformation of experience.' Kolb's model is based on a cycle that includes active learning and passive learning. These provide both concrete and abstract experience. Kolb's experiential learning cycle identifies how individuals prefer to learn.

- DO – concrete experience – where people would describe themselves as 'receptive, feeling, accepting, intuitive, present-orientated.'

- OBSERVE – reflective observation – where people would describe themselves as 'tentative, watching, observing, reflecting, reserved.'

- THINK – abstract conceptualisation – where people would describe themselves as 'analytical, thinking, evaluative, logical, rational.'

- PLAN – active experimentation – where people would describe themselves as 'practical, doing, active, responsible.'

However, Gibbs (1988) argues that 'it is not enough just to do, and neither is it enough just to think. Nor is it enough simply to do and think. Learning from experience must involve linking the doing and the thinking.' Further Zuber-Skerritt states that 'learning is a process as well as an outcome' (1992). If learning is to last and be transferred into practice in order to effect improvement it is important to complete the learning cycle regardless of where you may prefer to initially engage with learning.

Earlier in this chapter you looked at two different learning style questionnaires, so hopefully you now have a better understanding of the development activities you prefer and which suit your learning style. If you use this understanding when choosing development activities, you are more likely to enjoy the experience and maximise your learning. It will also help you retain your learning and your ability to transfer that into your work practice.

You will have learnt from your research and undertaking of the questionnaires that most people can use a mixture of learning styles and may or may not show a strong preference for one style. Being able to adapt your learning style to the task in hand will encourage creativity and improve your learning. Being able to learn from a wide variety of opportunities is preferable because what you need to learn varies, e.g. factual information or a new skill, and so the way you learn each of these would be different.

Rory manages supported living accommodation for people with mental health problems. He has worked in mental health for the past five years. The organisation he works for is introducing new assessments, risk assessments and person-centred plans. He has identified the need to familiarise himself with these new recording processes and his service manager has suggested two potential learning opportunities to meet those needs. Rory can either:

■ attend a training day where the service manager will spend the morning going through each new document providing an explanation, followed in the afternoon by group-work activities in which he will have the opportunity to become more familiar with, and practise using, the new documents

■ receive two coaching sessions with a more experienced colleague, during which time he will complete the new documents with his colleague who will be available to provide advice, guidance and feedback on his work.

1. What are the potential benefits to Rory of each opportunity?

2. Which learning styles would be best met by each opportunity?

Think about two different things you have learnt recently, for example a skill and a new policy.

1. How did you learn each one (i.e. what did you do)?

2. How did each learning experience relate to learning styles?

2.3.2 Produce a plan for your own professional development using appropriate sources of support

Care Quality Commission regulations require health and social care organisations to have systems in place that enable employees to identify, record, monitor and review professional development needs and plans. Plans are often aligned to organisational as well as individual goals and aspirations. To be effective, any plan must clearly identify the starting point and the desired (and/or required) outcomes and what steps need to be taken along the way in order to reach that point.

An effective professional development plan will include:

■ SMART development needs (i.e. Specific, Measurable, Realistic, Achievable and Time-bound)

■ the anticipated outcome for each identified need (what will be achieved)

■ how the identified need will be met

■ sources of support to meet the identified need

- any potential risks or barriers to the need not being met
- contingency plans to overcome any identified risks and potential barriers
- how and when the plan will be monitored and reviewed
- modifications to the plan as a result of monitoring and/or review.

Activity

Use the criteria identified above to review and evaluate your own professional development plan.

1. How effective is it in describing your development needs?

2. Does it contain sufficient **quantitative** and **qualitative** information to enable you to plan, monitor and review your development effectively?

3. What modifications could you make to your professional development plan to make it more effective?

4. How could you improve the professional development planning process used in your workplace?

Key Terms

Quantitative means relating to quantity, using measurable numerical data.

Qualitative means relating to quality, using words and descriptions.

Anywhere Care Home

Social Activities
What activities would you like to be available?

_____

What type of outings would you be interested in going on?

_____

What hobbies or interests did you enjoy before coming to Anywhere?

_____

_____

Figure 2.4 Qualitative data

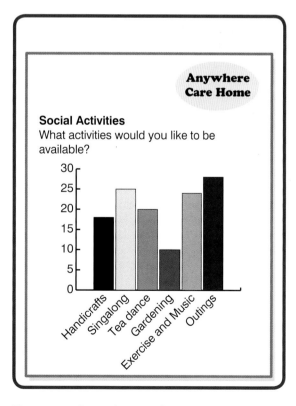

Figure 2.5 Quantitative data

2.3.3 Establish a process to evaluate the effectiveness of the plan

Planning is meant to be the start of a journey not the destination. Plans are therefore designed to be monitored, reviewed and modified as the situation changes. Perhaps the course you planned to attend was cancelled, but that doesn't mean the reason for attending is less of a priority. What it does mean is that you need to look at another way to meet that need. Professional development plans should be monitored and reviewed as part of regular supervision and given more time at appraisal. They should not be filed and forgotten.

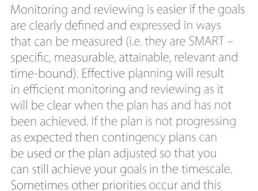

Remember

Monitoring and reviewing is easier if the goals are clearly defined and expressed in ways that can be measured (i.e. they are SMART – specific, measurable, attainable, relevant and time-bound). Effective planning will result in efficient monitoring and reviewing as it will be clear when the plan has and has not been achieved. If the plan is not progressing as expected then contingency plans can be used or the plan adjusted so that you can still achieve your goals in the timescale. Sometimes other priorities occur and this may be another reason why the plan requires adjustment.

Activity

1. Use your development plan as the basis for a professional discussion to demonstrate your understanding of your development needs and how to meet them.

Activity

1. Devise a set of evaluation criteria and evaluate the effectiveness of professional development plans in your workplace. Record your findings and implement improvements.

Be able to improve performance through reflective practice

2.4

2.4.1 Compare models of reflective practice

Reflective practice is not a new concept but one that is viewed as essential in health and social care where the only constant is change. Kottkamp (1990) defined reflective practice as 'a mode that links thought and action with reflection. It involves critically analysing one's actions with the goal of improving one's professional practice.'

To be effective, practitioners need to be able to assimilate new information and learn from every experience and interaction with others. Working with people requires high levels of knowledge, understanding and skill, as well as the ability to adapt and respond quickly to new situations. Reflection enables you to revisit a situation, examine and question it, and learn from it, as opposed to working in an inefficient and uncritical way, repeating mistakes.

Donald Schön introduced the concept of a 'reflective practitioner' as a person who consciously thinks about what they are doing. He considered the most effective practitioners to be those who were able to 'reflect-in-action' (i.e. during the activity) and 'reflect-on-action' (i.e. after the activity).

Schön's work has resulted in a number of other models of reflection being developed. These include:

- Kolb's Experiential Learning Model
- Gibbs's (1988) Framework for Reflection
- Borton's (1970) Framework for Guiding Reflective Activities

- John's (1995) Model of Structured Reflection
- Reynold's (1965) Progression of Competence
- Boud's (1985) Model of Experience-Reflection-Outcome
- Driscoll's (2000) Structured Reflection Model.

Activity

1. Research models of reflection and then complete the questions below. You may find it useful to use an internet search engine during your research, but remember to check that the information is from a credible source.

2. Complete the following table by briefly describing the key features of each of the following models of reflection (you may find it useful to use diagrams with your descriptions). The first one has been started for you.

Model of reflection	Key features
Schön	*Reflection-in-action – reflecting during the event* *Reflection-on-action – reflecting after the event*
Gibbs	
Boud	
Driscoll	

Figure 2.6 Taking time to reflect enhances your learning and practice

2.4.2 Explain the importance of reflective practice to improve performance

In your work role, one of the primary purposes of learning is to improve the quality of your work performance, whether that is direct service delivery or managing people. Regardless of the method of learning, reflecting on the experience will anchor that learning and help you to appreciate its value to your practice. You will find it easier to integrate learning into practice if you have reflected upon it before adding your learning to your existing knowledge bank. Sharing your learning with others will be easier, which in itself will reinforce your learning. Being able to

reflect will also enhance your appreciation of your knowledge and skills and is likely to lead to greater job satisfaction as your confidence increases.

2.4.3 Use reflective practice and feedback from others to improve performance

Although using what you learn through reflective practice is a valuable way of improving your performance it is limited to your own perception and interpretation of a situation. Seeking feedback from others will provide a more rounded perspective especially if you seek feedback from people who are both senior and junior to you. Seeking feedback from others will help to increase your self-awareness. Being self-aware will help you to understand the impact your behaviour has on others which is an important factor in having effective relationships with others. When your work role involves supporting and/or managing people this is even more important as a lack of self-awareness can lead to your being part of the problem rather than part of the solution in a situation.

A useful tool to both illustrate and improve self-awareness and mutual understanding between individuals within a group is Johari's window. This model was developed by Joseph Luff and Harry Ingram in 1955 and has four areas:

- the **open area**, which illustrates what the person knows about themselves that is also known by others

- the **blind area**, which illustrates what is unknown by the person but is known by others

- the **hidden area**, which illustrates what the person knows about themselves but is unknown by others

- the **unknown area**, which illustrates what is unknown by both the person and others.

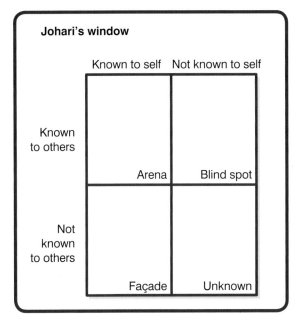

Figure 2.7 Johari's window

Seeking and accepting feedback from others, however, requires confidence, especially if what they tell you isn't what you would choose to hear. It is important therefore to consider feedback as another opportunity for learning and to ask questions of the other person so that you can use what they tell you to help you change if that is required.

To be useful and enable you to learn feedback needs to be specific and in sufficient detail for you to understand what you did well, what may need to change and how you can achieve that change. Using examples to illustrate what

you do so that you can explore the impact this has will help you to not only understand what needs to change but also how you might achieve this.

Activity | **In Practice**

Faith is the manager of a domiciliary care service. She has worked in social care for six years. She currently manages a team of twenty carers. She has just finished undertaking appraisals with four of the team with her manager. It is the first time she has conducted appraisals and has asked her manager to give her feedback on her performance. Before her manager gives Faith feedback, however, she asks Faith to reflect on the appraisals and her performance.

1. Why do you think Faith's manager asked for her reflection before giving feedback?

2. How might Faith's own reflection help the manager to give her feedback?

3. If you were in this situation what questions would you ask the manager to get feedback that you could use to reflect upon and improve your performance?

Figure 2.8 Everyone can benefit from feedback

2.4.4 Evaluate how practice has been improved through reflection on best practice, failures and mistakes

Reflecting on best practice is as important as reflecting on failures or mistakes so that you can transfer techniques into different situations. In each case the purpose is to increase your understanding of what works. However, people have a tendency to reflect only when things go wrong; although you can learn through this, it can create a reluctance to try new approaches. Reflecting on best practice initiatives means that you will analyse it to the extent that you are able to identify how and why something worked. This will not only give you a better understanding but also the confidence to try and apply the principles to your own area of work. Implementing a new process or practice without fully understanding its component parts is likely to lead to frustration and/or failure as you lack sufficient understanding to make the necessary adjustments required to fit your workplace situation.

Mezirow's (1991) 'perspective transformation' is the process of reflection where the person becomes critically aware of how and why their assumptions affect the way they think about themselves in relation to others. This perspective transformation is achieved through sudden insight or 'critical reflectivity'. Mezirow identified six stages of reflectivity through which the person is able to reflect upon and learn from a range of different situations, such as achievements, difficulties, positive feedback and new experiences, enabling them to revise their assumptions and make changes.

Activity

Think about a recent best practice initative that you have identified as potentially benefiting your workplace.

1. How do the main principles of the best practice initiative apply to your work situation?

2. What steps need to be taken to implement this best practice in your workplace?

3. What are the risks to successful implementation?

4. How would you overcome/manage those risks?

Mistakes or failures in practice do occur despite the existence of control measures. Working with people means that the potential for harm, both physical and emotional, as a result of mistakes and failures is considerable. It is imperative that practice changes as a result of what is learnt from mistakes and failures. This can be either those that occur in your workplace or in the wider health and social care sector. Failures in practice can often result in a government inquiry. This enables the facts of the situation to be uncovered as well as accounts of the situation from the perspectives of those involved or affected to be heard. This is followed by an analysis and evaluation of all the presented evidence. Those involved in leading the inquiry then use these to reflect upon and reach a conclusion on the lessons to be learnt. The resultant inquiry report will then contain recommendations for changes to practice to minimise the risk of failures continuing.

Activity

1. Identify government and other inquiry reports relating to mistakes and failures in health and social care practice that have been published in the past year that have had a direct impact on your area of work. For example:

   ■ The NHS Ombudsman report 'Care and compassion' which you can find at www.ombudsman.org.uk

   ■ The Care Quality Commission publishes reports including those relating to failures in practice. Visit the following for more information: www.cqc.org.uk

2. You may find it helpful to use an internet search engine to search for 'failures in care practice'. You can also read and refer to local reports, e.g. those internal to your organisation.

3. Reflect upon recommendations from one inquiry report that have resulted in changes in your workplace and then answer the following questions:

   ■ How have those findings/recommendations been implemented into policies and practices in your workplace?

   ■ How have you monitored the effectiveness of the changes implemented?

   ■ How has practice improved as a result of the changes implemented?

Remember

Your assessor will use the assessment criteria to provide you with specific feedback following observations of work practice as part of your Diploma, which will help you to recognise your knowledge and skills. Some of their feedback will relate to the way in which you relate to others, i.e. your values and attitudes, and this will help you to develop your self-awareness and improve your performance.

Are you ready for assessment?

✔ Do you know the potential barriers to professional development?

✔ Do you know the uses of different sources and systems of support for professional development?

✔ Do you know the factors to consider when selecting opportunities and activities for keeping knowledge and practice up to date?

✔ Do you know the importance of reflective practice in improving performance?

✔ Can you evaluate your knowledge and performance against standards and benchmarks?

✔ Can you prioritise development goals and targets to meet expected standards?

✔ Can you choose learning opportunities to meet development objectives and match your preferred learning style?

✔ Can you produce a professional development plan using an appropriate source of support?

✔ Can you establish a process to evaluate the effectiveness of a development plan?

✔ Can you compare reflective practice models?

✔ Can you use reflective practice and feedback from others to improve performance?

✔ Can you evaluate practice improvements achieved through reflection on best practice as well as failures and mistakes?

References

Borton, T. (1970) *Reach, Teach and Touch*. London: McGraw Hill.

Boud, D., Keogh, R. and Walker, D. (1985) Promoting Reflection in Learning: A Model in *Reflection: Turning Experience into Learning* (Eds, Boud, D., Keogh, R. and Walker, D.). London: Kogan Page.

Driscoll, J. (ed.) (2007) *Practising Clinical Supervision: A Reflective Approach for Healthcare Professionals (2nd Edition)*. Oxford: (Bailliere Tindall), Elsevier.

Gibbs, G. (1988) *Learning by Doing: a Guide to Teaching and Learning Methods* p9. London: Further Education Unit.

Imison, C., Buchan, J. and Xavier, S. (2009) *NHS Workforce Planning: Limitations and Possibilities*. London: The Kings Fund.

Johns, C. (1995) 'Framing Learning through Reflection within Carper's Fundamental Ways of Knowing in Nursing'. *Journal of Advanced Nursing*, Volume 22, pp226–34.

Kolb, D.A. (1984) *Experiential Learning: Experience as the Source of Learning and Development*, p38. Englewood Cliffs, New Jersey: Prentice-Hall.

Kottamp, R. (1990) *Means of Facilitating Reflection*. Education and Urban Society, 22.2, pp183–202. Sage Publications.

Leitch, S. (2006) *Leitch Review of Skills*. London: HM Treasury.

Mezirow, J. (1991) *Transformative Dimensions of Adult Learning*. San Francisco: Jossey-Bass.

Pedler, M. (2008) *Action Learning for Managers (2nd Edition)*. Surrey: Gower.

Reynolds, B. (1965) *Learning and Teaching in the Practice of Social Work* (2nd Edition). New York: Russell and Russell.

Rogers, J. (2007) *Adults Learning* (5th Edition). Maidenhead: Open University Press.

Schön, D. (1983) *The Reflective Practitioner*. New York: Basic Books.

Zuber-Skerritt, O. (1992) *Professional Development in Higher Education: a Theoretical Framework for Action Research* p103. London: Kogan Page.

Acts and Regulations

Data Protection Act (1998).

General Social Care Council (GSCC) Code of Practice.

National Occupational Standards (NOS).

The Care Quality Commission Essential Standards of Quality and Safety.

Websites and Web-based reports

Action Learning Associates. www.actionlearningassociates.co.uk, accessed 29 June 2012.

Department of Health. (2010) *A Vision for Adult Social Care: Capable Communities and Active Citizens*. DoH, London, www.dh.gov.uk, accessed 29 June 2012.

Care Quality Commission. www.cqc.org.uk, accessed 29 June 2012.

Care Quality Commission, www.cqc.org.uk/public/reports-surveys-and-reviews and www.cqc.org.uk/search/apachesolr_search/castlebeck, accessed 2 July 2012.

Care Quality Commission, www.cqc.org.uk/public/what-are-standards/standards/standards-care-homes, accessed 20 July 2012.

Equality and Human Rights Commission, www.equalityhumanrights.com/legal-and-policy/inquiries-and-assessments/inquiry-into-home-care-of-older-people/close-to-home-report/, accessed 20 July 2012.

NHS Ombudsman, *Care and compassion*, www.ombudsman.org.uk/improving-public-service/reports-and-consultations/reports/health/home, accessed 2 July 2012.

Parliamentary and Health Service Ombudsman. www.ombudsman.org.uk, accessed 29 June 2012.

Skills for Care. (2011) *Capable, Confident, Skilled: A Workforce Development Strategy for People Working, Supporting and Caring in Adult Social Care*. Skills for Care, Leeds

www.skillsforcare.org.uk/workforce_strategy/workforcedevelopmentstrategy/workforce_development_strategy.aspx, accessed 29 June 2012.

Chapter 3

Champion equality, diversity and inclusion

The purpose of this chapter is to assess the knowledge, understanding and skills required for a whole-systems approach to equality, diversity and inclusion. The chapter explores models of practice and requires a demonstration of skills and understanding of systems and processes.

By the end of this chapter you will:

1 Understand diversity, equality and inclusion in your own area of responsibility

2 Be able to champion diversity, equality and inclusion

3 Understand how to develop systems and processes that promote diversity, equality and inclusion

4 Be able to manage the risks presented when balancing individual rights and professional duty of care

Understand diversity, equality and inclusion in your own area of responsibility

Your role requires you to support individuals from a diverse range of backgrounds. This necessitates an egalitarian approach. You should uphold and promote equitable practice and offer equality of opportunity while taking into account people's political, economic, social and civil rights. As a manager in the social care sector you will be supporting people from a diverse range of backgrounds and cultures.

Equality is ensuring that everyone is treated equally and fairly regardless of their ability, religion, beliefs, race, gender, age, social status or sexual orientation.

Diversity is recognising people's differences, and valuing the contribution these make to an inclusive society for all. Inclusion therefore is the idea that every individual has the right to be 'included' without restriction or limitation and that everyone has the right to a sense of belonging in life and to feeling valued.

Activity

explain

1. Research and provide a clear definition of:

   ■ equality

   ■ diversity

   ■ inclusion.

3.1.1 Explain models of practice that underpin equality, diversity and inclusion in your own area of responsibility

At the heart of recent public sector reforms and the ethics of the personalisation agenda lies the promotion of an inclusive society, whereby people have the right to control the support they receive, make their own decisions about their lives and have the right not simply to be present within their own communities, but to participate actively and positively contribute. As a manager you will need to consider your own areas of responsibility within your workplace and how your practice can underpin the values and principles of equality, diversity and inclusion. In addition to this, your role will be to support and influence the practice of your staff, to ensure that everyone is treated equally and fairly without discrimination.

The policies and procedures within your workplace will be underpinned by a wide range of legislation and current codes of practice. These will provide you with a framework for working to ensure you uphold the principles and ethics of equality, diversity and inclusion.

There is a wide range of legislation and current codes of practice that provide a framework to model the policies and practice within your workplace.

Activity

1. To promote the values and principles of care and support successfully, consider whether you:

   - ensure equal access to opportunities to enable the people you support to participate fully in all activities

   - equip people with the skills to challenge inequality and discrimination

   - ensure that all policies, procedures and processes are non-discriminatory

   - ensure all resources are allocated fairly and equally.

It is important that you work within the code of practice in your area of responsibility and that you take into account the code when considering the conduct of your team. You need to lead your team to ensure they consider their own belief systems and the impact they may have. Policy updates can be shared through team meetings and in supervision, as well as training and personal development reviews.

Figure 3.1 It is important that you support your team to gain knowledge of equality, diversity and inclusion issues in the workplace and for the individuals you care for

You must demonstrate that you actively promote individuals' rights and choices and the equality of opportunity, as well as the values of privacy and dignity, confidentiality, individuality, independence and empowerment.

For example, consider how accessible information is about the organisation: is it suitable for people with sensory loss, i.e. are promotional leaflets available in Braille, or in voice-recorded formats? Are your complaints procedures clear and accessible? Are people supported in accessing independent advocacy services in order to have their views heard?

Activity

Consider codes of practice relevant to your area of responsibility.

1. Identify your responsibilities in relation to equality, diversity and inclusion.

2. For each area that you identify, give two examples of how you would meet your responsibility.

Activity

1. Do you promote a working environment that supports the values and principles of your organisation?

2. Demonstrate, by giving at least three examples, how you manage and lead your team to promote the following values and principles in your workplace:

   - Dignity
   - Privacy
   - Choice
   - Independence
   - Individuality

   - Empowerment
   - Confidentiality
   - Diversity
   - Equality
   - Inclusion

A person-centred approach is a model of practice that ensures individuals are central to the planning of their support; it is an opportunity to discover an individual's personal history and diversity. It ensures individuals are empowered to identify personal choices about how they wish to live their lives.

3.1.2 Analyse the potential effects of barriers to equality, diversity and inclusion in your own area of responsibility

Barriers that prevent equality and inclusion can be based on individuals' ethnic origin, sexual orientation, age, beliefs, gender, religion, disability, mental or physical health (including communication and language).

Table 3.1 Barriers that prevent equality and inclusion

Barrier	Examples
Physical	Buildings and access, personal physical health, sensory loss
Attitudinal	Personal feelings, thoughts, behaviours
Structural	Economic, environmental, social systems
Institutional	Policies and procedures where some people are disadvantaged over others, e.g. maternity leave/paternity leave

Activity

1. Consider three activities within your work setting and identify barriers that could potentially impact on these. For example, when supporting two people to go to a restaurant for lunch: if one person uses a wheelchair and the other person makes loud noises to communicate, potential barriers to ensuring that both have equal opportunities to benefit from the activity could include:

   - restaurant accessibility for people who use a wheelchair (physical barrier)

   - negative responses of other diners towards a person's method of communication (attitudinal barrier).

Oppression is the consequence of five different factors. This is best explained using the example below of the 'cycle of oppression'. It is the momentum of the different factors that keeps the cycle going.

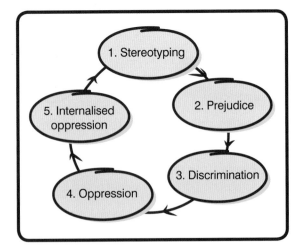

Figure 3.2 The cycle of oppression

The five factors are as follows:

1. Stereotyping: This is a preconceived generalisation about a group of people and their individual differences. Stereotypes form the basis of our prejudices. An example is the preconceived generalisation that all young people who wear hooded tops have anti-social behaviours.

2. Prejudice: A conscious or unconscious negative belief about a group of people and its individual members. Discrimination is the result of the person in power denying opportunity and resources to others.

3. Discrimination: This occurs when prejudice and power combine. Discrimination can take many forms including racism, sexism, ableism, ageism, etc. Many acts of discrimination build up over time. Perpetuated against one relatively less powerful social group, this leads to the less powerful group being forced into a state of oppression.

4. Oppression: This is the systematic subjugation of a group of people by a more powerful group, the result of which benefits one group over the other; it is maintained by social beliefs and practices. Target group members often believe the messages, and internalise the oppression.

5. Internalised oppression: 'Buying into' the elements of oppression by the target group who conform to the perceived stereotypes of the more powerful group.

Activity

1. Look at the 'cycle of oppression' in Figure 3.2, explain how each stage is perpetuated. Relate these stages to an example from your own area of responsibility. Consider:

   ■ direct discrimination

   ■ indirect discrimination

   ■ dual discrimination.

Failure to uphold equality, diversity and inclusion through your practice will breach European and UK law and codes of practice and incur penalties including loss of registration and significant damage to reputation.

Consequences for the individual range from low self-esteem, poor mental and physical health and risk of harm and abuse. If people are treated in a negative and oppressive manner, they can lose confidence and become isolated. This in turn could lead to an experience of **learned helplessness** and disempowerment.

Key Term

Learned helplessness means the act of giving up trying as a result of consistent failure to be rewarded.

Effects of discrimination include:

■ diminished life chances

■ social exclusion

■ marginalisation

■ poor interpersonal interactions and communication

■ disempowerment

■ low self-esteem and self-identity.

Activity | In Practice

You manage a house for three adults with mental health needs. The home is in a small residential suburb at the edge of a busy town.

In the town is a hospital, which was the main treatment centre for people with mental health needs. The site is to close and the 24 people who still live there are to be supported to find suitable accommodation in the local area.

The local media has run a series of features over the past few days providing a forum for local people to share their views on the announcement. Headlines have included: 'Mental patients to run loose in our town' and 'Are you concerned about your new neighbours?'

1. How will you support the people who live in the house you manage?

Activity

1. Research the relevant Acts, regulations, guidance and codes of practice currently informing policy and best practice in your area of responsibility.

2. Consider:

   ■ the impact of these on your practice and how they shape the policies and practices within your area of responsibility

   ■ your own and your team's development and improvement needs.

3.1.3 Analyse the impact of legislation and policy initiatives on the promotion of equality, diversity and inclusion in your own area of responsibility

You will need to be familiar with the Acts of Parliament, regulations, guidance and codes of practice currently informing policy and best practice in your area of responsibility. These include:

■ The Disability Discrimination Act (1995)

■ The NHS and Community Care Act (1990)

■ The Mental Health Act (1983)

■ The Equality Act (2010).

Be able to champion diversity, equality and inclusion

3.2.1 Promote equality, diversity and inclusion in policy and practice

As a leader, you will have an important role to play in championing diversity, equality and inclusion within your workplace. You should articulate your own values and beliefs regarding diversity, recognising equality, respect and tolerance, and encourage non-judgemental attitudes and anti-discriminatory practice in order to inspire and lead your team. You will need to consider how you can actively demonstrate anti-discriminatory practice and the importance of challenging overt and covert discrimination with the use of legislation and codes of practice.

Activity

1. What processes do you have in place to promote equality, diversity and inclusion in your workplace?

2. What processes do you need to develop?

Think about quality assurance systems, record keeping, monitoring and evaluating process, auditing and inspections.

Consider whether you and your team keep up to date with new developments by asking yourself the following questions:

- Do you discuss equality, diversity and inclusion in supervision, staff training and meetings?

- Are staff clear on their roles and accountability and the principles of promotion?

- Is there a clear management structure that supports and promotes through enforcement and compliance?

- Are there activities and opportunities for promotion?

3.2.2 Challenge discrimination and exclusion in policy and practice

When discrimination and exclusion occur in policy and practice, you have a duty of care to challenge it. You should review and monitor situations and identify and give examples of best practice. You can promote and exemplify good practice by:

- undertaking supervision

- encouraging reflective practice to consider individual roles and accountability

- maintaining quality assurance systems and record keeping

- monitoring and evaluating processes.

Figure 3.3 You have a duty of care to challenge discrimination and exclusion, and promote best practice

It is important that you challenge barriers, prevent exclusion and work to promote equality and diversity by tailoring support to individual preferences. A vital part of this is ensuring that the individuals you support are themselves involved in the design and review of their support plan and care programme.

Activity

1. Outline your response to the following situations:

   - You have received a complaint from a member of your staff regarding a service user who has reportedly refused to accept support from them on the grounds that they are 'not white'.

   - A service user has complained to you that they are not being included in meal planning and they believe that this is because they are a vegan.

   - A member of your staff has requested not to work on Sundays due to religious preferences.

Activity

1. Research the following and give **three** examples for each bullet point.

   - Why is it essential to challenge discrimination and exclusion?

   - What are the positive and negative effects of discrimination and exclusion?

   - What are the short- and long-term effects of discrimination and exclusion?

3.2.3 Provide others with information about the effects of discrimination, the impact of inclusion and the value of diversity

It is often necessary to provide others with information, for example about their roles and responsibilities or about policy and practice reforms.

1. Research and develop a presentation for your team that considers the following:

   ■ The positive and negative effects of discrimination, for example unemployment and inequality.

   ■ The impact of inclusion on self-esteem, health, equality, and team and partnership working.

   ■ The value of diversity, for example increased knowledge of other cultures and increased opportunities.

3.2.4 Support others to challenge discrimination and exclusion

It is important that you consider how you can encourage a positive culture within the workplace that promotes the principles of good practice and where working in an inclusive way is the norm. Examples of opportunities include:

■ developing and delivering training and Continuing Professional Development (CPD) reviews so that you and your team keep up to date with new developments

■ identification of your own and others' contributions through reviewing practice, undertaking **SWOT** analyses and updating policies and procedures

■ providing a safe environment where people feel empowered and supported to challenge discrimination and poor practice

■ identifying dilemmas and applying a risk–benefit analysis approach by supporting others to identify and consider risks, resource implications and differing priorities between stakeholders and partners.

1. Does your organisation promote an environment that values diversity and the ethics of inclusion?

2. Undertake a SWOT analysis of your organisation's commitment to anti-discriminatory practice.

3. What steps could you take to improve your practice, for example implementing an action plan?

SWOT stands for:

Strengths

Weaknesses

Opportunities

Threats.

Understand how to develop systems and processes that promote diversity, equality and inclusion

3.3

3.3.1 Analyse how systems and processes can promote equality and inclusion or reinforce discrimination and exclusion

Every organisation's procedures and policies are informed by legislation and national guidelines that promote anti-discriminatory practice. Your organisation will have a Mission Statement (or similar) that will detail the ways in which it intends to create a positive working environment whereby the shared principles and values of good quality support are upheld throughout the organisation.

The effectiveness of this approach will need to be monitored:

■ A regular review and audit of policies and practice will identify areas to be addressed.

■ Individual and family questionnaires can identify areas that require improvement, but also highlight areas of good practice and provide the benchmarks for reviewing and monitoring practice within the workplace.

■ Complaints procedures can contribute to providing evidence in particular cases.

Remember

Developing and maintaining effective complaints procedures will enable you to identify areas relating to diversity and equality, which require improvement.

■ Look at your own internal auditing processes for identifying complaints, recognising key issues, recording relevant actions and tracking resolutions.

■ Consider how this process can be fully inclusive by producing and collecting complaint information in accessible formats for service users as well as providing them with feedback on progress.

Sometimes organisations can discriminate inadvertently through policies and procedures that lead to disadvantages for certain groups. This is referred to as institutional discrimination.

Activity | *In Practice*

The following is an excerpt from an article published in February 2012 on the Public Service website (www.publicservice.co.uk):

'Institutional Discrimination "caused NHS deaths"'

The mental health charity Mencap has accused the NHS of continuing to practise 'institutional discrimination' and to have caused the deaths of 74 people with learning disabilities. ('Death by indifference: 74 deaths and counting': Mencap). The charity found that many health professionals were still failing to provide adequate care to people with a learning disability… The new report highlighted the deaths of 74 people over the last 10 years which were 'a direct result of institutional discrimination'.

Typical mistakes made by healthcare professionals… included failing to abide by disability discrimination law, ignoring crucial advice from families, and failing to meet even basic care needs. Mencap reckoned this situation was 'underpinned by an assumption by some health care professionals that people with a learning disability are not worth treating'.

1. Read Mencap's report 'Death by indifference: 74 deaths and counting' (www.Mencap.org.uk). Consider the steps you could take to ensure institutional discrimination does not occur within your own organisation.

Activity

Equality Impact Assessments review a service, policy, procedure or initiative to establish whether there is a negative impact on particular social groups (whether employee or service user). The purpose of Equality Impact Assessments is to identify:

- the extent of any impact on particular social groups

- whether that impact is negative

- other ways of working, which can remove or reduce the negative impact.

1. Undertake an equality impact assessment of a service, policy, procedure or initiative in your workplace.

3.3.2 Evaluate the effectiveness of systems and processes in promoting equality, diversity and inclusion in your own area of responsibility

Reflecting on the effectiveness of systems and processes that are in place to promote equality, diversity and inclusion will identify the improvements required to contribute to the health, self-esteem and happiness of the people you support as well as your staff. It is essential that you are able to identify good practice and improve or eliminate poor practice.

Activity

1. Undertake checks to ensure that your policies and procedures are current, up to date and reflecting current legislation.

2. Identify the gaps and plan and implement any necessary improvements. Think about what you need to measure and how you can do this.

3.3.3 Propose improvements to address gaps or shortfalls in systems and processes

Once you have evaluated the policies, procedures and practices of your organisation and identified any gaps, you will need to plan how you will improve these.

You will need to involve your team and the people you support through consultation processes and meetings. Be clear of the changes required to benefit the people you support and the organisation as a whole. Give timescales for these improvements to be made, and identify how you can monitor and audit them, to ensure that any amendments to systems and processes have a positive impact.

An inclusive workplace requires an approach to action planning that involves everyone. Key steps are to:

- identify what it is that you want to achieve and what the benefits are for the people you support, the organisation, staff and external partners (for example family members)

- identify areas of good inclusive practice and areas requiring improvement

- prioritise and devise a plan of action

- communicate with relevant parties and delegate tasks and responsibilities so that everyone involved takes 'ownership' of the plan

- detail how you intend to allocate resources within the organisation to meet your recommendations

- review, monitor and evaluate any impact that the plan has, and use this as the basis for future service planning.

Be able to manage the risks presented when balancing individual rights and professional duty of care

3.4

3.4.1 Describe ethical dilemmas that may arise when balancing individual rights and duty of care

Ethical dilemmas arise frequently throughout the social care sector. There are a number of areas where you will find your own views may be different from other people's, including the following:

- Confidentiality versus disclosure ('the right to know'): In certain circumstances, you may have to break confidentiality and share information with someone else. You will need to do this when there is a significant risk of harm, exploitation, abuse or significant financial gain or loss. All local authorities and providers of social care support are required to have a Safeguarding Vulnerable Adults Procedure for organisations and individuals to follow. Do you know yours? Familiarise yourself with the Mental Health Act and **Mental Capacity Act 2005 and Best Interest Assessment**.

Key Term

The Mental Capacity Act 2005 (MCA 2005) and Best Interest Assessment

The MCA 2005 provides a framework for decision making when a person lacks capacity to make a particular decision or take a particular action for themselves.

The five principles of the Assessment are:

1. Presume capacity unless established otherwise.

2. Take practical steps to enable decision making.

3. Accept that people can make unwise decisions.

4. Act in the person's best interest.

5. Use the action least restrictive of the person's rights and freedom of choice.

Activity

1. Consider, in relation to your own working setting, where potential rights and responsibilities may clash. How would you respond to the following examples?

   ■ A person you work with may choose not to eat for 24 hours as they wish to take part in a religious fast; however, they have a medical condition that requires they eat regularly so it is safe to take their medication.

   ■ A resident likes to have friends over to chat late into the night; another resident likes to go to bed early and does not like 'strangers' in their house.

   ■ An individual you support has epilepsy and chooses to lock their door at night. You are concerned as they could be at risk from seizures and staff need to access their room through the night to check they have come to no harm.

■ Own beliefs and values: Each of us have a unique set of values and beliefs, and strive to live our lives by these. The same is true for the people that you support. Occasionally, your own values and beliefs may be different from those of the people that you are supporting.

Activity

1. Think of **three** situations where your own values and beliefs may be different from those of the people that you support.

2. What are the implications for your own practice and for the organisation?

■ The management of resources: The principle of good quality support is to enable people to maintain their independence. Support costs financially (money) and in personnel (support workers). Balancing good support with available resources can be a challenge.

Activity

1. Consider where management of resources challenges your own practice within your workplace.

■ Organisational policy: It may be an organisation's policy that, in line with safety at work procedures, a member of support staff is never left alone in the building in which they work. While there will be solid reasoning behind these policies, they may also impact negatively on the supported person.

Activity

1. Consider an organisational policy within your workplace that presents you with an ethical dilemma.

■ Balancing the needs of the family and the needs of the individual: Social care and support should take into account the views of an individual's family. However, your key responsibility is to ensure that the individual is in control of their own lives, and at the centre of all decisions made about their support. Sometimes you may need to support the person to challenge their family's views, or to work with an advocate.

Activity — In Practice

Melanie wants to move out of her parents' house and into her own flat with support. Her parents are very reluctant and believe that Melanie does not have the skills to live independently. They are worried that Melanie will be very vulnerable due to her mental health support needs.

1. As the manager of Melanie's support team, how can you work with the individual and family to balance their needs while also meeting your duty of care and valuing Melanie's rights?

3.4.2 Explain the principle of informed choice

For some people, making complex decisions and choices requires additional support. There are different processes for decision making when considering long- or short-term choices. An informed choice is when an individual is supported to make a decision. You will have a responsibility to provide someone with all the necessary information to make those decisions. The individual accepts a shared responsibility for the choice that they make, and a shared responsibility for the outcome.

Figure 3.4 You have a responsibility to support all individuals in your care to make decisions about their lives

You should be mindful of the range of accessible information the individual requires, in order for them to be able to make the decision and this information must be unbiased and evidence based. Evaluate the nature of the decision being considered, how the individual communicates and who else may need to be involved, such as family members or an advocate. It is important that the individual's values are respected, and that you promote an enabling environment that empowers the decision maker.

It is vital that you have informed consent, which should be based on a clear appreciation and understanding of the facts and the implications and future consequences of an action.

3.4.3 Explain how individual capacity may affect informed choice

Issues of individual capacity may affect informed choice. This could be because of someone's physical or mental health, statutes of the law or diversity issues, for example in relation to someone's culture, religion, age or communication skills.

The Mental Capacity Act (2005), code of practice states:

- Every adult has the right to make their own decisions if they have the capacity to do so. You must assume that a person has capacity unless it can be established otherwise.

- Individuals should receive support to help them make their own decisions and all possible steps should be taken to try to help them reach a decision.

- Individuals have the right to make decisions that others might think are unwise. Making an 'unwise' decision does not mean that a person lacks capacity.

Activity

1. Identify how issues of capacity affect informed choice.

Activity **In Practice**

April has terminal cancer and has started to refuse her medication. There is general concern among your team that due to April's learning disability and the effects of her illness, she may not have the capacity to make decisions about her medication and end-of-life care.

1. What strategies do you need to put into practice?

3.4.4 Propose a strategy to manage risks when balancing individual rights and duty of care in your own area of responsibility

If individuals make 'unwise decisions', how will you manage this? As a manager, you will frequently need to consider strategies for managing risks when balancing individual rights and your duty of care.

Risk assessment and appropriate procedures should be part of your organisation's policy framework.

■ Risk management to enable risk (referred to as 'positive risk taking') considers current relevant legislation and devises action plans to manage, mitigate and where necessary eradicate risk.

■ Action plans consider the potential benefits and potential harm caused as a consequence of the risk being carried out (or not being carried out).

Activity

1. Consider individual beliefs. How can these impact on risk assessments?

Risk management must be a continuous process within your organisation. You will need to highlight this through team meetings, and by undertaking regular monitoring and review to identify current and potential risks. Ensure everyone is clear about their responsibilities for managing risks. Create and encourage a culture of mutual accountability, whereby the individual you are supporting, their family and friends and other relevant partnerships, work cohesively to manage positive risk assessment.

Remember

The principles of positive risk taking in self-directed care:

■ Balance the risk of harm with the benefits of increased independence and choice.

■ Enable people to make informed choices.

■ Support people to manage risks.

■ Ensure mutual accountability for all choices and decisions.

■ Keep people informed before, during and after assessment and support planning.

■ Promote flexibility and innovation when managing risk.

Are you ready for assessment?

- ✔ Do you know the models of practice that underpin equality, diversity and inclusion in your own area of responsibility?

- ✔ Do you know the potential effects of barriers to equality and inclusion in your own area of responsibility?

- ✔ Do you know the impact of legislation and policy initiatives on the promotion of equality, diversity and inclusion in your own area of responsibility?

- ✔ Do you know how systems and processes can promote equality and inclusion or reinforce discrimination and exclusion?

- ✔ Do you know how effective systems and processes are in promoting equality, diversity and inclusion in your own area of responsibility?

- ✔ Do you know how to propose improvements which will address gaps or shortfalls in systems and processes?

- ✔ Do you know the ethical dilemmas that may arise in your own area of responsibility when balancing individual rights and duty of care?

- ✔ Do you know the principles of informed choice?

- ✔ Do you know how issues of individual capacity may affect informed choice?

- ✔ Can you promote equality, diversity and inclusion in policy and practice?

- ✔ Can you challenge discrimination and exclusion in policy and practice?

- ✔ Can you provide others with information about the effects of discrimination, the impact of inclusion and the value of diversity?

- ✔ Can you support others to challenge discrimination and exclusion?

- ✔ Can you propose a strategy to manage risks when balancing individual rights and duty of care in your own area of responsibility?

References

Council of Europe (2010) *European Convention on Human Rights*.

Acts and Regulations

Disability Discrimination Act (1995).

Equality Act (2010).

Mental Health Act and Mental Capacity Act (2005).

Mental Health Act (1983).

NHS and Community Care Act (1990).

Websites

Care Quality Commission, www.cqc.org.uk, accessed 29 June 2012.

Equality and Human Rights Commission, www.equalityhumanrights.com, accessed 29 June 2012.

General Social Care Council, www.gscc.org.uk, accessed 29 June 2012.

Government Equalities Office, www.equalities.gov.uk, accessed 29 June 2012.

Improvement and Development Agency, www.idea.gov.uk, accessed 29 June 2012.

Joseph Rowntree Foundation, www.jrf.org.uk, accessed 29 June 2012.

Mencap, www.mencap.org.uk, accessed 29 June 2012.

National Minimum Standards, www.dh.gov.uk, accessed 29 June 2012.

Social Exclusion Task Force, www.cabinetoffice.gov.uk/social_exclusion_task_force.aspx, accessed 29 June 2012.

The Nursing and Midwifery Council, www.nmc-uk.org, accessed 29 June 2012.

Public Service, www.publicservice.co.uk, accessed 29 June 2012.

Develop health and safety **and risk management** policies, procedures and practices in health and social care settings

This chapter will help you understand your responsibilities relating to health and safety, of which a significant aspect is managing risks (in modern terms this now translates as enabling risks). In order to do this, you will need to ensure you have a sound understanding of the legislation that informs your policies and procedures, so you can implement them and ensure compliance within your service. A key to enabling risks is balancing choices with the potential for harm, and there are close links to safeguarding. Finally, evaluation and improvement of practice is an ongoing task in order to ensure safe practices.

By the end of this chapter you will:

1 Understand the current legislative framework and organisational health, safety and risk management policies, procedures and practices

2 Be able to implement and monitor compliance with health, safety and risk management requirements

3 Be able to lead the implementation of policies, procedures and practices to manage risk to individuals and others

4 Be able to promote a culture where needs and risks are balanced with health and safety practice

5 Be able to improve health, safety and risk management policies, procedures and practices

Understand the current legislative framework and organisational health, safety and risk management policies, procedures and practices

4.1

Health and safety is a legal requirement, closely monitored by the Health and Safety Executive (HSE), and it applies to all health and social care environments. As a manager, it is your responsibility to ensure you have adequate policies, procedures and practices in place. Breaches of health and safety requirements can have serious consequences, both for individuals and organisations. This brings into sharp focus the responsibility to take all reasonable measures to keep individuals safe, whether service users, staff or any individuals visiting a service.

4.1.1 Explain the legislative framework for health, safety and risk management in the work setting

The Health and Safety at Work Act (1974), sets out the duties of employers to take measures to protect the safety of others 'so far as is reasonably practicable'. The Management of Health and Safety at Work **Regulations** (1999) (the Management Regulations) are more explicit and, like the Act, apply to every work activity. The main requirement on employers with five or more staff is to carry out risk assessments. As health and safety is a legal requirement it will form the basis of many of your policies and procedures. As a manager, it is important that you understand the links between legislation, policy and

practice as this will help you to implement them and ensure compliance, which is your responsibility.

Key Term

Regulations are the law, and prescribe a specific course of action, which must be complied with.

Figure 4.1 Keeping up to date with legislation and its implementation in your policies and practice will ensure compliance

1. Create a table like the one below (which has been started for you) and complete it using the following list of regulations:

- Health and Safety at Work Act (HSAWA) (1974).

- Management of Health and Safety at Work Regulations (1999) (amended 2003).

- Personal Protective Equipment at Work Regulations (1992).

- Provision and Use of Work Equipment Regulations (1998).

- Manual Handling Operations Regulations (1992).

- Health and Safety (First Aid) Regulations (1981).

- Health and Safety Information for Employees Regulations (1989).

- Reporting of Injuries, Diseases and Dangerous Occurrences Regulations (RIDDOR) (1995).

- Electricity at Work Regulations (1989).

- Control of Substances Hazardous to Health Regulations (2002) (COSHH).

- Food Safety Act 1990 and Food Hygiene Regulations (2006).

- Regulatory Reform (Fire Safety) (2005).

- The Human Medicines Regulations (2012).

Regulation	Policies and procedures within the workplace	Examples of how they are implemented in practice	Examples of how compliance is monitored	How does it meet requirements?
Manual Handing Regulations (1992)	Risk assessments policy Manual handling policy Moving and handling policy Health and safety policy	Risk assessment in place Relevant training and updates Appropriate equipment, suitably maintained.	Monthly reviews of risk assessments Audits for training Spot checks Monthly health and safety audits covering equipment Supervision	Direct links to specification stated in regulations Compliant with HSAWA

2. As you complete the table, consider how your policies, procedures and practices meet the legal requirements.

Further information can be found via the Health and Safety Executive website, www.hse.gov.uk

Chapter 4 | **Develop health and safety and risk management policies, procedures and practices in health and social care settings**

59

4.1.2 Analyse how policies, procedures and practices in own setting meet health, safety and risk management requirements

Undertaking the above activity should enable you to analyse and reflect upon how well your service meets requirements in terms of legislation. If you are in a regulated service then you will also be subject to the Care Quality Commission's (CQC) Essential Standards of Quality and Safety. Health and safety impacts on many areas of practice, and as such is reflected over a number of CQC outcomes. The main outcomes relating to health and safety are listed in Table 4.1.

Table 4.1 CQC's Essential Standards relating to health and safety

Regulation	Outcome	Title and summary of outcome
9	4	Care and welfare of people who use services: people experience effective, safe and appropriate care, treatment and support that meet their needs and protect their rights.
10	16	Assessing and monitoring the quality of service provision: people benefit from safe, quality care because effective decisions are made and because of the management of risks to people's health, welfare and safety.
11	7	Safeguarding people who use services from abuse: people are safeguarded from abuse, or the risk of abuse, and their human rights are respected and upheld.
12	8	Cleanliness and infection control: people experience care in a clean environment, and are protected from acquiring infections.
13	9	Management of medicines: people have their medicines when they need them, and in a safe way. People are given information about their medicines.
14	5	Meeting nutritional needs: people are encouraged and supported to have sufficient food and drink that is nutritional and balanced, and a choice of food and drink to meet their different needs.
15	10	Safety and suitability of premises: people receive care in, work in or visit safe surroundings that promote their well-being.
16	11	Safety, availability and suitability of equipment: where equipment is used, it is safe, available, comfortable and suitable for people's needs.

This is a press release issued following an inspection by the CQC taken from their website.

The Care Quality Commission (CQC) has told an NHS Foundation Trust that if it does not take immediate steps to improve standards of its mental health services, enforcement action may follow. The demand for action comes as the regulator publishes a responsive review report and a Mental Health Annual Statement (December 2010) report which highlight findings and recommendations for improvements to care. The responsive review was triggered by concerns which led the regulator to examine the trust's compliance with their essential standards of quality and safety through assessing information held about the trust and carrying out three visits to the trust.

CQC inspectors found the trust to be in breach of five regulations covering:

- care and welfare
- safeguarding people
- safety and suitability of premises.
- staffing
- assessing and monitoring service provision

The Mental Health Act Annual Statement report 2010 outlines a series of MHA Commissioners' recommendations on how the trust must continue to comply with the Mental Health Act and Codes of Practice when detaining patients under the Act. The Annual Statement reflects the findings of Commissioners during visits over eight months between February and October 2010. Commissioners reported that the trust had responded constructively to the findings from those visits. However, some concerns had not been fully addressed and these have been taken into account in CQC's recent review.

Failing to meet five essential standards

The CQC inspectors found that the trust was not meeting five essential standards and has concerns in these areas:

Care and welfare of people who use services

- Not all care plans were person centred or included information regarding each individual's wider care and inclusion needs.
- The seclusion suite on one ward is not meeting environmental requirements or the requirements of the Mental Health Act (1983) Code of Practice.

Safeguarding vulnerable people who use services from abuse

- Policies in relation to adult safeguarding and incident reporting do not clearly set out arrangements that ensure consistent reporting, investigation and dissemination of learning in relation to matters regarding cases of abuse allegations and incidents.
- Incident reporting and auditing systems are not robust.

Safety and suitability of premises

- Poorly designed fixed furniture and the presence of potential ligature points in some parts of the premises pose a risk to people who use services.
- The standard of décor and maintenance of one ward does not promote the dignity and well-being of people using services.

continues

Staffing

- There are not always sufficient numbers of staff with the right competencies, knowledge, qualifications, skills and experience available to meet the needs of patients.

Assessing and monitoring the quality of service provision

- There is a lack of consistency in grading of incidents and no safety mechanism to ensure that inconsistencies are identified and resolved.

- There are delays in the time it takes between staff reporting incidents and their managers signing off the processes.

CQC East Regional Director Frances Carey said: "The trust has already positively responded and submitted action plans which set out how they intend to meet essential standards."

"We will be monitoring this trust closely and won't hesitate to use our enforcement powers if these improvements are not made swiftly."

1. Consider how these failings occurred.

2. What could be put in place to ensure such failings do not recur?

Be able to implement and monitor compliance with health, safety and risk management requirements

4.2

4.2.1 Demonstrate compliance with health, safety and risk management procedures

A key aspect of your role as manager is to ensure that:

■ all staff comply with policies and procedures, are vigilant for risks and understand their role and responsibilities

■ induction and training is robust and covers all aspects of health and safety

■ all staff know what records and reports to complete and when to make checks

■ regular audits are undertaken to monitor compliance

■ systems are in place to ensure all risk assessments are updated either by a dedicated health and safety officer for general risks or by a key worker for service user risks.

Figure 4.2 A key aspect of management is ensuring proper training and induction processes in health and safety

Remember

Make health and safety part of the set agenda for both staff meetings and supervisions. Ask staff to read out a health and safety policy at every staff meeting as a reminder for all. If you do not already subscribe, sign up for updates from the HSE at: www.hse.gov.uk

The Management Standards (available at www.hse.gov.uk/stress/standards/index.htm) represent a set of conditions that, if present, reflect a high level of health well-being and organisational performance. They cover six key areas of **work design** that, if not properly managed, are associated with poor health and well-being, lower productivity and increased sickness absence. In other words, the six Management Standards cover the primary sources of stress at work. These are:

■ Demands   ■ Relationships

■ Control   ■ Role

■ Support   ■ Change.

Key Term

Work design means to improve both job satisfaction and quality, and to reduce employee problems such as absenteeism or grievances.

Chapter 4 | **Develop health and safety and risk management policies, procedures and practices in health and social care settings**

63

1. Reflect on how your service supports staff in relation to the six points on page 63 and complete a table to note how this is done.

4.2.2 Support others to comply with legislative and organisational health, safety and risk management policies, procedures and practices relevant to their work

As well as staff who must follow health and safety regulations, there are also the service users and various other visitors to the provision such as family, friends and professionals who must comply as well. There will also be the less frequent visitors, such as contractors or even inspectors and regulators. You need to have the systems in place to ensure everyone's health and safety.

We have focused already on how staff can be supported to comply with health and safety regulations.

1. Consider how all the others listed can be supported and whether you have the systems in place to ensure this happens. Examples of areas to reflect on are security, fire safety, infection control, electrical safety, COSHH and challenging behaviours.

4.2.3 Explain the actions to take when health, safety and risk management policies, procedures and practices are not being complied with

The starting point as a manager is for you to feel sure that adequate time and training has been dedicated to health and safety so there can be no excuse for non-compliance by staff. Non-compliance might be picked up in an audit or via a report or directly observing something of concern. It might also be highlighted during an inspection from the HSE or Environmental Health, Fire Brigade, CQC or Supporting People. It is always preferable to have the systems in place, such as regular audits, to identify potential issues before inspectors arrive!

However non-compliance is identified, action will be needed to address it. As a manager you need to consider how effective the systems you have in place are; is it a system fault or that of an individual? The latter might lead to a standard setting exercise to monitor an individual staff member's practice with additional training, mentoring and shadowing being put in place. However, if the issue was serious enough it could also lead to a staff disciplinary. If it is the system that is at fault, this needs to be quickly remedied and then communicated to all relevant staff.

Dealing with service user non-compliance of health and safety needs more careful consideration. If it is a straightforward case of a breach of health and safety law then action is clear, but if it surrounds managing individual risk you need to be balancing this with choice.

1. Consider the following scenarios and the actions you would take as a manager:

   ■ A care assistant is doing the laundry on the ground floor and is wearing disposable gloves. The front door bell rings and she answers the door with her gloves still on.

   ■ A wheelchair battery is being charged in a hallway as the plug in the normal room used is out of action.

   ■ You notice a support worker helping a service user up after she has tripped and fallen on a step. The service user does not appear hurt but is keen to get back to her room and asks the support worker to 'give her a hand'.

   ■ The cleaning trolley and laundry collection bin is left unattended in the hall while the cleaner goes with a care assistant to show her where a service user's clothes have been hung.

   ■ A service user has been removing her soiled pads and placing them in her bedroom waste bin.

Despite the decline in proactive inspections, various enforcement actions could still be taken by the HSE – depending on the gravity of the non-compliance – but these would obviously be for larger, systemic breaches than lapses in procedure. These would include informal guidance, an improvement notice, a prohibition notice or prosecution if no actions are taken.

All this is once again a reminder of the potential consequences of not meeting health and safety requirements. If a fatality were to occur as a result of a breach and possible negligence then the Corporate Manslaughter and Homicide Act (2007) could be used. This was introduced to hold individuals, generally at a senior level, accountable in the event of a death occurring.

4.2.4 Complete records and reports on health, safety and risk management issues according to legislative and organisational requirements

In order to effectively manage health and safety and ensure compliance, records are vital. They should be in good order and follow the principles of the Data Protection Act (1998).

As with any written record, health and safety records could potentially be used in a court of law as evidence. Also, as regulations are a legal requirement, it is necessary to show evidence of compliance to the relevant authorities. Completion of accident and incident reports is critical as a way to both record and monitor anything of concern. It is good practice to ensure also that any actions are documented. Some organisations will also record 'near misses' as a way to highlight potential issues.

Additionally under RIDDOR (1995), anything of a serious nature must be reported. This could be matters such as a serious injury or even a death, anything listed as a reportable disease or any other major incident that causes danger.

Undertaking regular audits is an additional safeguard to ensure that relevant records are being completed and are accurate, legible and fit for purpose. Remember, the clearer your recording systems are, the more likely they are to be completed appropriately.

Chapter 4 | **Develop health and safety and risk management policies, procedures and practices in health and social care settings**

65

This is an example of a health and safety breach taken from the (Health and Safety Executive (HSE) website.

A care home company has been fined £150,000 following a prosecution by the HSE after a pensioner died at a nursing home in Birmingham. Seventy-four-year-old Brigid O'Callaghan, known as Vera, died after being strangled by a lap belt when she was left strapped in a wheelchair overnight. Birmingham Crown Court heard today that staff at one of the company's nursing homes, did not properly check on Mrs O'Callaghan on the night of 27 October 2005, leaving her in a wheelchair in her room rather than helping her to bed. She was discovered dead the next morning by a member of staff, having slipped from the seat of the wheelchair to the floor, with the lap belt strap around her neck.

An HSE investigation into safety standards at the home following Mrs O'Callaghan's death found more than 15 failings in her treatment. The court heard that the home had failed to carry out a proper risk assessment and care plan for Mrs O'Callaghan's stay, did not communicate her needs to staff, failed to ensure she could call for help and did not monitor whether night-time checks were carried out. HSE inspectors also identified more than ten further potential hazards that put residents at risk, ranging from a cluttered corridor to dirty conditions. These included the absence of window restraints; excessive water temperature in two bathrooms; failure to secure a laundry room; tripping hazards and charging a battery in a corridor; storing lifting slings over a handrail; inappropriate treatment of waste items and laundry; dirty conditions of a shower and toilet; inappropriate storage of items in bathrooms; failure to secure a housekeeping room; a cluttered corridor; insufficient resources for an adequate maintenance programme; insufficient monitoring of the management of the home; and lack of staff training.

The care home company pleaded guilty to two breaches of Section 3(1) of the Health and Safety at Work Act (1974). The first charge focused on the issues most closely connected to Mrs O'Callaghan's death and the second on the potential hazards for the other residents. The company was fined £150,000 in total and ordered to pay £150,000 in costs.

HSE inspector Sarah Palfreyman said:

"Mrs O'Callaghan's death was a preventable tragedy caused by a shocking case of mismanagement. The managers of this, and indeed all care homes, have a duty of care for their residents. At the very least they should be making sure that residents are comfortable and safe at night, not left in a wheelchair. There were some awful conditions for the elderly residents to live in and hazards that could easily have caused them serious injury. The home's managers were not given appropriate monitoring or supervision and as a result the staff were not being properly trained or monitored. Working in a care home is a specialised job and it's vital that all employees have the correct training in place, which in this instance, they did not."

1. What failings occurred within this home to contribute to this tragedy?

2. What systems could have been implemented to help prevent such a tragedy?

Further examples can be located at 'the EHP' website theehp.com by searching for 'prosecutions in brief'.

Be able to lead the implementation of policies, procedures and practices to manage risk to individuals and others

4.3

4.3.1 Contribute to development of policies, procedures and practices to identify, assess and manage risk to individuals and others

As previously stated, as a manager it is your responsibility to identify and take action to limit any risks within your setting. The key tool to managing **risks** is your risk assessment system. There are many different formats in use and it is for you to consider if they are fit for purpose and relevant for your service. The HSE recommend 'Five steps to risk assessment' (see Figure 4.3), but this is just one method.

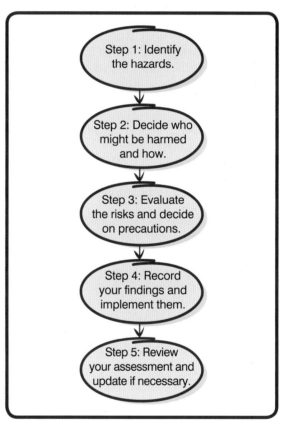

Figure 4.3 The HSE's 'Five steps to risk assessment'

There are many potential risks in a health and social care environment such as:

- using equipment
- contact with hazardous chemicals or waste
- handling medication
- environmental **hazards**.

Chapter 4 | **Develop health and safety and risk management policies, procedures and practices in health and social care settings**

67

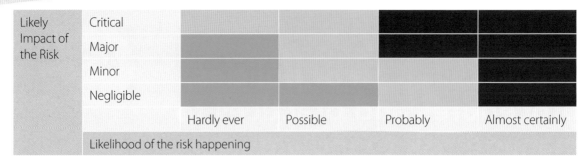

Likely Impact of the Risk	Critical				
	Major				
	Minor				
	Negligible				
		Hardly ever	Possible	Probably	Almost certainly
	Likelihood of the risk happening				

Figure 4.4 A standard matrix based on traffic lights to assess risk

Furthermore, there may be individual risks posed by service users, such as moving and handling, or managing behaviours.

Depending on the nature of your service and the needs of individuals within the setting, you might need to consider a more in-depth approach. Services may have two types of risk assessments:

1. general risks of the service for all, for example COSHH

2. risks specific to service users, for example self-medication or complex behaviours.

Again, this reminds us of the links between assessing and managing risks and safeguarding; managing a risk inappropriately could be seen as neglect.

Another system in use is a matrix that rates the severity of the risk versus the likelihood of it occurring. This can take the form of a 'traffic light' system with the red area being high risk and high likelihood (see Figure 4.3). This can be used in conjunction with the 'Five steps to risk assessment'.

4.3.2 and 4.3.3 Work with individuals and others to assess and manage potential risks and hazards

There are a number of risk screening tools that are appropriate for some situations, such as for falls, nutrition, pressure sores and mental health assessments. These operate on a scoring system

to identify whether someone is at risk and, if so, how any risks will be managed. With other areas of risk, though, the HSE five-step model is a useful framework. You will no doubt have risk management systems in place, and it is for you to decide whether these are fit for purpose in assessing and then managing risks or if a new template is needed. Furthermore, the service does need to ensure that all risks are identified in the first place and managed appropriately.

Activity

As we know, health and safety covers a vast area and it is impossible to hold all areas in your head at all times when working to assess and manage risks.

Developing a screening tool is an effective way to identify potential risks when working with individuals so these can be assessed and managed. This can be a simple list of the most common types of hazards likely to exist within your service and for your client group, which can then be used as a checklist. Consider areas like mobility, sight/hearing, cognition, and the environment.

1. Develop a screening tool for the key factors relating to the people who use your service.

2. Implement the tool.

3. Monitor its use.

4. Review its effectiveness in managing risks.

Be able to promote a culture where needs and risks are balanced with health and safety practice

4.4

4.4.1 Work with individuals to balance the management of risk with individual rights and the views of others

Risk management is now better termed 'risk enablement' when related to service users. This change in terminology reflects how practice and thinking is evolving within health and social care.

It is important to remember that the role of any support or care service is to work with individuals, with capacity, in a way that promotes their choices, even if this entails elements of risk. This is the complex task of balancing choices and rights with duty of care and safeguarding. It can be made even harder with 'well-meaning' families who might want you to take a more protective stance. However, you need to prioritise the individual you are supporting, and your role in this scenario would be to manage the tensions that might arise.

Positive risk taking entails carefully thought-through plans where risks are identified, discussed and then planned for. In the past, and possibly still currently in some organisations, a risk-averse culture has kept service users safe but also restricted their opportunities to live life to the full. Risk assessment should be there to enable a task to happen rather than list a set of reasons why it shouldn't. Fear of negligence can be a potential issue when managing risks, so to guard against this, ensure:

■ all reasonable steps have been taken

■ reliable assessment methods have been used

■ information has been collated and thoroughly evaluated

■ decisions are recorded, communicated and thoroughly evaluated

■ policies and procedures have been followed.

(Department of Health (2010), *Risk Guidance for People with Dementia*.)

Key Term

Positive risk taking is part of the process of measuring risk and involves balancing the positive benefits that are likely to follow from taking risks against the negative effects of attempting to avoid risk altogether.

Chapter 4 | **Develop health and safety and risk management policies, procedures and practices in health and social care settings**

69

Figure 4.5 Risk enablement can support individuals to live full and active lives

4.4.2 Work with individuals and others to develop a balanced approach to risk management that takes into account the benefits for individuals of risk taking

In order to create a positive risk-taking ethos, policies need to be carefully devised. Furthermore, to then implement these requires a skilled and well-trained staff team who believe in the benefits of positive risk taking. Service users may well require support in some areas of their lives, however this does not preclude them from having choices and the right to take risks as we all do in life. Implementing a person-centred approach with the individual's wishes central and a 'can-do' attitude looking at the benefits of something rather than focusing on the risks will improve the quality of life and put the individual in control.

4.4.3 Evaluate your own practice in promoting a balanced approach to risk management

Skills for Health and Skills for Care have devised 'Common Core Principles to Support Self-Care' as a resource for practice change. Self-care could also be redefined as the individual taking responsibility and being in control. The vision of empowerment and increased independence and choice will 'only be achieved by significant cultural change and changing the attitudes, behaviours and skill base of all people working in health and social care' (www.dh.gov.uk).

Principle 7 of 'Common Core Principles to Support Self-Care' is: 'Support and enable risk management and risk taking to maximise independence and choice'. This is of particular relevance to this unit. The context for Principle 7 is: 'The worker encourages and supports individuals to make choices about how to live their lives and manage any identified risks. The worker promotes choice and independence while supporting individuals to manage risks proportionately and realistically.'

Below are a range of statements relating to organisational behaviours taken from this section.

- It uses a 'can-do' attitude with managing perceived risks and involves individuals in finding solutions.

- Perceived risks are assessed against the likely benefits of taking part in the community, learning new skills and gaining confidence.

- The service is not risk averse; risks are broken down into smaller aspects to manage them better.

- There is an understanding that risks cannot be removed entirely no matter how much support is given.

- A balance is met between enabling individuals to lead independent, dignified lives while avoiding and preventing unnecessary harm.

- Safeguarding procedures are understood and implemented when needed.

- The potential impact of any risk is fully assessed and accurately recorded detailing the risk, context and action taken to reduce the risks.

- Individuals understand that with rights come responsibilities and making choices might mean taking risks.

- There is clarity between the difference of putting an individual at risk and enabling an individual to manage risks.

- The service will work with others, be they families or other professionals, to develop common approaches to risk taking, seeking agreed solutions where conflicts exist.

- The service has relevant policies and procedures which are adhered to.

- All know and understand the legal implications of individuals' choices and risk taking and will seek advice when needed.

1. Rate your service out of 10 against each area and come up with an action plan if needed on how to implement changes. Score 10 as being excellent down to 1 as being not present.

2. How does the service support and enable risk management and risk taking to maximise independence and choice?

3. Identify areas to work on with an action plan. Remember to make objectives SMART; state what specifically needs to happen, how it will be measured, how it is achievable and realistic, and the timescales within which it will happen.

4.4.4 Analyse how helping others to understand the balance between risk and rights improves practice

The previous activity should have given you insight into some of the areas related to this learning outcome.

Getting a good balance between managing risks and promoting choices is key to person-centred practice and is an ideal that all health and social care workers need to be committed to. Enabling a person to have autonomy and control in their life has positive effects on self-image, their sense of well-being and overall quality of life. Should you need more ideas, ask your service users.

Chapter 4 | Develop health and safety and risk management policies, procedures and practices in health and social care settings

71

Be able to improve health, safety and risk management policies, procedures and practices

4.5

4.5.1 Obtain feedback on health, safety and risk management policies, procedures and practices from individuals and others

Obtaining feedback on your health and safety systems is vital to ensure you meet requirements and offer a high-quality service. There are a number of different ways that you might receive feedback:

■ CQC Inspections or from other regulatory bodies

■ HSE advice, Environmental Health, Fire Brigade

■ visiting professionals, such as a district nurse or physiotherapist or occupational therapist

■ feedback questionnaires completed by service users and their families

■ quality assurance systems, such as regular audits

■ comments and complaints

■ service user meetings/forums

■ supervisions and staff meetings.

Activity

1. Review the bulleted list above (on how you may receive feedback) and reflect on how well they identify health, safety and risks.

4.5.2 Evaluate the health, safety and risk management policies, procedures and practices within the work setting

Evaluation is key to ascertaining how well your service is managing health, safety and risks and will inform your future management of this area. You can devise an audit suitable for your particular service to make evaluations against covering areas such as whether:

■ the amount of incidents and accidents are recorded

■ all regular checks such as as fire safety, food hygiene, water checks, first-aid boxes or medication audits are undertaken on time

■ all COSHH statements are present and all products stored safely

■ all pieces of electrical equipment have had the Portable Appliance Test

- all pieces of moving and handling equipment have a valid and current safety check

- all risk assessments are up to date and relevant and whether service users have been involved in the process

- personal protective equipment such as gloves and aprons are readily accessible and available and correct hand-washing guides are available for everyone

- all cleaning rotas are followed

- health and safety issues were reported and how was this done – via written communication, via a team meeting, via a supervision or highlighted via an audit

- all staff have current health and safety training.

You can also undertake visual checks of the environment, e.g. checking carpets are not worn or fraying, or whether exits and corridors are kept clear.

You can also analyse any qualitative feedback from staff, service users and significant others via the previous feedback mechanism.

4.5.3 Identify areas of policy, procedures and practices that need improvement to ensure safety and protection in the work setting

It is hoped that by looking at the area of health and safety you will have identified areas for improvement already. This could be as a result of a change you were unaware of or a better understanding of how to implement or monitor aspects of health and safety. It might be that you can see additional areas of training needed for staff or a change to induction procedures. Changes in legislation do occur and this will always impact on your service. Also, local authorities may issue good practice guidelines related to health and safety, which will change the way things are done.

Remember

Ensure you create an action plan to implement any changes you have identified with time scales for completion.

All of this can seem quite onerous, but having a regular system to monitor health and safety such as a monthly audit, and having health and safety as a regular staff meeting and supervision agenda item does help.

4.5.4 Recommend changes to policies, procedures and practices that ensure safety and protection in the work setting

Health and safety clearly has high priority within any organisation, and if changes have been identified that are required to meet regulations then these must be undertaken as a matter of urgency. If there are other areas that you feel are compliant yet could still be improved, these might form part of a quality assurance cycle process. Remember that any changes that are implemented then need to be cascaded back to staff to ensure they are fully informed.

Chapter 4 | **Develop health and safety and risk management policies, procedures and practices in health and social care settings**

73

Are you ready for assessment?

✔ Do you know the legislative framework for health, safety and risk management in the work setting?

✔ Do you know how policies, procedures and practices in your own setting meet health, safety and risk management requirements?

✔ Do you know the actions to take when health, safety and risk management policies, procedures and practices are not being complied with?

✔ Do you know how to evaluate your own practice in promoting a balanced approach to risk management?

✔ Do you know how helping others to understand the balance between risk and rights improves practice?

✔ Can you demonstrate safety compliance with health and risk management procedures?

✔ Can you support others to comply with legislative and organisational health, safety and risk management policies, procedures and practices relevant to their work?

✔ Can you complete records and reports on health, safety and risk management issues according to legislative and organisational requirements?

✔ Can you contribute to development of policies, procedures and practices to identify, assess and manage risk to individuals and others?

✔ Can you work with individuals and others to assess and manage potential risks and hazards?

✔ Can you work with individuals to balance the management of risk with individual rights and the views of others?

✔ Can you work with individuals and others to develop a balanced approach to risk management that takes into account the benefits for individuals of risk taking?

✔ Can you obtain feedback on health, safety and risk management policies, procedures and practices from individuals and others?

✔ Can you evaluate the health, safety and risk management policies, procedures and practices within the work setting?

✔ Can you identify areas of policy, procedures and practices that need improvement to ensure safety and protection in the work setting?

✔ Can you recommend changes to policies, procedures and practices that ensure safety and protection in the work setting?

References

Care Quality Commission (CQC) (2008) *Essential Standards of Quality and Safety*.

Department of Health, (2010) *Risk Guidance for People with Dementia*. London: Department of Health.

Health and Safety Executive (2001) *Health and Safety in Care Homes*. Sudbury: Health and Safety Executive.

HM Treasury (2004) Orange Book, *Management of Risk: Principles and Concepts*. London: HMSO.

Supporting People: a government programme for funding, planning and monitoring housing-related support services for vulnerable adults.

Acts and Regulations

Control of Substances Hazardous to Health Regulations (2002) (COSHH).

Data Protection Act (1998).

Electricity at Work Regulations (1989).

Food Safety Act 1990 and Food Hygiene Regulations (2006).

Health and Safety at Work Act (HSAWA) (1974).

Health and Safety (First Aid) Regulations (1981).

Health and Safety Information for Employees Regulations (1989).

Management of Health and Safety at Work Regulations (1999) (Amended 2003).

Manual Handling Operations Regulations (1992).

The Human Medicines Regulations (2012).

Mental Health Act (1983) Code of Practice.

Personal Protective Equipment at Work Regulations (1992).

Provision and Use of Work Equipment Regulations (1998).

Regulatory Reform (Fire Safety) (2005).

Reporting of Injuries, Diseases and Dangerous Occurrences Regulations (RIDDOR) (1995).

Websites

Cambridgeshire and Peterborough NHS Foundation Report,

www.cqc.org.uk/media/care-quality-commission-demands-action-after-report-identifies-failings-cambridgeshire-and-pet, accessed 29 June 2012.

Department of Health, (2008) *Common Core Principles to Support Self Care*. www.dh.gov.uk, accessed 29 June 2012.

Health and Safety Executive, (2009) *How to Tackle Work Related Stress*, www.hse.gov.uk/pubns/indg430.pdf, accessed 29 June 2012 and www.hse.gov.uk/stress/standards/index.htm, accessed 2 July 2012.

Health and Safety Executive, www.hse.gov.uk/news/subscribe/index.htm, accessed 2 July 2012.

Health and Safety Executive, www.hse.gov.uk/press/2011/coi-wm-32911.htm, accessed 2 July 2012.

Chapter 4 | **Develop health and safety and risk management policies, procedures and practices in health and social care settings**

75

Safety and Health Practitioner Online: www.shponline.co.uk/news-content/full/government-wields-axe-over-safety-inspections, accessed 29 June 2012.

Skills for Care, www.skillsforcare.org.uk, accessed 2 July 2012.

Skills for Care, (2011) *Learning to Live with Risk*, www.skillsforcare.org.uk, accessed 29 June 2012.

Skills for Health, www.skillsforhealth.org.uk, accessed 2 July 2012.

'theEHP' website, theehp.com/2012/02/17/health-safety-hse-prosecutions-in-brief-13-february-17-february/, accessed 29 June 2012.

Updates on HSE prosecutions, www.hse.gov.uk/enforce/prosecutions.htm, theehp.com/category/health-safety/, accessed 29 June 2012.

Chapter 5

Working in
partnership
in health
and social care settings

Since the 1980s it has been widely acknowledged that it's not possible for one professional group to deliver all the complex health and social care needs required by most of the service users (Sullivan and Skelcher, 2002). The formal requirement for cooperation between the different workforces has become essential to ensuring that effective integrated and efficient services are delivered for the mutual benefit of all involved.

The aim of this chapter is to assess the learner's knowledge, understanding and skills required to implement and promote effective partnership working.

By the end of this chapter you will:

1 Understand partnership working

2 Be able to establish and maintain working relationships with colleagues

3 Be able to establish and maintain working relationships with other professionals

4 Be able to work in partnership with others

Understand partnership working

5.1

While the idea of partnership is often accepted as understood, there is in fact very little theoretical underpinning of the concepts involved (Le Riche and Talor, 2008). In health and social care, it could be said that partnerships are those relationships between the services, with users and carers. They are formed between individuals or groups that have a responsibility to cooperate in undertaking mutually agreed service goals.

5.1.1 Identify the features of effective partnership working

In a genuine partnership, no one has full control in every situation and it needs to be accepted at the outset that some health and social care partners will be more independent and exert more power and influence than others. Acknowledging the fact that a true partnership empowers the service user, their carers and professionals is crucial to eliciting the necessary management and behaviour changes on the part of the service providers.

Health and social care partnerships have not been formed in a vacuum: they emerged as a result of the 1980s policy drivers for joined-up services (Ling, 2000). This push for collaboration between health and social care services led to a plethora of White Papers in the late 1990s detailing various proposals on quality and partnership, culminating in the Health Act of 1999. This Act imposed a new duty on health and social services to cooperate and the operational flexibility to enable joint working. There was pressure on services to support well-being rather than illness and dependence, resulting in more policy changes. These policies were developed to ensure that the individual was at the centre of any partnership and would therefore have a stronger voice and more choice about how services were to be delivered (Department of Health, 2006).

Activity

Go to www.legislation.gov.uk and find the Health Act (1999).

1. What information can you find on partnership working within the detail of the Act?

2. Do you implement aspects of the Act in your daily working practice?

Activity

Reflect on the variety of partnerships you experience in your own professional practice.

1. How are they different?

2. How do you feel your role varies with each one?

5.1.2 Explain the importance of partnership working with colleagues and other professionals

Community empowerment was one of the main strands of the Conservative Party leader David Cameron's views on the 'Big Society'. So much so, that following the election of 2010, the coalition government introduced its White Paper *Equity and Excellence: Liberating the NHS* (Department of Health, 2010). One of the main aims of the policy was to empower clinicians so that they could improve the quality of collaborative services. Given that aim, in the Health and Social Care Bill (2011) that followed, Health and Well-Being Boards were established to guide and monitor the commissioning of local integrated services across the NHS, public health and social care. It is envisaged that ultimately they would not monitor and guide the commissioning groups but would take over the responsibility for the joint commissioning of specific services, for example for people with dementia.

Activity

Go to the Department of Health website (www.dh.gov.uk) and search for the term 'Health and Well-Being Boards'.

1. Read the information provided and consider the impact they could have on your practice.

2. Would you consider these changes beneficial to you and your service users?

5.1.3 Analyse how partnership working delivers better outcomes

According to Jo Webber (2011), the principles involved in ensuring Health and Well-Being Boards work are the same principles as for making any constructive relationships work between organisations. This will depend on the ability of the boards to develop a strategy that the providers can agree upon. However, the key relationships must remain those between the service users and those that care for them. Everything else needs to be considered secondary to that focus. The shared sense of purpose has to be the quality of the service from the users' perspective.

Although many of today's service users are sophisticated and articulate consumers, the funding and organisational arrangements more often than not support a dependent agency relationship despite initiatives to move towards personalised budgets. However, it can be argued that it is the **personalisation agenda** itself that affords the service users the opportunity for self-directed support and that it could transform types of partnership engagement.

Key Term

The **personlisation agenda** is the building of a system of care and support in which individuals define their own requirements.

John is a sophisticated and articulate service user who, because of his depression, is supported by you and regularly attends your day-care service. However, he would be more suited to a lower level of personalised care and self-directed support but because of the local funding model, this cannot happen.

1. What would be the ideal model of support for John?

2. Which of your health care colleagues would still need to be involved in John's care?

3. How could you ensure John continues to receive appropriate support if his needs change?

Figure 5.1 Partnerships work best when they agree priorities, delegate roles, share values, communicate effectively and train together

5.1.4 Explain how to overcome barriers to partnership working

Partnerships face a multitude of potential difficulties. Some of these are associated with the day-to-day issues involved in coordinating the disparate (unrelated) organisations and personnel. Others relate to the lack of planning in order to bring together people with different responsibilities, values and expertise.

Due to the fact that partnerships are formed as the primary means of solving complex health and social care problems, it is all too easy for their good intentions to end in failure. To avoid failure, they should agree priorities, delegate roles, share values, communicate effectively and train together.

In setting organisational priorities, the partners should also make sure that they are focused on clear objectives and the extent to which these can be achieved. Partnerships may lose sight of their overall objectives in a hustle and bustle of everyday activity, or assume that implicit objectives or a shared desire to work together are enough. Doctors, social workers, therapists and nurses will all claim their ethical commitment, which necessitates putting the interests of the service users and their carers first. This means there is a level of consistency in the stated values they share. However, they all have an interest related to their own position and job security. In other words, there is an expectation that health and social care workers are capable of internalising the conflicts that inevitably arise in their partnership working in order to focus solely on their users' needs. Remember that not all staff are professionalised or regulated, so the assumption of shared values cannot be taken for granted and ought to be clarified at the outset.

Be able to establish and maintain working relationships with colleagues

Empowering the workforce to work in partnership with others is assumed to benefit everyone by increasing their satisfaction and well-being. It is also expected to be a cost-effective way of delivering services (Audit Commission 1998).

> ### Key Term
>
> **Empowerment** means to give (someone) more power, usually making them more confident in controlling their own life and claiming rights.

5.2.1 Explain your own role and responsibilities in working with colleagues

Colleagues are any people who work with you in providing health and social care services.

They can be in a similar profession or have an entirely different status and employment situation. However, most service users now rely upon health and social care colleagues to cooperate in the delivery of integrated services. While health and social care colleagues have disparate perspectives, they may share many professional values, such as supporting people in difficulty and treating people with respect for their privacy and dignity.

To work in any partnership, you must be compassionate and committed to working collaboratively with colleagues, reporting your concerns and being able to record the information you deem relevant to ensuring the safety of the service user.

A number of different partnership models exist depending on the purposes of the undertaking and the era in which they first emerged. Table 5.1 summarises the three main models and their main characteristics.

Table 5.1 Models of partnership working (Adapted from Lowndes and Skelcher, 1998)

Model	Characteristics					
	Basis for forming partnership	Means of user communication	Methods of conflict resolution	Degree of working flexibility	Cooperative climate	User role/ working preferences
Hierarchy 1940s–70s	Employment relationship	Routines	Administrative and supervisory	Medium	Formal; bureaucratic	Dependent
Market 1980s	Contract	Prices	Haggling and legal action	Low	Precision and/or suspicion	Independent
Network 1997	Complementary strengths	Relational	Norm of reciprocity concerned with reputation	High	Open-ended; mutual benefits	Interdependent

Neither the Hierarchy nor the Market Partnership models empowered service users or their carers, so a flexible and user-responsive approach was required. Since the late 1990s, contracting networks of joined-up services working across agencies has become the model of partnership working. Users appear in control of how services are shaped and improved. Networking is seen as a means for people using health and social care services to increase credibility and visibility.

Activity

1. Evaluate the processes in place for changing the ways your service is administered or practised.

5.2.2 Develop and agree common objectives when working with colleagues

The exercise of power at institutional, household and personal level is at the root of the term empowerment and therefore at the root of meaningful partnerships. Remember that fundamental to developing successful working partnerships is the ability of everyone involved to recognise their different roles and to share control and influence.

Key considerations need to be made that will determine how much responsibility the workforce should assume and the level of informed decision making required. These include:

■ the degree of social vulnerability of the service user

■ the complexity level of the health care need

■ the level of variability in the support required.

Devolving responsibility to the health and social care workforce either by the service user or providers depends on mutual trust. Involving all the staff from the outset in agreeing their working roles and responsibilities signals that trust. However, according to Pastor (1996), the process of empowering the workforce involves issues of **accountability** and risk taking. Pastor suggests it operates on five different levels and is modified to prevent unnecessary risk to service users. It requires moving from a stage where the manager makes all the decisions but consults and informs the team through various forms of relationship building. This can eventually lead to the forming of completely autonomous teams who may or may not decide to consult the manager.

Key Terms

Devolve means to transfer or delegate power to a lower level.

Accountability refers to being answerable for something, or having responsibility for it.

Whatever the complexity of relationship building, it is nevertheless a process that Moss Kanter (1994) has endeavoured to simplify into eight components. She suggests there are eight 'I's that create the successful 'We's of true partnership working, which can be applied to health and social care practice as follows:

1. Partnerships are built first on *individual* excellence. This would mean that organisations fully appreciate and respect the expertise of all their workforce, and that users have real rather than token choice.

2. The relationship should be *important* to both partners. In other words, users must be assured of the continuity of professional services rather than uncertainty that the provision will end.

3. Relationships are *interdependent*; that there is an assumption that all professionals want it to work.

4. There is mutual *investment* in skills. The partners invest in a service aimed at maintaining and developing team-working skills.

Activity

Think about the funding and investment that your work setting receives.

1. How is the investment shared between different areas/functions?

2. Which areas receive the most and what are the main shortfalls in your opinion?

5. *Information sharing* is central to the partnership process. (This is the single biggest cause for complaint in health and social care.)

6. *Integration* of service provision. This is so that professional partners learn from each other and their service users.

7. There is *institutionalisation* of the process. This is to ensure that service-user involvement is given formal status.

8. Partners behave towards each other with *integrity*. Users are reliant on the care values promoted by the service providers being reflected in the working practices.

Activity

1. Select one of Moss Kanter's eight 'I's listed above.

2. Assess an area of your practice and explain how it provides evidence of that element of successful partnership working.

5.2.3 Evaluate your own working relationships with colleagues

The benefits of professional partnership working are that they enable staff to share ideas and efforts in order to bridge the gaps in delivering services. Different degrees of collaboration can exist across agencies or organisational boundaries, extending from autonomy through to complete integration of services (Edwards *et al*, 2009).

When evaluating your partnership working relationships with colleagues, it may be important to consider Reed *et al*'s (2005) forms of integration. These will allow you to consider your successes and areas for improvement when dealing with:

■ service sector providers in health and social care

■ professions such as nurses, social workers, doctors, therapists

■ institutions and communities (primary and secondary)

■ organisation types, for example public, private or voluntary

■ care groups for acute and long-term care, children, adults, those with mental health issues or learning disabilities.

5.2.4 Deal constructively with any conflict that may arise with colleagues

Due to the fact that a wide range of personnel are required to cooperate for partnership working to take effect, a number of roles and responsibilities have to be formally agreed. This ensures that everyone in the partnership understands the contribution they are expected to make. Conflict could result if these are determined by skills and expertise rather than personal qualities. Sometimes it is beneficial for roles to overlap or merge so that boundaries between the partners become blurred. However, there will be times when maintaining distinct roles becomes important so that individuals can make their unique contribution from a particular service perspective.

Activity

1. Did you meet resistance to a blurring of role boundaries?

2. Had you expected to encounter such resistance?

3. How did you ensure that your appropriate power in the partnership was not undermined while still respecting the position of the others involved?

4. What could you have done differently?

Figure 5.2 Sharing ideas about service improvements

Diploma in Leadership in Health and Social Care | Level 5

Be able to establish and maintain working relationships with other professionals

One of the benefits of partnership working with other professionals is the joint learning that comes from the enhanced understanding of diverse people and organisations coming together. Joined-up working requires an integrative style of leadership development to nurture and develop skills for partnership working. Such leadership requires the adoption of a different mind-set in which the effective functioning of a team or partnership as a whole is the main purpose.

5.3.1 Explain your own role and responsibilities in working with other professionals

While everyone in a partnership shares responsibility for safeguarding and promoting the welfare of the service users, they also need to appreciate each other's role and responsibility. While these will vary depending on the individual's area of expertise and practice, all health and social work professionals will share an imperative to protect service users' rights and promote their interests and independence.

All health and social care workers need to have a respect for others and a compassionate nature. They must be able to:

- communicate effectively with others in the interest of their service users
- identify and challenge discriminatory practices
- apply interviewing, listening and observation skills to the joint assessments process and shared reports

- negotiate and organise skills that enable good team working
- deal with difficult situations and manage conflict.

5.3.2 Develop procedures for effective working relationships with other professionals

Building strong professional partnerships requires effective people and team skills, where all the participants respect each other and consider the interests of their partners as well as themselves. Creating an atmosphere of trust between partners, where people are listened to and where they listen to others, requires considerable skill and attention. Healthy professional relationships can only be built on open, honest and sensible approaches to dealing with people, with the intention to cooperate being upmost in everyone's mind and reinforced by common policies and procedures.

Effective mechanisms for internal and external communications are vital to the success of all forms of collaboration. General skills of listening, negotiating and compromising are a given in any relationship, but service users can be placed at unacceptable risk if professional partners have not worked out their joint communication protocols. In order to share information on policy, available resources, user needs and service standards requires compatible data sets and where possible IT systems. Shared structures and data systems needs to be backed up with a culture of avoiding specialist language that is exclusive and excluding.

Figure 5.3 It is essential to create an atmosphere of trust between partners

5.3.3 Agree common objectives when working with other professionals within the boundaries of your own role and responsibilities

Effective professional partnerships are built on a shared commitment where all partners have specialist skills and can be relied upon to be accountable for their specific responsibilities and will be equally affected by the benefits and disadvantages arising from their alliances.

To gain that sense of unity requires considerable effort and time agreeing the partnerships' aims and objectives before moving on to action. The objectives need to be agreed in an inclusive way and must be specific, detailing deadlines, roles and responsibilities. The process of clarifying objectives requires careful assessment of priorities and agreement on what would constitute their successful outcomes. Ensuring they conform to the SMART acronym (see p28) could be helpful at this stage.

5.3.4 Evaluate procedures for working with other professionals

The effectiveness of any professional partnership in health and social care can be judged on its failures and successes. The ability to be clear about the purpose of professional partnerships and monitor their actions and the resources they use is essential for any organisation. So once objectives are agreed, it is crucial that professionals discuss how their partnership actions will be measured and specifically how information on those actions will be collected and collated.

Activity

Consider the professional partnerships you are involved with.

1. What do the other professionals want from working with you?

2. What do you want from working with the other partners?

Appropriate governance (SCIE, 2011) structures need to cover issues such as:

- professional regulation and accountability

- supervision and performance appraisal

- the management of risk and the audit of accidents and incidents

- organisational learning and continuing professional development (CPD)

- complaints and compliments.

The evaluation should help professional partners to remain focused on the outcomes of their joint actions, on how well they are progressing and what needs to change to improve services further.

5.3.5 Deal constructively with any conflict that may arise with other professionals

A strong professional partnership can be expected to have conflicting interests, so disagreements will arise on how best to get things done. Professional diversity, which can be a partnership's greatest strength, may also present a barrier to good working relationships. Successful professional relationships distinguish between control and influence. In a genuine partnership, no single professional has complete control even though some partners may be able to exercise more power than others. Being able to influence the partnership outcomes on the other hand is different and requires sensitivities and leadership skills that may be exercised by professional groups perceived to be less powerful.

Inter-professional differences of perspective, such as those arising from the medical model and the more holistic social model, may create differences such as their divergent view on what is acceptable risk.

It has been suggested that as multi-disciplinary working becomes the *modus operandi* for health and social care delivery, the consequence is ultimately that roles converge. Robinson and Cottrel (2005) suggest that as professional identities are threatened, professionals will either be reluctant to collaborate or will revert to using their own professional language to ensure they maintain their separate identity.

Activity In Practice

Mohammed is an experienced social worker. A service user with full mental capacity has refused support to help her organise repairs to her home and consequently faces the harsh winter with a draughty house and only a small electric fire for heating. Mohammed was contacted by the community matron, as she felt that the cold and the state of disrepair of the house left this woman at unacceptable risk during the winter months.

1. What can Mohammed do to help the community matron understand the service user's choices?

2. How do the divergent perspectives on risk affect this partnership?

Be able to work in partnership with others

Linden (2002) suggests that collaboration happens when people from different agencies decide to produce services from the sharing of efforts and resources. Policies advocating multi-agency working acknowledge the interrelatedness of community needs for health, social services, law enforcement, welfare, housing and education.

5.4.1 Analyse the importance of working in partnership with others

Given that policy and local practices have focused on joined-up working initiatives since 1997, inter-agency partnership working is central to everyone's work in health and social care. Not only is this considered essential to delivering improvements in care to service users, it is also seen as adding value, for instance by introducing innovation and change. Examples of this include early interventions with people who have first episodes of psychosis or the Prince's Trust helping vulnerable adults with education and employment.

Tait and Shah (2007) suggest that voluntary sector involvement brings a number of benefits, such as:

- possessing complementary skills to those of the statutory bodies
- offering practical advice and help on issues such as housing and finance
- having advocacy and campaigning experience
- providing employment, education and leisure opportunities

- having experience of user-led and managed delivery being trusted by the wider public because of their independence.

The government's support for the role of the voluntary sector in delivering public services was signalled by the fact that it set up the National Strategic Partnership Forum (Department of Health, 2012) to identify good partnership ideas and provide guidance on overcoming the many barriers to successful inter-agency partnerships.

Activity

Consider the inter-agency partnerships you are involved with.

1. What do the agencies want from working with you?

2. What do you want from working with them?

5.4.2 Develop procedures for effective working relationships with others

Emerging forms of health and social care are required to develop collaborative services with service users and their carers over extended periods. However, it cannot be assumed that all service users want to be active participants in their care. They may be reluctant to be a partner and prefer for service providers to make the decisions for them (Roberts, 2002).

In order to become active in the management of their care services, users need to be knowledgeable, motivated and confident. They can do this through enlisting the support of advocates to act on their behalf or by engaging with project work, such as Devon County Council's *Learning to Involve*, which trains service users to speak out for the services they want.

While process issues such as agreeing objectives, building up trust, or dealing with budgets, need to be clarified, the criticism of inter-agency partnerships has been the over-emphasis of this activity rather than concentrating on the quality of outcomes. In response, the government has introduced the new 'Outcomes Framework for Adult Social Services' (Department of Health, 2011), which details four domains for developments in future services. These are:

■ enhancing quality of life for people with care and support needs

■ delaying and reducing the need for care and support

■ ensuring that people have a positive experience of care and support

■ safeguarding people whose circumstances make them vulnerable and protecting them from avoidable harm.

Agencies with different backgrounds, training and understanding of their service users' issues need time to work together effectively on such outcomes. For example, they have to develop a shared vision based on common values of service delivery. They function best when everyone understands and can appreciate the diverse skills of each other's organisation no matter what their status.

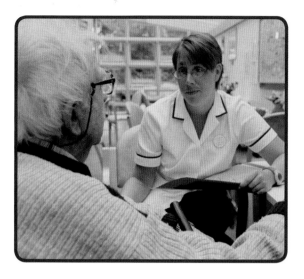

Figure 5.4 Different agencies need to work together to develop a shared vision of service delivery

5.4.3 Agree common objectives when working with others within the boundaries of your own role and responsibilities

While each agency may have a different service delivery system, a joint management structure must emerge to clarify the roles of authority, responsibility and mutual accountability. Joint working cannot happen without all parties perceiving a mutual benefit in a shared vision and common service goals. Staff in multi-agency teams face issues concerning the balance between specialist and generalist skills and status, with specialists from different agencies being required to redefine their roles.

Having a clear justification that a partnership is needed for service users helps to realise the values upon which they can create a shared vision and a rationale for action. The key issues around which realistic, reliable and valid objectives for the partners must be built are:

- agreeing specific policy and procedures
- determining agreed boundaries
- agreeing accountability in respect to commissioning, purchasing and providing
- identifying agreed staff and finance resource pools
- agreeing leadership
- providing joint training and development needs with specific attention to mutual trust and attitude
- developing mechanisms for communication and sustaining good personal relationships.

5.4.4 Evaluate procedures for working with others

Monitoring and **evaluation** processes should ensure partners receive regular and relevant information regarding the impact of their efforts. This allows collaboration participants at governance, management and practice levels to assess their effectiveness and adjust their plans based on outcomes. The assessment can be considered from various perspectives, such as:

- the overall purpose
- value for money
- responsiveness
- sustainability
- flexibility.

Yet according to the Audit Commission (2009), partnership agreements do not always include outcome measures, and when they do they are not often monitored.

Hambleton *et al* (1996) suggests that inter-agency working may leave the public unclear about where responsibility and accountability for delivering services lies. So clear governance structures are needed for:

- strategic planning
- policy and procedures
- practice changes
- monitoring
- financing.

However, inter-agency working can result in ambiguity that may cause risks to organisational accountability. The Audit Commission (2005) needs reassurance that public money is spent wisely and the quality of life for service users will improve as a consequence of this type of working.

Activity

1. From your own experience of inter-agency working, and using the key issues listed in 5.4.3 above, judge the effectiveness of the collaboration.

5.4.5 Deal constructively with any conflict that may arise with others

Conflict between agencies can occur when there are issues related to trust, openness and good will between key people. Bhutta (2005) suggests that the statutory service may become anxious if it believes its staff resources may be removed or reduced by its increasing involvement with the voluntary sector. Such tensions between agencies can create barriers to collaboration. It is clearly up to the voluntary sector to reassure their partners that they are not a cheaper service option.

Establishing common understandings within and across agencies, although essential, is not always easy to achieve. Conflicts can also arise when partners have unrealistic expectations combined with inadequate resourcing and misunderstanding of roles. For example, Secker and Hill's (2001) study of inter-agency working found that the police service often felt dumped upon by mental health services. Dealing with conflicts of this kind challenges the different agencies involved to remain responsive to those that hold different views on how services are being delivered and who is bearing the burden of responsibility.

Sharing our differences honestly and openly and looking for positive solutions enables us to move to a new understanding of the appropriate way to manage a particular issue. Dealing positively with conflict helps to challenge what Janis (1982) calls 'group think', which happens when a group becomes so insulated that norms develop where certain ways of behaving become accepted practice and can go unchallenged, even when they are dysfunctional.

Are you ready for assessment?

- ✔ Do you know how to form effective partnerships?

- ✔ Can you establish and maintain effective working relationships with colleagues?

- ✔ Can you establish and maintain effective working relationships with other professionals?

- ✔ Can you establish and maintain effective working relationships with others?

References

Audit Commission (1998) *A Fruitful Partnership: Effective Partnership Working.* London: Audit Commission Publications.

Audit Commission (2005) *Governing Partnerships: Bridging the Accountability Gap.* London: Audit Commission.

Audit Commission (2009) *Means to an End.* London: Audit Commission.

Bhutta, M. (2005) *Shared Aspirations: The Role of the Voluntary and Community Sector in Improving the Funding Relationship with Government.* London: National Council for Voluntary Organisations.

Department of Health (2006) *Our Health, Our Care, Our Say: A New Direction for Community Services.* London: HMSO.

Department of Health (2010) *Equity and Excellence: Liberating the NHS.* London: HMSO.

Department of Health (2011) *Transparency in Outcomes: A Framework for Quality in Adult Social Care.* London: HMSO.

Edwards *et al*, (2009) *Improving Inter-professional Collaborations: Multi-agency Working for Children's Well-being.* London: Routledge.

Glasby, J., Dickinson, H. (2008) *Partnership Working in Health and Social Care.* Bristol: The Policy Press.

Hambleton, R., Essex, S., Mills, L., Razzaque, K. (1996) *Inter-Agency Working in Practice.* York: Joseph Rowntree Foundation.

Janis, I. L. (1982) *Groupthink: Psychological Studies of Policy Decisions and Fiascoes.* Boston: Houghton Mifflin.

Le Riche, P., Talor, I. (2008) *The Learning, Teaching and Assessment of Partnership Work in Social Work Education* (pp1–69). London: Social Care Institute for Excellence.

Linden, R. M. (2002) *Working Across Boundaries: Making Collaboration Work in Government and Non-profit Organizations.* San Francisco: Jossey-Bass.

Ling, T. (2000) *Unpacking Partnership: The Case of Health Care* in Clarke, J. *et al* (Eds) *New Managerialism New Welfare?* (pp82–101.) London: Sage Publications.

Lowndes, V. and Skelcher, C. (1998) *The Dynamics of Multi-Organisational Partnerships: An Analysis of Changing Modes of Governance.* Public Administration (76), pp313–333.

Moss Kanter, R. (1994) 'Collaborative Advantage: The Art of Alliances'. *Harvard Business Review*, July–August, pp94–108.

Pastor, J. (1996) *Empowerment: What It Is and What It Is Not.* http://www.jpa-international.com/.

Reed, J, *et al.* (2005) 'A Literature Review to Explore Integrated Care for Older People'. *International Journal of Integrated Care*, 5(17) pp1–8.

Roberts, K. (2002) 'Exploring Participation: Older People on Discharge from Hospital'. *Journal of Advanced Nursing* (40), pp413–20.

Robinson, M, Cottrell, D. (2005) 'Health Professionals in Multi-Disciplinary and Multi-Agency Teams: Changing Professional Practice'. *Journal of Interprofessional Care* 19(6), pp547–60.

SCIE (2011) *Social Care Governance: A Workbook Based on Practice in England*. London: Social Care Institute for Excellence.

Secker, J, Hill, K. (2001) 'Broadening the Partnerships: Experiences of Working Across Community Agencies'. *Journal of Interprofessional Care* 15 (4), pp341–50.

Sullivan, H., Skelcher, C. (2002) *Working Across Boundries: Collaboration in Public Services*. Basingstoke: Palgrave Macmillan.

Tait, L., Shah, S. (2007) 'Partnership Working: A Policy with Promise for Mental Healthcare'. *Advances in Psychiatric Treatment* (13), pp261–71.

Webber, J. (2011) 'Why the Success of Health and Well-being Boards Depends on Relationships'. *HSJ*, 16 November.

Acts and Regulations

Health Act (1999)

Health and Social Care Act (2012)

White Paper *Equity and Excellence: Liberating the NHS* (Department of Health, 2010)

Websites

Department of Health, www.dh.gov.uk, accessed 2 July 2012.

Department of Health (2012) National Strategic Partnership Forum – Statement of Purpose, http://www.dh.gov.uk, accessed 2 July 2012.

Prince's Trust, www.princes-trust.org.uk, accessed 2 July 2012.

Social Care Institute for Excellence (SCIE), www.scie.org.uk, accessed 2 July 2012.

Chapter 6

Lead and manage
a team within
a health and **social care setting**

Team working is a central tenet of health and social care policy (Maslin-Prothero and Bennion, 2010). The term 'team' is often confused with the idea of multidisciplinary working, whereas it primarily relates to a group of people with complementary skills committed to a common goal.

The aim of this chapter is to ensure that you have the knowledge, understanding and skills required to lead and manage a team in a health and social care setting.

By the end of this chapter you will:

1 Understand the features of effective team performance

2 Be able to support a positive culture within the team

3 Be able to support a shared vision within the team

4 Be able to develop a plan with team members to meet agreed objectives

5 Be able to support individual team members to work towards agreed objectives

6 Be able to manage team performance

Understand the features of effective team performance

6.1

Although you will not always need to work in a team, it is important that you understand the features of effective team performance.

6.1.1 Explain the features of effective team performance

Bruce Tuckman's 'Forming Storming Norming Performing' theory (1965) helps to explain the predictable phases of team behaviour (see Table 6.1). Tuckman suggests this understanding is required in order for teams to reach maturity and deliver results.

Table 6.1 Bruce Tuckman's phases of team development

Forming	The individual roles and responsibilities are unclear and people are concerned to avoid conflict and gather information.
Storming	People begin to vie for position and power in relation to others. Conflict arises as people open up and their ideas are challenged.
Norming	A consensus is reached with roles and responsibilities assigned and accepted. Ground rules of conduct are agreed; tolerance and respect of difference now becomes the norm.
Performing	The team has a shared goal and strategic direction. Disagreements may still happen but they are resolved quickly and decisions are made without direction.

Tuckman continued to refine his theory and added a fifth phase which he called 'Adjourning'. It is about the loss felt when moving on or leaving a team (Tuckman and Jensen, 1977). Another later classical perspective on team development was postulated by Syer and Connolly (1996), who consider teams to be a form of an enclosed system. They see the team *inputs,* such as the structure and size of the team, transformed into service *outputs* over time through robust *structural processes* as a result of planning, problem solving and decision making.

Activity

1. Examine the Syer and Connolly (1996) model of team development and reflect on how it compares to Bruce Tuckman's (1965) model.

2. What are the main differences between the models?

3. How do they help you understand your own team's stage of development?

6.1.2 Identify the challenges experienced by developing teams

Developing teams often requires organisational change so are often subject to the kinds of challenges that occur during any form of change. Staff may be fearful of working with people they do not know and may be resistant to moving or joining a new team. But building a successful team requires health and social care organisations to have appropriate staffing procedures and not be unduly influenced by personality issues.

Health and social care organisations need to identify what skills and expertise they require and recruit and staff accordingly. The skills mix and diversity within the team should reflect the service plans. Therefore newly appointed members must be inducted in such a way that they understand and conform to the group's values and purpose. Their role and support mechanisms should be clarified so that they can contribute as quickly as is reasonably possible.

6.1.3 Identify the challenges experienced by established teams

The main challenge to established teams is to maintain enthusiasm and momentum. This can be achieved by promptly overcoming workload obstacles, resolving conflict between individuals and giving timely feedback on performance. Teams cannot be expected to maintain their efforts without recognition for the good work they do, but once momentum is built, it is easier to maintain and transfer across a number of activities.

Figure 6.1 Effective team members communicate trust and enthusiasm and work efficiently

Overall team performance relies heavily on the individual commitment and contribution of all its established members. The effective established teams are characterised by team members who are enthusiastic, communicate trust to their co-workers, and manage their time efficiently by concentrating on the most important work assignments (Chong, 2007).

6.1.4 Explain how challenges to effective team performance can be overcome

It can be difficult to ensure effective team working in health and social care. Dawes and Handscomb (2005) suggest this is due to competing professional interests. They also suggest that in some specialist areas, such as accident and emergency, care was effective despite poor team working. However, in areas where long-term services are required and in multiple settings, for example mental health or learning disabilities, then quality care outcomes are synonymous with effective team working.

The main challenge is to select and support the appropriate people who are capable of sharing the organisational goals, and then become committed to the service outcomes. In return, West (1994) suggests that organisations need to be transparent about their values in relation to service users and staff, and then communicate a clear vision of what the health and social care teams are expected to achieve in a reasonable timeframe.

6.1.5 Analyse how different management styles may influence outcomes of team performance

Management and leadership are said to be inherently different but complementary tasks (Zalenznick, 1992). Managers are usually appointed to their post and the skills they require are generalised but also specific to the position they hold in the organisation. Management styles can be divided into three main catagories of autocratic, paternalistic or democratic, and they reflect the ways managers make decisions relating to their subordinates.

On the other hand, a leader can be anyone in the team who has the ability to influence others. A leader's major role is to create the underlying conditions that will support the effective functioning of the health and social care team. According to Alimo-Metcalfe *et al* (2007), this is achieved by health and social care organisations adopting a servant-leadership style.

Activity

Leadership abilities are important qualities in managers as they build commitment from staff and thus enable them to help people to work effectively together.

1. How do people influence others?

2. In your team(s), which members would you say have the ability to influence staff and why?

3. In your organisation, are there managers who also have the skills to build staff commitment?

Managers need to begin by setting clear goals, establishing rules and assigning responsibilities. They can then move on to the more onerous tasks of organising the resources, motivating the team members and creating a spirit of cooperation. The more complex the team's task, the more the leadership and management style needs to reflect the team's stage of development so that roles can be delegated appropriately and support provided as required (Wheelan, 2005).

As teams mature and develop confidence, the style of management and leadership will change to enable team members to take on the leadership functions themselves.

6.1.6 Analyse methods of developing and maintaining trust and accountability

Stephen Covey (Covey and Merrill, 2006) claims that in ethical management, the primary focus of a leader is to establish trust, and that this arises from the two 'dimensions' of character and competence. The team's character relates to its motive and intent, whereas its competence relates to its skills and results.

Activity

Trust and respect within health and social care teams is often assumed by managers and the public alike.

1. Consider a time when a service user naively trusted you or another team member.

Service users who require complex care will be vulnerable and will need to have confidence in the teams that provide their services. While staff registered with professional bodies will have sytems of accountability, the vast majority of health and social care is provided by unregulated team members.

People who arrange their own care through the use of personal budgets and direct payments may be particularly vulnerable when they have to employ their own team to deliver services. Thus, *Enabling Excellence* (Department of Health, 2011) sets out the government's plans to reform workforce regulations and proposes a system of assured voluntary registration for unregulated workers.

6.1.7 Compare methods of addressing conflict within a team

Arguments can arise in teams over pressure with workloads, particularly at key times in the year, for example when staff with young families want extra time off in school holidays. The pressure of working unsocial hours, lone working, transport problems or the stress of working with abusive families may give rise to stress.

While conflict can be an inevitable result of working within any team, allowing the disputes to get out of hand can cause unnecessary disruption. However, when teams focus on service users' problems rather than their own differences, disagreements can be openly acknowledged. Disputes may also provide a means of stimulating team discussions and improve decision-making (Loxley, 1997).

Fisher and Ury (1983) argue that almost all disputes can be resolved with principled negotiation. They suggest a four-stage process to reach a win-win solution:

1. separate the people from the problem
2. focus on interests rather than positions
3. generate a variety of options before settling on an agreement
4. insist that the agreement be based on objective criteria.

Activity *In Practice*

Jayne's social-work team had recently been reorganised, with the result that there were more negative comments circulating about her team. After several weeks of listening to these comments, which she felt were unfair criticisms, Jayne was becoming increasingly demotivated. She planned to raise the issue of the negative comments and how they were being spread at the next team meeting.

1. How should Jayne approach this situation and what are the possible outcomes?

Belbin (1993) saw the managers' ability to select their own team members as one of the major constraints to team effectiveness. He demonstrated that although the strength of a team lay in the individual differences of the members, people with very similar or very different ways of working will not perform well together.

Activity

Visit the Belbin website (www.belbin.com) and review the team roles. Pay particular attention to the contribution and allowable weaknesses attributed to each role.

1. Does this help to explain your role in the team?

2. Does it explain some of the behaviours of other team members?

Be able to support a positive culture within the team

6.2

According to Hackman (2002), an effective team has a stable membership of approximately six to eight people, with clearly described tasks and agreements over the authority to manage the work in a reasonable amount of time.

6.2.1 Identify the components of positive culture within your own team

Health and social care teams develop patterns of working based on shared values and beliefs, and this determines how members interact with each other and their service users. There must be a cultural readiness to address concerns of equity and justice for the team members, as well as a tolerance of difference and diversity (NHS Executive, 2000).

Team **culture** therefore encompasses the professional values of the members as well as giving meaning to the context in which decisions are made by them. For example, when you join a new team you are usually helped by other team members to understand and adapt to the unwritten cultural norms that are important in uniting the team spirit. Indeed, Mintzberg (2009) suggests that culture represents the meaningful soul of any community.

Key Term

Culture is described by Mead (2000) as a complex pattern of shared behaviours that distinguishes people from each other and is transmitted over time.

Activity

Consider the unwritten rules in your team.

1. How many and what are they?

2. How are they passed on to new team members?

3. How do these shared norms help you work and play?

Health and social care work is generally accepted to be based on the ideals of altruism. In caring for others, staff can in return expect to be cared for at work. To do this, managers need to create a workplace community culture where talented staff are valued and retained. This will also ensure that service users get the access, responsiveness and relevance of services they have a right to expect.

6.2.2 Demonstrate how your own practice supports a positive culture in the team

Individual team members will bring a unique cultural perspective to their health and social care work. The more experienced and self-confident they are, the more they can contribute to the team goals and ultimately to the success of the team in meeting service targets. Cultural norms and practice values, such as service user choice and anti-discriminatory practice, can be shared with the other members of the team and these values can be become implicitly accepted as part of everyday practice.

When health and social care workers are considering their own practice, the two most important collaborative skills they need to have as a team member are to:

- appreciate and understand their own responsibilities within the team
- communicate from a service user perspective.

According to Suter *et al* (2009), both these skills are proven to deliver positive service user and provider outcomes. Reflection on and in practice allows the individual to consider their performance in relation to others in the team. As Cooper (2011) suggests, it is your own internal supervisor; a means of examining your intuitive feelings about your performance in the team and coming to a reasoned understanding about your strengths and weaknesses.

6.2.3 Use systems and processes to support a positive culture in the team

It is important that there are mechanisms in place to support the free flow and exchange of information on effective working practice that can be exchanged beyond the team itself (Lawler and Bilson, 2004).

Hackman (2002) describes four types of teams:

1. Manager-led teams: health and social care staff are given team instructions and time limits.

2. Self-managing team: the health and social care task is assigned but is led and managed by the team.

3. Self-designing team: the health and social care team work strategically but can modify the service delivery plans.

4. Self-governing team: the health and social care team develop the strategy, and design and modify the service plan accordingly.

In an organisational context, self-managing and self-designing teams are genuine teams. Manager-led teams are in effect just groups of co-workers rather than effective teams. Self-governing teams are normally confined to health and social care management boards rather than teams providing front line services.

Activity

Think about the teams you work in and cooperate with in your organisation.

1. How do they compare to Hackman's types?

2. How many would you categorise as genuine teams?

Once appropriate team structures are in place and staff have been appropriately inducted, then the team processes need to ensure the combined inputs translate into the required service outcomes. The processes need to be explicit to all and structured to maintain formal but agreed systems of team communication, with shared data, record keeping and coordination of practice. There must also be support for team building and staff development based on individual appraisals and supervision outcomes.

6.2.4 Encourage creative and innovative ways of working within the team

The extent to which a team will be creative and promote innovation in practice will depend on the climate for change within the group and the extent to which staff feel free to challenge the status quo. The proactive early identification of service users at risk of requiring hospitalisation, residential or nursing home care and early interventions have already led to more service users taking control over their own well-being.

The rollout of the personalisation agenda and further integration of health and social care has required new approaches to both the commissioning and delivery of services. New role development and new ways of working continue to be called for by the Coalition Government (Department of Health, 2010a; 2010b).

Most health and social care organisations have employees who promote innovation as a consequence of their work roles. Rosenfeld and Servo (1991) classified them as follows:

- Ideator: A person who generates countless possibilities but only in the realm of fantasy.

- Inventor: The practical, pragmatic person who likes to solve problems.

- Technological gatekeeper: The expert that is used for a reality check as they are always at the cutting edge of new developments.

- Champion: The conventional person with influence who can support and legitimise the unconventional ideator or inventor.

- Sponsor: The high status individual with control of the resources to apply to the development.

- Entrepreneur: The calculated risk taker whose interest is in making a thriving product and profit.

Figure 6.2 Effective teams work together

Be able to support a shared vision within the team

A team that supports a service user perspective requires systems and processes that consider the needs of service users and their families as paramount. They need to produce services that are accessed easily and maintain independence and choice for their service users.

6.3.1 Identify the factors that influence the vision and strategic direction of the team

Strategy is about planning. Setting a vision for that direction is about ensuring service users and staff, as well as other professionals and organisations, have clear ideas about what social care should look like in the future. The final strategic direction is likely to be influenced by shared values, empowerment of staff and service users, together with openness and honesty in practice.

In assessing the future planning direction of any health and social care team, leaders should address several key questions:

- What service targets do we want to meet?

- What level of services do we provide now?

- What could we do better for our service users?

- What do service users say we need to stop doing?

- What service provision do we need to preserve?

- What do we need to do to maintain motivation within our team?

According to Beresford *et al* (2005), the vision for service users is clearly about assisting communities to live fulfilling independent lives as well as providing people with choice and control over the services they receive. The leadership imperative, therefore, is to translate or transform that vision so that the whole team is motivated to deliver services that meet those aspirations, for example the kinds of services based on principles outlined in *A Vision of Adult Social Care* (Department of Health, 2010a).

6.3.2 Communicate the vision and strategic direction to team members

Communication systems are vital in health and social care teams because they not only provide them with clarity of purpose, they also help to reinforce and check for a common understanding among team members. There should therefore be transparent structures and protocols for how information is transmitted between team members.

The main formal communication channel is regular team meetings, although informal links that develop over time between individuals are also important. Team meetings should be positive events with a clear agenda to which team members can contribute (RCN and NHS Institute for Innovation and Improvement, 2007). The aim should be meaningful discussions that produce ideas and solutions to service problems in the minimum amount of time.

Activity

Effective teams have communication methods that clearly assign roles and responsibilities. They do this best when they meet regularly to coordinate their work and discuss problems they are experiencing openly and without fear.

1. How often are your team meetings?

2. Do you understand all the different roles in your team?

3. Do you feel comfortable and confident enough to raise your concerns during team meetings?

Figure 6.3 Team members need to be able to engage positively across other groups and agencies

As well as team meetings, group cohesion and focus on objectives can be supported by the use of IT technology solutions such as mobile phone services, texting, voicemail messaging, teleconferencing, email and the developing of shared intranet databases. These methods are efficient for team members and also help in maintaining communications with service users and other teams. However, these systems are not always available to teams or service users and there may be incompatibility problems that limit their use (Jelphs and Dickinson, 2008).

6.3.3 Work with others to promote a shared vision within the team

In addition to working collaboratively within the immediate team and with service users, team members must also engage positively across other groups and agencies, such as the police force and the education system. This provides the opportunity to share ideas and perspectives, as well as tap into a number of alternative views and experiences. It also enables us to question our own knowledge and abilities.

In the case of vulnerable adults, a quality service is heavily dependent on the team's ability to inform, consult and incorporate the views of service users and their advocates (Atkinson *et al*, 2007). The public trust in health and social care teams is contingent upon their understanding the ability of health and social care staff to act and advise with the needs and interests of service users uppermost.

Service users and their carers or advocates need to engage fully in service development plans by responding to consultations. Informal unpaid carers and voluntary sector staff can also play their part in any team development. The value of their contribution is being acknowledged increasingly and they are viewed as fundamental to the success of an inter-professional workforce (Tope and Thomas, 2007).

6.3.4 Evaluate how the vision and strategic direction of the team influences team practice

The acceptance of team working as an effective means of delivering quality health and social care services has been evident in policy since 1993 (Borrill *et al*, 1999). However, unless teams are set specific measurable, achievable and relevant targets, then it is not possible to make a realistic value judgement on their performance, that is, an evaluation (Latham and Locke, 2002).

Activity

Visit www.mindtools.com, look up 'team management' in the toolkit, and find out what methods are used to evaluate your team's performance.

1. Complete the team performance questionnaire and check the score and interpretation.

2. What have you learnt about your team's performance from completing this activity?

Whether targets are set by the team or by the organisation, they should be reviewed as part of any team development activity. The process of review also raises issues around how the team works together and highlights what will enable the team to grow and develop their practice.

If targets are set by involving the team members and critically have a service user focus, then they are more likely to be achieved, as staff will be motivated towards ensuring a successful outcome. In addition, accurate and timely feedback about the team's performance is required by the team members collectively and individually as service issues occur. Not only can feedback be a means of acknowledging and rewarding success, it also helps the team to take charge of problems and correct any misunderstandings or mistakes promptly.

Be able to develop a plan with team members to meet agreed objectives

6.4

When planning services you will require team leaders to be proactive and predict demand, rather than just simply responding when it arrives. It may appear that effective planning is an unrealistic goal. This is because change, particularly in health and social care, does not occur in a vacuum; the smallest plan has risks and benefits that are not always predictable.

6.4.1 Identify team objectives

A team needs to know what is expected of it, and objectives are statements that define the purpose of the team. These are often referred to as targets or goals. Since 1990, health and social care organisations have been required to conform to a central strategic framework, with the planning of most services based on an assessment of local need. For example, in services for older people, the objective is to ensure that they receive appropriate and timely packages of care regardless of health and social services boundaries (Department of Health, 2007).

All health and social care services are now expected to be responsive to the individual, person-centred and delivered with the support and involvement of carers (Department of Health, 2010c). Therefore, team objectives need to be aligned with national and local service priorities, such as increasing the use of personal budgets, while identifying development objectives to ensure the staff have the ability and resources to deliver the results.

Activity

Consider your own team objectives.

1. How responsive are they to the individual?

2. How do they align to the national and local service priorities?

6.4.2 Analyse how the skills, interests, knowledge and expertise within the team can meet agreed objectives

A health and social care team that employs the right mix of people, with the right values and experience to deploy in support of people with complex needs, is more likely to be able to deliver successful outcomes.

Team members will start off with different levels of experience and ability, from the novice to the highly specialised practitioner, but not all health and social care staff have the same self-development opportunities.

Despite some limitations to opportunities, practice settings provide an ideal setting in which teams can learn and reflect on their experiences (Eraut and Hirsh, 2008).

Kolb's (1984) model of experiential learning was modified by Honey and Mumford (1992) to describe a learning cycle. If applied to health and social care practice, team members can examine and review their experiences to learn from them and plan appropriate responses to future situations.

Activity

1. Find a learning styles questionnaire. Complete it either as a team exercise or as a solo task.

2. What have you learnt about your learning style from completing this activity?

3. What have you learnt about your colleagues?

4. How will what you have found out alter your interactions within the team?

6.4.3 Facilitate team members to participate actively in the planning process

The task of team planning is to create an organisation that responds to the needs of its service users (Dowling *et al*, 2006). A collaborative team planning approach uses interventions with service users and their carers that are based on humanistic and democratic values.

The plans produced should cover all the team's objectives and each one should specify:

■ focus: the services to be provided

■ shared values: guiding principles

■ outcomes expected: results the service users and carers need

■ steps to achievement: priorities

■ resources required: funding, people, equipment and information

■ timeline: reasonable end date

■ leadership: named key worker.

Moss Kanter (1983) provides a useful checklist of criteria for designing plans. She suggests that they develop in such a way that they appear to the participants to be triable, reversible, divisible, concrete, familiar, congruent, and have publicity value. The last criterion would perhaps be better expressed in the health and social care sector as having public value.

6.4.4 Encourage the sharing of skills and knowledge between team members

It is self-evident that individual team members must have knowledge and experience before they can share it with others. The NHS Futures Forum (Moore, 2011) believes that education and training is not only the key to consolidating skills in teams, it also affords them the opportunity to appreciate each other's roles.

One of the most important ways in which new members of any health and social care team are empowered to share their understanding of each other's roles is via a system of induction that has a consistent format (Skills for Care, 2010a). Once established, team members benefit from learning from the more experienced team members, who can help the less experienced by mentoring and coaching them to become more confident and thus more capable of handling their practice problems.

As the workforce will be expected to deliver more integrated services across traditional social care and health boundaries, they will also find themselves employed by different kinds of organisations. In addition to joint-working arrangements, fostering inter-agency understanding can be achieved by setting up work-shadowing schemes (Atkinson *et al*, 2007).

6.4.5 Agree roles and responsibilities with team members

All team members should have interesting and valued roles to perform. In order for them to appreciate each other's unique contribution, individual roles need to be clear and unambiguous. This prevents misunderstanding within the team in relation to protocols to be followed and the types of information to be shared.

Team roles need to be flexible enough to accommodate individual differences, personal development needs and membership changes. Ideally, individuals should be able to negotiate their roles and responsibilities. However, many health and social care teams are unable to choose who they work with. In addition, as the concepts of personalisation are adopted, then service users need to be accepted as core members of the team (Bamford, 2011).

Although there is not an 'I' in the word 'Team', there cannot be a team without individuals. To flourish, a team must nurture and build confidence and skills in the individuals.

Figure 6.4 Team roles need to be flexible enough to accommodate individual differences

Activity

1. What factors did your managers consider when they agreed your roles and responsibilities?

2. What factors may they consider when agreeing your colleagues' roles and responsibilities?

Be able to support individual team members to work towards agreed objectives

6.5.1 Set personal work objectives with team members based on agreed objectives

Health and social care teams are subject to regular supervision and annual individual performance reviews (Morrison, 2005). These ought to be an ideal opportunity for individual team members to reflect on their performance and agree a feasible number of their personal objectives for the coming year.

Individuals need to be able to consider how they relate to service users and be able to assess their team-working strengths and weaknesses. They also need to review the threats and opportunities there are in cooperating with other agencies (Payne, 2000).

Ideally, personal team objectives should be negotiated between the line manager and/or team leader. They need to be agreed and endorsed to ensure they support the team aims and be written in such a way that they are realistic and are capable of being evaluated.

Activity

1. How do you ensure personal team objectives are SMART (Specific, Measurable, Achievable, Relevant and Time-bound)?

Activity In Practice

One of Jayne's service users who has mild dementia is refusing to let the care worker into her house to give her medication. Jayne arranges to visit the service user on the care worker's next visit. She realises that people with dementia often refuse to take their medication if they have forgotten what it is for and they do not trust the care worker. They may refuse help from some care workers but not others and refusing to accept particular care workers may be the service user saying they do not trust them or know who they are.

Jayne knew it was important for the care worker to give a clear explanation in words and symbols each time they offered the medication. The service user had to take several different tablets so they should be reminded what each tablet is for. Jayne talked to the service user to try to clarify what was happening and what she would be prepared to accept.

After discussing the problems they were having, she agreed with the care worker and service user which of them would take responsibility for the administration of the medication. As well as the administration, a record of any refusal to cooperate would be documented.

It was agreed with the care worker's organisation that there was a need for the same care worker to attend to the service user, so that a closer relationship could be built with the service user's preferred care worker. There would be a review of the new arrangements after a month, and the care worker or service user could contact Jayne by text if there were

any other problems during that time.

1. Why is it important for this service user to have the same care worker visiting?

2. Why do people with dementia need to be reminded about their medication every time?

3. How will documenting the refusal help Jayne to monitor the situation?

6.5.2 Work with team members to identify opportunities for development and growth

West (2012) suggests that many clinicians are often so overloaded with work that it stops them from evaluating their practice. Yet all practice settings or situations provide learning opportunities and everyone within the team should have the desire to develop and grow their existing role.

Continuing Professional Development (CPD) is the umbrella term used to cover a range of activities that help individual team members prove they remain fit to practice. Indeed, for individual health and social care professionals, registration is aligned to a portfolio of evidence to show that they have engaged in meaningful development and update practice (Health Professions Council, 2011; Nursing and Midwifery Council, 2010).

Activity

Access Lifelong Learning Accounts (www.lifelonglearning.co.uk), which is one of the ways the government hopes to empower adults to take more control over their own lifelong learning. This website aims to provide clear information and advice on skills, careers and financial support tools.

1. Use the site to store your personal information.

2. Use the skills diagnostic tool to identify your strengths and development needs.

3. Find local training and education courses.

4. Build your curriculum vitae.

5. Check your eligibility for government funding.

6.5.3 Provide advice and support to team members to make the most of identified development opportunities

All team members need time to reflect and opportunities to discuss their concerns. To do this openly and honestly, individuals require a safe and supportive environment that values their contribution. Team structures that provide peer support are particularly helpful when practitioners are involved in complex and sometimes distressing cases, for example when dealing with cases of domestic violence or people with lack of capacity.

Mentorship or shadowing is one way in which leaders can appoint, or individuals can select, a trusted colleague to guide them on both personal and career development (PACEC, 2008). While mentoring by peers may not always be appropriate for new or inexperienced team members, it is often useful when team members hold leadership or line management posts. Individuals can start the process of managing themselves by forward planning their future. They may need to enlist others' opinions when considering their working relationships, but they should also consider their career aspirations and personal needs before they start to put together their personal development plans (Cottrell, 2008).

6.5.4 Use a solution-focused approach to support team members to address identified challenges

Positive change approaches are ways of communicating positive outcomes that can help individuals envision a gradual change in their practice (Myers, 2008). Solution-focused management focuses on solutions rather than practice problems. It was first developed in the 1980s by Steve de Shazer and Insoo Kim Berg as an approach to family therapy. Since then it has been adopted and adapted to coaching, and in team working. The approach depends on believing that the individual team member has the necessary strengths and resources to change what is not working, to doing what does work and to move forward (Fowler, 2011). The process involves helping the individual envision a preferred practice outcome, using scales to measure and develop progress towards that outcome and identifying the small practical steps towards their successful future.

Activity

1. Read the list of questions found at www.northwestsolutions.co.uk in the resources section under 'solution focused questions'.

2. Working with a colleague with a similar problem, use the questions to arrive at a satisfactory solution.

Be able to manage team performance

Team performance management is about establishing a formal, rigorous system of gathering information that will measure service delivery against the team's targets.

6.6.1 Monitor and evaluate progress towards agreed objectives

Monitoring a health and social care team's performance is essential so that any threats to its service delivery are identified early and corrective actions taken. According to Martin (2002), some people can become suspicious of the idea of controlling performance; however, it is essential to ensuring quality outcomes, on time and within budget.

An evaluation of the team's performance will entail a close examination of the available qualitative and quantitative evidence on outputs at an organisational, team and individual level. West (2004) suggests there are two dimensions of team functioning: the tasks the team is required to do, and the social climate that impacts on how they operate. Of the two, the social climate will determine how team members cope with diversity of opinions, accept difference and resolve conflict.

When you encourage a climate in which people communicate openly and share information, this can cause problems when personal data, either about team members or service users, needs to be kept confidential. However, generally teams rely on the free flow of good management information, which needs to be:

- relevant, in other words needed by the team in order to function

- clear, in that it is unambiguous and in a style agreed by the team

- complete and accurate, so that it is factual and specific rather than opinionated

- timely and up to date, and available to the team when they need it.

6.6.2 Provide feedback on performance to individuals and teams

Feedback on individual performance should be based on how well individuals have completed their work assignments and cooperated with other team members. It will require frank discussions around the person's performance in relation to their team and service objectives. It is also an ideal opportunity to motivate by giving praise where deserved.

Figure 6.5 Feedback provides an ideal opportunity to recognise individual achievements

The feedback may be formal in that it is undertaken by the line manager or team leader, or informal in that other team members provide feedback, for example during mentoring sessions or compliments made by service users and carers. It could focus on particular issues, such as the quality of the written case reports or workload management.

Alongside other forms of appraisal, the model of **360 degree feedback** has become increasingly popular in health and social care settings. According to Richardson (2010) it helps employees identify learning needs, reduces absenteeism and improves client-focused delivery.

One method of team feedback is to have one team member observe or audit the team and keep a careful record of what members say in team interactions and the effects on team behaviour. This would include how well the team runs meetings so that everyone can contribute and all disparate opinions can be heard before agreeing decisions and reaching a consensus.

Teams should be able to agree on realistic performance indicators. These help them to see whether they will achieve their targets and what actions to take if they are failing. If the team needs to change to meet new demands from service users, this may involve challenging issues of access to appropriate data and resources as well as support arrangements.

Key Term

360 degree feedback is a process in which people who know and understand the work of the team rate the team member's performance. The feedback can include reports by peers, line managers, service users or carers.

Activity

1. Visit www.youtube.com and watch the video on 360 degree feedback.

2. What are the benefits of 360 degree feedback?

3. How should this type of feedback be used?

4. How can honest feedback be collected?

6.6.3 Provide recognition when individual team objectives have been achieved

People feel valued and motivated if they are rewarded for their efforts. Rewards need not necessarily be financial; in health and social care work, making a difference to service users' well-being can be intrinsically motivating. Organisations that encourage learning from practice and within teams will share the benefits with their employees, because it increases their feelings of inclusiveness and autonomy (Senge *et al*, 1994). Away days, celebratory events and announcements in staff magazines are other forms of marking success whether big or small. They can also be used as a way to increase team motivation and employee engagement (MacLeod and Clarke, 2011). However, team rewards are more effective when they do not focus on any individuals but on the whole team. Keeping the whole team's morale high requires fairness and equal opportunities, so that everyone's voice – including that of service users and carers – is heard.

Activity

Consider how you and your team deals with success and failure.

1. What kinds of praise do you receive and who from?

2. How do you and your team deal with praise?

3. How do you deal with criticism?

4. Is that criticism constructive?

6.6.4 Explain how team members are managed when performance does not meet requirements

If clear objectives have been set, it's much easier for team leaders to notice someone who is underperforming or coasting along within a team. Some individuals – often experienced or those of higher status – will put in less effort when working in a team than they would do if they worked alone. In a team dynamic known as 'social loafing', they calculate that the other team members' efforts will compensate for their lack of commitment (Levi, 2007; West and Field, 1995).

If issues of poor performance are to be discussed, either individually or with the team, then there must be clear evidence that standards of service were not met. If discussions are conducted openly and without blame, more information may come to light and solutions are more likely to be achieved.

In the event of the worst-case scenario, team leaders will have to deal with poor performance. In doing so, they ought to have well-understood policies and procedures in place to ensure that if they need to discipline staff they do so in a way that is legal, fair and transparent (ACAS, 2009). Actions taken need to be reasonable and justifiable given the circumstances.

Are you ready for assessment?

✔ **Do you know the main features of an effective team?**

✔ **Do you know how to build a positive team culture?**

✔ **Do you know how to create a shared team vision?**

✔ **Can you develop a plan to meet the team objectives?**

✔ **Can you support other team members to work towards their objectives?**

✔ **Can you manage the team's performance?**

References

Advisory, Conciliation and Arbitration Service (ACAS) (2009) *Disiplinary and Grievance procedures*. Middlesex: HMSO.

Alimo-Metcalfe, B., *et al* (2007) *The Impact of Leadership Factors in Implementing Change in Complex Health and Social Care Environments*. London: Department of Health.

Atkinson, M., *et al* (2007) *Multi-Agency Working and its Implications for Practice: A Literature Review* pp1–108. London: CfBT Education Trust.

Bamford, T. (2011) *The Team Approach in Person-Centred Health Care: The Social Work Perspective*. The International Journal of Person-Centred Medicine 1(1), pp23, 26.

Belbin, M. (1993) *Team Roles at Work*. Oxford: Butterworth.

Beresford, P., *et al* (2005) *Developing Social Care: Service Users' Vision for Adult Support*. Bristol: Social Care Institute for Excellence, pp1–47.

Borrill, C., *et al* (1999) *The Effectiveness of Health Care Teams in the National Health Service*. Aston University, Aston Centre for Health Service Organisation Research.

Chong, E. (2007) *Role Balance and Team Development: A Study of Team Role Characteristics Underlying High- and Low-Performing Teams*. Victoria University of Wellington, pp202–17.

Cottrell, S. (2008) *Skills for Success: Personal Development and Employability*. Basingstoke: Palgrave Macmillan.

Covey, S., Merrill, R. (2006) *The Speed of Trust: The One Thing That Changes Everything*. New York: Simon and Schuster.

Dawes, D., Handscomb, A. (2005) *A Literature Review on Team Leadership*. Manchester: The European Nursing Leadership Foundation.

Department of Health (2007) *National Service Framework for Older People*. London: HMSO.

Department of Health (2010b) *Healthy Lives, Healthy People: Our Strategy for Public Health in England*. London: HMSO.

Department of Health (2010c) *Personalisation through Person-Centred Planning*. London: DH Publications, pp1–57.

Department of Health (2011) *Enabling Excellence: Autonomy and Accountability for Health and Social Care Staff*. London: Department of Health.

Dowling, S., *et al* (2006) Person-Centred Planning in Social Care: A Scoping Review. York: Joseph Rowntree Foundation, pp1–64.

Eraut, M., Hirsh, W. (2008) *The Significance of Workplace Learning for Individuals, Groups and Organisations*. Centre on Skills, Knowledge and Organisational Performance, Oxford and Cardiff Universities, pp1–97.

Fisher, R., Ury, W. (1983) *Getting to Yes: Negotiating Agreement Without Giving In*. New York: Penguin Books.

Fowler, J. (2011) *Solution-Focused Clinical Supervision: Using Solution-Focused Techniques Within Clinical Supervision* in Cutcliffe, J., Hyrkas, K., and Fowler, J. (Eds), *Routledge Handbook of*

Clinical Supervision: Fundamental International Themes. Oxford: Routledge, pp102–11.

Hackman, J. (2002) *Leading Teams: Setting the Stage for Great Performances.* Boston: Harvard Business School Press.

Honey, P., Mumford, A. (1992) *The Manual of Learning Styles.* Maidenhead: Peter Honey Publications.

Kolb, D. (1984) *Experiential Learning.* New York: Prentice Hall.

Jelphs, K., and Dickinson, H. (2008) Working in Teams. Bristol: Policy Press.

Latham, G., Locke, E. (2002) 'Building a practically useful theory of goal setting and task motivation'. *American Psychologist,* 57(9), pp705–17.

Lawler, J., Bilson, A. (2004) 'Towards a More Reflexive Research Aware Practice: The Influence and Potential of Professional and Team Culture'. *Social Work and Social Sciences Review,* 11(1), pp63–80.

Levi, D. (2007) *Group Dynamics for Teams.* Thousand Oaks: Sage.

Loxley, A. (1997) *Collaboration in Health and Welfare.* London and Philadelphia: Jessica Kingsley Publishers.

MacLeod, D., Clarke, N. (2011) *Engaging for Success: Enhancing Performance Through Employee Engagement.* HMSO, Office of Public Sector Information.

Martin, V. (2002) *Managing Projects in Health and Soial Care.* London: Routledge.

Maslin-Prothero, S., Bennion, A. (2010) 'Integrated Team Working: a Literature Review'. *International Journal of Integrated Care* (10), pp1–11.

Mead, M. (2000) *The Study of Culture at a Distance.* New York: Berghahn Books.

Mintzberg, H. (2009) 'Rebuilding Companies as Communities'. *Harvard Business Review* July–August, pp300ff.

Morrison, T. (2005) *Staff Supervision in Social Care: Making a Real Difference for Staff and Service Users.* Brighton: Pavillion.

Moss Kanter, R. (1983) *The Change Masters: Corporate Entrepreneurs at Work.* New York: Simon & Schuster.

Myers, S. (2008) *Solution-Focused Approaches.* Dorset: Russell House Publishing.

NHS Executive (2000) *The Vital Connections: An Equalities Framework for the NHS.* London: Department of Health.

PACEC (2008) *Models of Mentoring across Social Care in the West Midlands.* Cambridge: Public and Corporate Economic Consultants, pp1–66.

Payne, M. (2000) *Teamwork in Multiprofessional Care.* Hampshire: MacMillan Press.

RCN, NHS Institute for Innovation and Improvement (2007) *Developing and Sustaining Effective Teams.* London: Royal College of Nursing.

Richardson, R. (2010) '360-Degree Feedback: Integrating Business Know-How with Social Work Values'. *Administration in Social Work,* 34(5), pp 259–74.

Rosenfeld, R. Servo, J. C. (1991) *Facilitating Innovation in Large Organisations* in Henry, J, and Walker, D. *Managing Innovation.* London: Sage Publications (pp28–39).

Senge, P., Kleiner, A., Roberts, C., Ross, R. B., Smith, B. J. (1994) *The Fifth Discipline Fieldbook: Strategies and Tools for Building a Learning Organisation.* New York: Doubleday.

Suter, E. *et al* (2009) 'Role Understanding and Effective Communication as Core Competencies for Collaborative Practice'. *Journal of Interprofessional Care* (23), pp41–51.

Syer, J., Connolly, C. (1996) *How Teamworking Works: The Dynamics of Team Development.* London: McGraw-Hill.

Tope, R., Thomas, E. (2007) *Health and Social Care Policy and the Interprofessional Agenda*. London: CIPW (pp1–113).

Tuckman, B., Jensen, M. (1977) *Stages of Small-Group Development Revisited*. Group and Organisation Studies 2(4).

Tuckman, B. W. (1965) 'Developmental Sequence in Small Groups'. *Psychological Bulletin*, pp384–99.

West, M., Field, R. (1995) 'Teamwork in Primary Health Care. 1. Perspectives from Organisational Psychology'. *Journal of Interprofessional Care*, 9(2), pp117–22.

West, M. (1994) *Effective Teamwork*. London: Blackwell.

West, M. (2012) *Effective Teamwork: Practical Lessons from Organisational Research*. London: Blackwell.

Wheelan, S. (2005) *Creating Effective Teams: A Guide for Members and Leaders*. London: Sage.

Zalenznick, A. (1992) *Managers and Leaders: Are They Different?* Harvard: Harvard Review.

Websites and Web-based articles

Community Care, *The Need for More Critically Reflective Social Work*, www.communitycare.co.uk, accessed 2 July 2012.

Department of Health (2010a) A Vision for Adult Social Care: Capable Communities and Active Citizens, www.dh.gov.uk, accessed 2 July 2012.

Health Professions Council (2011) Continuing Professional Development. www.hpc-uk.org/registrants/cpd/index.asp, accessed 3 July 2012.

Lifelong Learning Accounts, www.lifelonglearning.co.uk/ln11105.htm, accessed 2 July 2012.

Moore, J. (2011) Education and Training – next stage: A report from the NHS Future Forum. www.dh.gov.uk/en/Publicationsandstatistics/Publications/PublicationsPolicyAndGuidance/DH_127443, accessed 3 July 2012.

Nursing and Midwifery Council (2010), www.nmc-uk.org/Registration/Staying-on-the-register/Meeting-the-Prep-standards/, accessed 2 July 2012.

Skills for Care (2010a) *Common Induction Standards*, www.skillsforcare.org.uk/cis, accessed 2 July 2012.

Chapter 7

Develop professional **supervision** practice in health **and social care settings**

In health and social care settings, skilled people are assigned the responsibility of overseeing the work of others in order to ensure they meet their organisational, professional and personal objectives (Morrison, 2005).

The aim of this chapter is to assess the knowledge, understanding and skills required to undertake professional supervision of others.

By the end of this chapter you will:

1 Understand the purpose of professional supervision

2 Understand how the principles of professional supervision can be used to inform performance management

3 Be able to undertake the preparation for professional supervision with supervisees

4 Be able to provide professional supervision

5 Be able to manage conflict situations during professional supervision

6 Be able to evaluate your own practice when conducting professional supervision

Understand the purpose of professional supervision

7.1

While supervision is traditionally associated with social care, it has also been increasingly seen as essential for all the 'helping' professions. The ideal method of professional supervision is seen as supportive. However, since the 1980s, public sector concerns for quality and risk avoidance have grown, and so has the widespread adoption of private sector management supervision practices.

7.1.1 Analyse the principles, scope and purpose of professional supervision

A principle is essentially a value precept or guideline and, applied to supervision, it provides us with the conditions for the process. Morrison (2005) suggests there should be underpinning beliefs to supervision, some of which are that:

- staff are entitled to the highest standards
- supervision is the most important relationship
- supervision is about reflection as well as action
- supervision must attend to both process and content
- good supervisors bring about change
- supervising is a complex and demanding task that requires training
- supervisors should be a role model for their staff.

Morrison also goes on to describe the scope of supervision as a process involving complex relationships between the supervisor, the supervisee, the organisation and the service users.

Activity

Consider the functions of your supervision.

1. How does it ensure your accountability for practice?

2. How does it support you in practice?

3. What are your training needs it has identified?

4. In what way does it help you to deal with difficult practice issues?

7.1.2 Outline theories and models of professional supervision

A supervision model is a theoretical framework to guide the delivery of clinical supervision. It outlines the important stages within the process, its functions and the roles of the supervisor and supervisee (Fowler, 2007).

There are numerous models of supervision from a range of theoretical backgrounds, such as sociological, management, psychoanalysis and counselling, feminism and education. The three most often cited are functional, internationalist and practice (centred and solution-based).

1. 'Three-function interactive model' (Cutcliffe and Proctor, 1998) is a process where the supervisor and supervisee are jointly responsible for completing formative, normative and restorative supervision sessions.

2. 'Intervention analysis framework' adapted from Heron's work (Sloan and Watson, 2001) consists of two intervention approaches:

- authoritative interventions, where the supervisor controls the process using interventions that are prescriptive, informative and confronting

- facilitative interventions, where control lies with the supervisee and the interventions are cathartic, catalytic and supportive.

3. 'Solution-focused approaches' (Myers, 2008) focus on the positive through goal identification rather than why problems arise.

More recently, Davys and Beddoe (2010) have developed the functional model to integrate management and development aspects of the process. They represent it as a triangle with each point of the triangle having a supervisor function connected by lines of tension. In the centre of the triangle are the core conditions under which supervision should occur: values, respect, safe climate, conflict resolution and anti-discriminatory practice.

Activity

1. Examine Davys and Beddoe's model (2010) in detail. Note the similarities and differences with the three most commonly cited models.

2. How does their model integrate the management and developmental aspects of supervision?

3. How does this differ from the other models?

4. Identify the possible tension in your own experience of supervision.

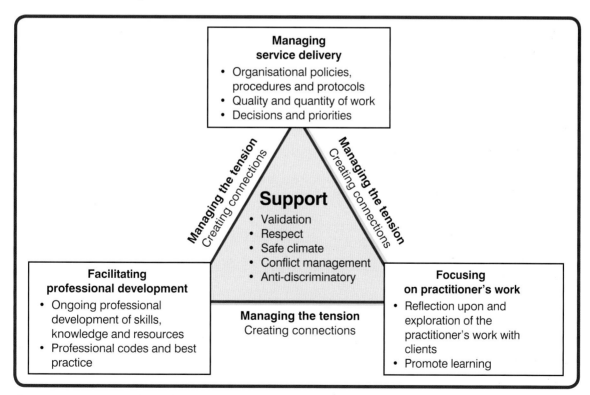

Figure 7.1 Davys and Beddoe's supervision model

7.1.3 Explain how the requirements of legislation, codes of practice and agreed ways of working influence professional supervision

The focus of any supervision is to develop the supervisee's professional practice in line with the expectations of the employer, service users and carers as well as the legal dictates of the eleven individual Professional Councils' standards (The Law Commission, 2012).

From the employers' perspective, the Department of Health has set clinical supervision as a key target to be achieved. They describe it as: 'a formal process of professional support and learning which enables individual practitioners to develop knowledge and competence, assume responsibility for their own practice and enhance consumer protection and safety of care in complex clinical situations' (Department of Health, 1993, p15).

Similarly, all the professional regulators state quite categorically that health and social care workers are responsible for keeping their knowledge and skills up to date throughout their working life and maintaining and improving their performance.

Staff should have realistic workloads, enabling management systems and access to continuing development opportunities. Managers have a duty of care to provide good quality supervision (Department of Health, 2010b).

7.1.4 Explain how findings from research, critical reviews and inquiries can be used within professional supervision

Health and social care workers come from different professional backgrounds, and this may impact on the types of research they produce. Whatever the evidence, it should produce knowledge that is useful in everyday practice (Marsh and Fisher, 2005).

Evidenced-based research is a multi-professional approach to an organisational effort to bridge the theory–practice divide. The research outcomes are then used to produce guidelines, **protocols** and standards to which all professionals are expected to conform. The National Institute for Health and Clinical Evidence was established in 1999 to help in this process and has gone on to provide free access to best evidence.

Evidence-based health and social care practice will make use of current research and critical reviews of the literature when making decisions relating to the well-being of service users and carers. It requires a five-stage method:

1. A focused question.

2. Finding the information related to the question.

3. Critically appraising the information.

4. Applying the answers to practice.

5. Evaluating and sharing results.

> **Key Term**
>
> **Protocols** are codes of behaviour.

7.1.5 Explain how professional supervision can protect individuals, supervisors and supervisees

The purpose of professional supervision from an employer perspective is to ensure public protection. Link this to regulation in health and social care and appointing supervisors is a means of increasing professional accountability and avoiding risk by increasing surveillance of the workforce (Beddoe, 2010). From a purely individual professional perspective, supervision is a means of reflection on and in practice as a way to identify your continuing professional development needs (Godden, 2012).

Activity

Visit the newly formed College of Social Work (www.collegeofsocialwork.org) and review the Professional Capabilities Framework.

1. How will this help you plan your career development?

2. How will this help to protect the public?

Activity   *In Practice*

Caroline understands that the philosophy behind the personalisation agenda for all services is the way forward, but she is concerned that the uptake among elderly service users is very low. She is also concerned that the programme used to calculate the budgets seems to favour the less dependent service user and penalise the highly dependent, which does not give her confidence in the process.

Staff express concern during supervision that since Caroline has been given the responsibility for calculating the budgets, the costs of even the basic services are not comparable to those under the direct payment system. This has generated more work stress as Caroline now spends additional time getting support to find the funding required to meet the assessed level of need.

During supervision, Caroline suggests that she is demotivated about personal budgets and it's no wonder the uptake is low. She suspects that it is the organisation's way of cutting funding for social services.

1. Does Caroline really understand personalisation?

2. Is Caroline right to suspect cuts in funding?

3. Is she protecting the public by her actions?

Understand how the principles of professional supervision can be used to inform performance management

Performance management in health and social care settings is vital to ensuring organisational quality. It links the work of teams and individuals to their stated objectives. There can only be service improvements if everyone understands what is expected of them and how that contributes to the organisation's vision of service delivery (Improvement and Development Agency (I&DeA), 2007).

7.2.1 Explain the performance management cycle

Three theoretical perspectives inform how performance management will be implemented (Buchner, 2007):

1. Control theory: This approach focuses on providing feedback as a means of shaping behaviour. It relies on the idea that feedback allows people to appreciate what they do well and what they need to do to correct their performance.

2. Goal theory: This approach emphasises setting and agreeing objectives which can then can be measured and managed.

3. Social cognitive theory: This is based on the idea that what people believe they are capable of impacts on their performance. Thus developing positive self-belief in employees is an important management task.

Whatever perspective is adopted or adapted, it is crucial that there is a shared understanding about what and how services are to be delivered. Therefore having an approach to managing all the people involved increases the likelihood of health and social care organisations achieving their aims.

According to Armstrong (2009), the performance management has five main elements to its implementation:

1. agreeing objectives

2. measurement of outputs

3. feedback related to performance

4. positive reinforcement

5. dialogue about development.

Armstrong suggests that performance management should be about line managers and subordinates working in partnership to get the best results for everyone involved. The cycle is a continuous and self-renewing process of annual agreements, oversight during the year and formal review. The I&DeA (2007) has a simpler model of 'plan, do, review and revise' (see Figure 7.1).

While the wider health and social care organisation needs to adopt a strategic approach to performance management, you and your team need to think about how you assure and monitor the quality of the services you provide (Morrison, 2005).

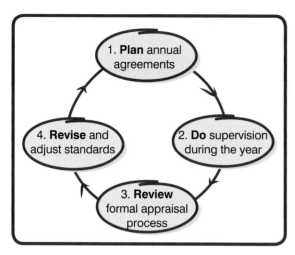

Figure 7.2 Performance management cycle (adapted from I&DeA and Morrison)

7.2.2 Analyse how professional supervision supports performance

All health and social care organisations should have an overall performance management framework that includes supervision. This is because professional supervision is believed to make a significant contribution to the way health and social care organisations achieve quality outcomes for service users. The aim of supervision is to support service users to lead healthy and independent lives (Department of Health, 2010a; Department of Health, 2010c).

By contrast, performance management is directed at improving the quality of the workforce outcomes or outputs. Within health care, there tends to be a clear division between performance management and clinical supervision (Butterworth and Faugier, 2012; Department of Health, 1998). In social care settings, the functions are integrated and it is these organisational and cultural differences that could be detrimental to joint working (Godden, 2012).

Effective supervision will not only deal with the normative managerial aspects of performance, it will also deal with the educative and pastoral features of staff

professional support. According to Skills for Health (2012), these features are:

- line management: accountability and quality of services to users and carers

- professional supervision: reflecting on and in practice issues and reviewing roles and responsibilities

- continuing professional development: using constructive feedback that helps staff to identify their learning and career development needs.

Activity

During your latest supervision sessions:

1. How did you handle accountability issues?

2. How did you review the professional aspects?

3. Were you able to agree on training and development needs?

7.2.3 Analyse how performance indicators can be used to measure practice

Performance indicators are measures that help health and social care teams understand what is happening in practice, compare themselves to others and make the necessary adjustments to improve. Most performance management requires some form of measuring standards or quality indicator. The data gathered can then be used for feedback during staff appraisals. A concern for all health and social care managers is that too many indicators will prevent them from focusing on real improvements (NHS IIIC, 2008).

Performance indicators are generally numerical in value and rely on facts rather than supposition. In order to avoid the idea that indicators are associated with finding fault with professionals, they must be understood in context of practice. Measurement of practice will always produce some variation and failure to understand, whether the cause is common or a special factor.

Some aspects of a team's performance may not be measurable quantifiably but can be assessed against agreed definitions that constitute good behaviour, for example anti-discriminatory practice.

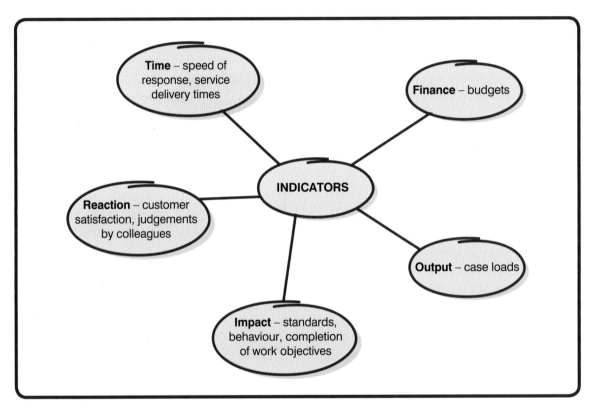

Figure 7.3 The most common types of performance indicators

Be able to undertake the preparation for professional supervision with supervisees

7.3

Good supervision is a regular two-way process in which the supervisor and supervisee meet to review practice and accept full responsibility for what occurs. In addition, all health and social care settings have an obligation to provide a positive culture of supervisory practice (CWDC and SfC, 2012).

7.3.1 Explain factors which result in a power imbalance in professional supervision

Power is often perceived as some form of control or influence exerted over someone or something, when in effect it is a resource that is available to everyone. However, some cultures or communities are deemed more powerful than others and so imbalances in power are inevitable in any kind of professional relationship (Hawkins and Shohet, 2007).

Richmond's (2009) view is that supervisory relationships are imbued with power sources that emerge from both managerial and professional authority. Thus both parties to supervision will have personal experiences and beliefs that will impact on their relationship.

According to Davys and Beddoe (2010), power imbalances are likely to emerge from three sources:

1. the legitimate role of the line manager as supervisor

2. the authority derived from professional knowledge and skill

3. the perceived personal attributes of the supervisor to exercise their authority in issues of unsafe practice.

7.3.2 Explain how to address power imbalance in your own professional supervision

Given that power permeates every supervisory relationship on a number of levels, it is important for supervisors to find ways to minimise the possible detrimental effects. The most important strategy is to establish and maintain a healthy relationship with a supervisee during supervision. It begins with negotiating and agreeing protected time and a safe space for supervision.

The success of the relationship depends on both parties having an open and respectful approach that enables honest disclosure of difficult practice issues. Supervisors should acknowledge their power base within the supervisory relationship with its inevitable bias in favour of the supervisor or line manager. The onus therefore lies with the supervisor to use that power imbalance wisely and ethically (Raven, 1993; Hughes and Pengelly, 1997).

7.3.3 Agree with supervisee confidentiality, boundaries, roles and accountability within the professional supervision process

All employers have a duty of care, which means that line managers or supervisors need to be concerned about the supervisees' physical, psychological and social well-being (Boorman, 2009). That means creating and agreeing a safe positive culture and climate which allows supervision to be:

- person-centred: focused on supervisees' practice to service users and carers

- based on an agreed agenda: related to supervisee set objectives

- private: free of interruptions

- ethical: based on professional values such as equal opportunities and anti-discriminatory practice

- a free flow of information: data needs to be available and accessible

- recorded: kept confidential unless judged otherwise.

7.3.4 Agree with the supervisee the frequency and location of professional supervision

Within many health and social care settings, supervision may not be entirely voluntary. Some professionals such as social workers and midwives have the requirements for supervision prescribed. In addition to determining how frequently supervision takes place, there may be other conditions about who is allowed to be a supervisor as well as what form supervision should take.

However, Northcott (2000) insists that clinical supervision should be voluntary and can only be effective in improving practice if it is embedded in the professional psyche. Yet whatever form the supervision takes – whether managerial or professional – the element of agreement is that all health and social care settings should arrange for supervision to be:

- regular: throughout the year, ideally eight times and *ad hoc* when necessary

- planned: the time and place negotiated and agreed by both parties.

Activity

1. Consider the challenges to creating a safe positive climate for supervision in your organisation. Using the bulleted points above, identify the potential conflicts that may occur.

2. How do you address health and well-being issues during supervision?

7.3.5 Agree with the supervisee sources of evidence that can be used to inform professional supervision

It is generally agreed that the focus of any supervision should be person-centred, whether conducted from an organisational, service user or professional perspective. To that end, the information used will directly relate to those three perspectives as well as concentrating on particular personal issues the supervisee may be experiencing.

The evidence that may be used to inform practice may come from several sources, but should be linked to the supervisee's practice objectives, such as:

- workload management
- monitoring of the quality of service provided
- reflection on and in practice
- team working assessments
- user satisfaction surveys
- multi-layered feedback (360°)
- performance measurements
- observation of practice.

7.3.6 Agree with supervisee actions to be taken in preparation for professional supervision

Effective supervision is an important employee right for people in health and social care settings, but it is also a responsibility.

The guidance given by the Effective Supervision Unit, which was developed in association with a wide range of employers, practitioners and partners, including the Department of Health and the Department for Education and Skills, is that supervisees should:

- prepare for each supervision meeting by reviewing notes from the previous meeting and thinking about the things they want to raise and discuss
- be ready to share thoughts and ideas in the meeting
- be open about what has gone well and what they have found difficult
- be ready to plan and undertake training and other development activities as agreed with their supervisor
- check and read the notes of their meetings to make sure they follow through and complete any actions as agreed.

(CWDC and SfC, 2012)

Activity

1. Do you think you prepare your supervisees adequately for their supervision?

2. Do you feel your supervisees can talk openly with you?

3. Do you and they follow through with all the actions you have agreed upon?

Be able to provide professional supervision

7.3

Professional supervision in health and social care settings may have different purposes and relevance (Driscoll, 2007). Some will be formal as part of the planned professional or managerial supervision, while others may be both. There will also be times when informal and *ad hoc* supervision is necessary to deal with particularly difficult practice or personal issues or problems.

7.4.1 Support supervisees to reflect on their practice

According to Morrison (2005), supervisors require both professional and managerial competence to negotiate the interface between the different supervisory systems and create a safe and secure climate for their supervisees.

How much support a supervisee will require may well depend on their level of professional maturity (Hawkins and Shohet, 2007). Initially, the novice practitioner will be dependent on the supervisor for encouragement with a structured approach to supervision and information giving. The more professionally mature supervisee, while requiring less structure to supervision, may still need facilitating to articulate their understanding of situations in their practice or personal relationships.

Activity

1. Consider your own stage of supervision support and how it corresponds to Hawkins and Shohet's (2007) stages of development.

2. Do you feel that your support is appropriate to your level of experience?

3. What needs to change?

4. What needs to remain the same?

7.4.2 Provide positive feedback about the achievements of the supervisee

Praising professional behaviour is important as it increases motivation and reinforces commitment. It has to be genuine as flattery will be quickly detected and reduce the impact of well-deserved praise. If positive feedback is an on-going activity in health and social care settings, then formal feedback situations will not normally cause any difficult conversations. However, the topic(s) and structure for feedback should be agreed prior to commencing any dialogue. It may range from simple questions and responses related to everyday practice through to the more formal written and verbal feedback.

Figure 7.4 Praising professional behaviour increases motivation and reinforces commitment

McKimm (2009) suggests that feedback should be linked to professional development and learning and focus on behaviours that can be changed. Whatever the scenario, the principles of giving positive feedback are the same: a safe and secure professional relationship with open dialogue helps the supervisee to receive messages appropriately. Positive feedback is then more likely to help the supervisee to make informed decisions about their practice and accept responsibility for their future learning and development.

7.4.3 Provide constructive feedback that can be used to improve performance

The aim of any form of supervision enables professionals to maximise their effectiveness. Constructive feedback and observation of practice should be part of the learning process for workers and supervisors. All feedback should be aligned to the professional's personal practice or team objective and be specific.

The feedback you give should focus on your supervisees' practice or performance strengths and particular development needs in both written and spoken forms. Some of your supervisees may need extra support to identify one or two areas for development.

Throughout, you will need to acknowledge what and how well they have achieved in a positive way.

Shohet (2006) provides a useful acronym for giving effective feedback: CORBS, which stands for:

- **C**lear: what and why
- **O**wned: use 'I' statements
- **R**egular: frequent
- **B**alanced: confirming corrective and reflective
- **S**pecific: related to an event or behaviour.

Activity

When you have to deal with staff who need extra support, practise using CORBS. For instance, you could use it when you feel someone is too quiet in team meetings and you need to encourage their contribution.

1. How was the constructive feedback accepted?

2. Would you consider using this technique for other issues?

3. In what other practice situations could this technique be useful?

7.4.4 Support supervisees to identify their own development needs

While informal support and advice from colleagues may be helpful to health and social care workers, it should not be considered a substitute for formal supervision sessions. On the other hand, peer support and supervision may be considered as part of a formal process.

A key aspect of enabling supervisees to identify their own development needs is to support them in reviewing and reflecting on practice issues. This may include reviewing roles and relationships, evaluating the outcomes of their work and exploiting opportunities for wider learning.

7.4.5 Review and revise professional supervision targets to meet the identified objectives of the work setting

To ensure effective clinical supervision, supervisees need to have prepared for their meeting and be active (rather than passive) participants within the supervisory relationship. When reviewing their targets related to their work, supervisees should consider:

- how their workload was managed and priorities set
- why management and professional policies and procedures should be used
- which service users planned outcomes they are expected to achieve and by when
- whether work is allocated according to their experience and skill
- when practice risks are identified and how they are addressed
- what their statutory responsibilities are and how they are addressed
- their case recording, including how they ensure daily records are of the requisite standard
- what continuing professional development has been completed and what further learning and development they require.

7.4.6 Support supervisees to explore different methods of addressing challenging situations

It is accepted that practitioners in health and social care settings can be affected by the stressful nature of the work (Godden, 2012). Thus, the opportunity to share experiences through a form of structured reflection during a clinical supervision session is held to be beneficial to practitioners' personal well-being.

Reflection is more than just thinking; it takes time, preparation and a willingness to learn that requires the commitment of the supervisee to engage fully in the process. Guided reflection is a form of focused conversations in and about practice and is a way of applying this form of learning to the supervision process (Davys and Beddoe, 2010).

In order to learn from challenging situations, the supervisee must examine the effect of events, the consequences and the interactions that occurred on themselves. To help them fully understand the events, they should also consider how they might have caused or influenced the situation.

7.4.7 Record agreed supervision decisions

While supervision is normally undertaken on a one-to-one basis, in private and in confidence, the records pertaining to that supervision are not confidential. It is normal practice for organisations and professions in health and social care to have agreed some general format for recording supervision.

Records should be made in a timely manner and signed; the content and decision have to be agreed and understood by both parties. The records are then filed, although health and social care workers should have access to their records and indeed copies of their reports. It needs to be made explicitly clear to employees that managers may also have access to the reports, normally for auditing the quality of the supervision.

Be able to manage conflict situations during professional supervision

7.5

Despite clarification of the supervisee roles and responsibilities before, during and after supervision, some staff may still remain anxious and conflicted about the process (Morrison and Wonnacott, 2010). This is where the experience of the supervisor is crucial – in picking up the clues in the supervisee's behaviour and in having the skills to manage and resolve conflict situations.

7.5.1 Give examples from your own practice of managing conflict situations within professional supervision

A conflict situation in supervision is any context in which there is opposition to the professional behaviour, values and goals of the process. With some employees the conflict might result in a sharp verbal dispute, while for others their might be a more deep-seated issue. According to Taylor (2011), people challenge because they care and so are motivated to be difficult. She suggests that just actively listening to people's emotions and affirming the person can help to turn around a difficult situation and engender more staff loyalty.

Thomas's (1992) five-stage model of conflict can be applied to supervision as follows:

1. an awareness of practice or performance problems

2. an expression of thoughts and emotions

3. the perceived intentions of the supervisee

4. the observed or reported behaviour

5. the resulting practice outcomes.

On other occasions, supervisors need to be more assertive with the supervisee. Here the DESC (Describe, Express, Specify, Clarify) model (Bower and Bower, 1991) is a particularly useful approach for giving corrective feedback. Confrontational feedback may not be a comfortable experience for the supervisee because they may feel powerless. However, the intention is not to devalue them but to help them learn by focusing on the problem behaviour and not on the person, as follows:

■ Describe: the behaviour/performance that creates problems.

■ Express: your emotions and feelings about that behaviour/performance.

■ Specify: what you want the supervisee to do.

■ Clarify: the consequences for failing to change or alternatively changing.

When feedback is given in a timely, respectful and honest manner with a chance for discussion, it can be an opportunity for reflection on past, present and future learning.

You are a new manager. Ranjeet, an experienced social worker, has come for her planned supervision session. You had agreed with her prior to supervision that you would discuss her case load. In particular you are keen to review her handling of one of her homeless service users, who was refusing to stay in a hostel that had agreed to take him on his discharge from hospital. The district nurse has also expressed some concerns to you that he may lack capacity and is requesting some proactive action to protect what she considers is a vulnerable adult.

As you are raising these issues about the service user, Ranjeet starts to raise issues related to her previous manager's style of supervision and complains about the lack of direction she received.

1. How can you use confrontational feedback to enable Ranjeet to focus on the service user issues?

7.5.2 Reflect on your own practice in managing conflict situations experienced during the professional supervision process

The interdependency of the supervisory relationship does not in itself create conflict situations; rather, the supervisory process provides the conditions under which it may happen. Therefore supervisors should be sensitive to the power dynamic within their supervisory relationships, particularly with regard to differences in gender, race or ethnic biases. By handling conflict appropriately and quickly, they will stop any potential damage or breakdown in their supervisory relationships.

According to Thomas and Kilmann (2002), no two people have identical expectations so conflict is a natural part of any human interaction. They believe that in any conflict situation, an individual's behaviour will range between the two dimensions of assertiveness or cooperativeness. These dimensions can be used by supervisors to reflect on how they believe they or the supervisee behaves when confronted by a conflict situation:

- Competing: assertive but uncooperative.
- Accommodating: cooperative but unassertive.
- Avoiding: unassertive and uncooperative.
- Collaborative: assertive and cooperative (also known as the win–win approach).
- Compromising: seeks a quick solution; neither overtly assertive nor cooperative.

The aim of conflict management is to empower both parties to reach a consensus on how the dispute can be resolved. It involves understanding and respecting the rights and interests of each party while at the same time acknowledging their respective responsibilities in the process.

All competent communications depend on the situation and context in which they occur. Adult-to-adult interpersonal transactions (Berne, 2010) that bring about a win–win or collaborative approach to conflict resolution leaves both parties feeling positive about the outcome. It avoids the 'Drama Triangle' of games in supervision where either one can be seen to be adopting the role of a persecutor, rescuer or victim (Morrison, 2005).

According to Adler and Proctor (2011), getting to a win–win solution involves several stages:

1. The first stage is that performance problems are identified and agreed.
2. Next, both give their perspective on the cause of the problem and it is discussed from each point of view.
3. Finally, a solution is negotiated and the follow-up action agreed.

Be able to evaluate your own practice when conducting professional supervision

7.6

Since it is generally accepted that health and social care work is stressful, effective supervision not only plays an important role in supporting and motivating staff but it also benefits employers with employee recruitment and retention by reducing stress and burnout (Hawkins and Shohet, 2007). Because of the importance of supervision to improving services in health and social care settings, it is essential to ensure the process is conducted ethically as well as equitably and consistently.

7.6.1 Gather feedback from supervisee(s) on your own approach to the supervision process

To evaluate is to determine the quality of the supervision and a supervisee's experiences. Evaluation ought to be based on what can be mutually agreed are the standards of supervision an employee is entitled to expect. The feedback from the supervisees will form only one part of that evaluation (SCIE, 2011). In addition, the feedback is more helpful to the supervisor if it is aligned to certain standards and gathered during supervision.

A standard is a level of performance that everyone should be able to achieve. The result of setting standards in supervision is to improve the consistency and accountability in the quality of all supervision. Being a supervisor is a significant responsibility, as the individuals you supervise often have high expectations of the process. While it is unrealistic of both parties to assume the process will be perfect, there are

some minimum standards that supervisees should expect (CWDC and SfC, 2012), and the supervisor can expect to ask if they have been fulfilled.

The standards require that:

- supervision should be regular, planned well in advanced and not changed except in exceptional circumstances
- the supervisees can also expect to have an agreed agenda that is well structured and that they have been encouraged to contribute towards
- the setting ought to be private so that it promotes a positive climate and an anti-discriminatory process. Furthermore, there should be time to discuss, uninterrupted, the pertinent issues around the three supervisory functions:

1. line management: ensure appropriate workload and performance management; maintain motivation and job satisfaction through clarity on work and team objectives

2. professional practice: support reflection in and on practice and give guidance on focus of case work; allow for discussion on methods used to deliver services and debrief after dealing with stressful cases

3. continuing professional development: use critical reflection and analysis of your own knowledge, values and skills and understanding of your own practice. Provide positive constructive feedback to assist learning and identification of development needs.

■ the supervisory records need to be promptly documented, stored securely and copied to the supervisee.

Activity

1. Use the above standards to audit your latest supervisory sessions.

2. Did you have to rearrange any of the planned session and why?

3. How many staff submitted agenda items? Of those that did, how many were from new staff?

4. How did the setting impact on the process?

5. Review the storage of records. Did the supervisees get a copy of their record?

Activity

There are several dimensions to well-being such as:

■ physical

■ emotional

■ social

■ intellectual

■ spriritual

■ environmental.

1. Using each of the dimensions, consider how your supervision supports or hinders your well-being.

7.6.2 Adapt approaches to your own professional supervision in light of feedback

According to the British Association and College of Social Workers research report on supervision (Godden, 2012), there is evidence that good supervision improves both practice and the well-being of social workers. They advise that employers in health and social care settings should therefore ensure that a supervision framework is in place, and ensure that effective supervision takes place.

Davys and Beddoes (2010) suggest that receiving feedback about supervision both enhances and tests the supervisory relationships. When it is used regularly within a supervisory session, it becomes accepted practice. The ability to learn from this feedback enables supervisors to develop, change and improve the quality of the process.

Davys and Beddoes go on to advocate that supervision is viewed as a skill-based activity in which there are intentional uses of interventions; they believe this is necessary for learning to occur. Therefore, it may help supervisors to use the interventions framework for exploring the feedback given during supervisory sessions. Using the framework, it is possible to consider your own supervisory performance in relation to the following interventions:

■ Facilitative: was it a confirmatory and reflective climate?

■ Catalytically: did it allow the supervisee the opportunity to self-reflect and reframe their practice?

- Conceptual: did it ensure the sharing of knowledge and performance information?

- Confrontational: was corrective feedback required and did it produce change?

- Prescriptive: was any immediate action needed on an issue that may progress to a formal complaint?

In all supervisory sessions, it is important that the supervisor acts as a role model for the supervisees so that the process is seen as legitimate and authority is exercised appropriately (Morrison and Wonnacott, 2010). To that end. it is helpful to reflect on whether all supervisees can expect to be treated impartially and alike. Finally, it is important to confirm with the supervisees that the recording of the session and action plans accurately and fairly reflect the discussions.

Activity

In the light of the feedback:

1. What aspects of your practice would you consider went well?

2. What aspects of the process need to change?

3. What are your development needs?

Are you ready for assessment?

- ✔ **Do you know the purpose of professional supervision?**

- ✔ **Do you know how professional supervision can inform practice?**

- ✔ **Do you know how to prepare for professional supervision with supervisees?**

- ✔ **Can you provide professional supervision?**

- ✔ **Can you manage conflict situations?**

- ✔ **Can you evaluate your own supervisory practice?**

References

Adler, R. and Proctor, R. (2011) *Looking OUT Looking In*. Boston MA: Wadsworth.

Armstrong, M. (2009) *A Handbook of Human Resource Management Practice*. London: Kogan Page.

Beddoe, L. (2010) 'Surveillance or Reflection: Professional Supervision in "the Risk Society"' *The British Journal of Social Work* 40(4), pp1279–96.

Berne, E. (2010) *Games People Play*. London: Penguin.

Boorman, S. (2009) *NHS Health and Well-Being*. London: Department of Health.

Bower, S. A. and Bower G. H. (1991) *Asserting Yourself: A Practical Guide for Positive Change*. Cambridge MA: Peresus Books.

Buchner, T. (2007) *Performance Management Theory: A Look from the Performer's Perspective with Implications for HRD*. Human Resource Development International 10(1), pp59–73.

Butterworth, C. and Faugier, J. (2012) *Clinical Supervision and Mentorship in Nursing*. London: Chapman and Hall.

Cutcliffe, J. and Proctor, B. (1998) 'An Alternative Training Approach to Clinical Supervision'. *British Journal of Nursing*, Vol 7, pp280–5.

CWDC and SfC (2012) *Providing Effective Supervision*. Leeds: Children's Workforce Development Council, and Skills for Care.

Davys, A. and Beddoe, L. (2010) *Best Practice in Professional Supervision: A Guide for the Helping Professionals*. London and Philadelphia: Jessica Kingsley Publishers.

Department of Health (1993) *A Vision for the Future: Report of the Chief Nursing Officer*. London: HMSO, Department of Health.

Department of Health (1998) *A First Class Service: A Quality Service*. London: HMSO.

Department of Health (2010b) *Building a Safe and Confident Future: Implementing the Recommendations of the Social Work Task Force*. London: HMSO.

Driscoll, J. (2007) *Practising Clinical Supervision: A Reflective Approach for Health Care Professionals*. Edinburgh: Bailliere Tindall.

Fowler, J. (2007) 'Solution-Focused Techniques in Clinical Supervision'. *Nursing Times* 103(22), pp30–1.

Godden, J. (2012) *Research on Supervision in Social Work, with Particular Reference to Supervision Practice in Multi Disciplinary Teams*. London: British Association of Social Workers, College of Social Work.

GSCC (2010) *Codes of Practice for Social Care Workers*. London: General Social Care Council.

Hawkins, P. and Shohet, R. (2007) *Supervision in the Helping Professions*. Maidenhead: Open University Press.

HPC (2008) *Standard of Conduct, Performance and Ethics*. London: Health Professionals Council.

Hughes, L. and Pengelly, P. (1997) *Staff Supervision in a Turbulent Environment: Managing Process and Task in Front Line Services*. London and Philadelphia: Jessica Kingsley Publishers.

I&DeA (2007) *Performance Management: the People Dimensions*. London: Improvement and Development Agency.

Marsh, P. and Fisher, M. (2005) *Developing the Evidence Base for Social Work and Social Care Practice*. Bristol: Social Care Institute for Excellence (SCIE).

McKimm, J. (2009) 'Giving Effective Feedback'. *British Journal of Hospital Medicine* 70(3), pp158–61.

Morrison, T. (2005) *Staff Supervision in Social Care : Making a Real Difference for Staff and Service Use*. Brighton: Pavillion.

Morrison, T. and Wonnacott, J. (2010) *Supervision: Now or Never: Reclaiming Reflective Supervision in Social Work*. Surry: In-Trac.

Myers, S. (2008) *Solution-Focused Approaches*. Dorset: Russell House Publishing.

NHS IIIC (2008) *The Good Indicators Guide: Understanding How to Use and Choose Indicators*. Coventry: NHS Institute for Innovation and Improvement.

Northcott, N. (2000) *Clinical Supervision: Professional Development or Management Control* in Spouse, J. and Redfern, L. (Eds) *Successful Supervision in Health Care Practice*. Oxford: Blackwell Science.

Raven, B. H. (1993) 'The Bases of Power: Origins and Recent Developments'. *Journal of Social Issues* (49), pp227–51.

Richmond, D. (2009) 'Using Multilayered Supervision Methods to Develop Creative Practice'. *Reflective Practice: International and Multidisciplinary Perspective* 10(4), pp543–57.

SCIE (2011) *Social Care Governance: A Workbook Based on Practice in England*. London: Social Care Institute for Excellence.

Sloan, G. and Watson, H. (2001) 'John Heron's Six-Category Intervention Analysis: Towards Understanding Interpersonal Relations and Progressing the Delivery of Clinical Supervision for Mental Health Nursing in the United Kingdom'. *Journal of Advanced Nursing*, 36(2), pp206–14.

Taylor, R. (2011) *Confidence at Work: Get It, Feel It, Keep It*. London: Kogan Page.

The Law Commission (2012) *Regulation of Health Care Professionals and Regulation of Social Care Professionals in England*. London: The Law Commission.

Thomas, K. W. (1992) *Conflict and Negotiation Processes in Organisations* in Dunnette, M. D., and Hough, L. M. (Eds) *Handbook of Industrial and Organisational Psychology*. Palo Alto: Consulting Psychologists Press.

Thomas, K. W. and Kilmann, R. (2002) *Thomas-Kilmann Conflict Mode Instrument*. Mountain View CA: CPP Inc.

Websites

Department of Health (2010a) *A Vision for Adult Social Care: Capable Communities and Active Citizens*. www.dh.gov.uk, accessed 3 July 2012.

Department of Health (2010c) *Healthy Lives, Healthy People: Our Strategy for Public Health in England*. www.dh.gov.uk, accessed 3 July 2012.

The College of Social Work, www.collegeofsocialwork.org, accessed 3 July 2012.

Chapter 8

Manage health and
social care practice
to ensure positive
outcomes for individuals

The aim of this chapter is to enable you to understand the importance of positive outcomes for individuals. With the growing importance of personalisation in health and social care services, increasing emphasis is being placed on achieving outcomes that meet the expressed needs of people using health and social care services. This means responsibility for planning and managing your service in ways that enable you to recognise the key aspects of outcome-based practice. To achieve this aim, you need to ensure that you are aware of current evidence for best practice to inform the interventions in your service.

By the end of this chapter you will:

1 Understand the theory and principles that underpin outcome-based practice

2 Be able to lead practice that promotes social, emotional, cultural, spiritual and intellectual well-being

3 Be able to lead practice that promotes individuals' health

4 Be able to lead inclusive provision that gives individuals choice and control over the outcomes they want to achieve

5 Be able to manage effective working partnerships with carers, families and significant others to achieve positive outcomes

Understand the theory and principles that underpin outcome-based practice

8.1

8.1.1 Explain outcome-based practice

Outcome-based practice is of growing importance in health and social care services. It is a key policy driver at a time when there is increasing concern that the UK is falling behind other EU countries in several aspects of health care. Social care services, particularly those serving older people, are under increased pressure due to demographic changes.

> ### Activity
>
> 1. Familiarise yourself with some of the policy documents on outcome-based approaches by accessing the Department of Health website (www.dh.gov.uk), which has a series of documents both on outcomes in the NHS and social care services.

> ### Key Term
>
> **Outcome-based practice** is an activity or process that has a beneficial impact on the individual's life. It can be an action taken or a service delivered. Another way to describe it is to say that the 'output' is the *effort* made and the 'outcome' is the *effect* on the individual.

With the growth of personalisation and individual budgets, the priorities of individuals have become an important focus for service providers, and how different treatments and support processes can lead to positive outcomes. Outcome-based approaches place the needs of the individual at the centre of service delivery, contrasting those designed by service providers.

8.1.2 Critically review approaches to outcome-based practice

As outcome-based practice is increasingly recognised it is important to listen to the individual and tailor services to their needs. This means developing flexible person-centred approaches that will deliver meaningful outcomes. The recent developments in social care such as person-centred planning is an example of a new approach concerned with positive outcomes for individuals.

Drivers for outcome-based approaches include:

- rising demand for health and social care services.

- delivering best outcomes for individuals with limited resources.

- treatment and care processes evaluated through evidence-based research and practice.

Activity

1. What do these drivers mean for your service?

2. What will be the main impact?

8.1.3 Analyse the effects of legislation and policy on outcome-based practice

Recent reforms of the NHS, alongside proposed changes in social care, are based on the need to improve services using outcomes as a measure of performance. A focus on outcome-based practice is a recognition that services must adjust to limited growth in resources while still delivering high quality.

Activity

The government's vision for health and social care can be found in two documents produced by the Department of Health. To access these documents, go to *www.dh.gov.uk* and search for: *Transparency in Outcomes, a Framework for Adult Social Care* and *The NHS Outcomes Framework 2012/2013*.

1. Read these documents and reflect on the implications for your service.

2. What will be the most challenging aspects of implementing a more outcome-based approach in your service?

3. What are some of the specific changes you would have to make to current practices to ensure that you could implement some of the recommendations?

8.1.4 Explain how outcome-based practice can result in positive changes in individuals' lives

Outcome-based practice is concerned with providing services that respond to the goals, priorities and aspirations identified by individuals. A shift in attitudes is taking place in services with professionals increasingly seen in **facilitator** roles rather than managing the process and making all the decisions. This does not mean ignoring professional expertise, but ensuring that knowledge is available to support individuals' own decisions.

Key Term

Facilitators encourage and support individuals to take control of their own assessment and support plan, so that it is tailored to their particular needs and circumstances. They support and empower the individual by providing ideas and information on service options.

Research by Harris *et al* (2005) on an outcomes approach to assessment and review for people with disabilities found that assessment based on the **social model of disability** identified three dimensions that supported positive change:

■ change outcomes, such as improving self-care skills or building self-confidence

■ maintenance outcomes, such as slowing down the deterioration in the quality of life of the individual

■ outcomes associated with the process of receiving services, such as feeling valued, being respected or listened to.

What this research found was that service users who were assessed using an outcome model were:

- more satisfied with the process as it allowed for a broader assessment of their needs

- provided with enhanced choice and control over the assessment process

- service users who had no difficulty identifying a broad range of outcomes.

Furthermore:

- most professionals valued it as it allowed them to be more creative and imaginative as they moved from an assessor to a facilitator role

- the assessment approach was one where the user's perspective was central to the process

- the findings of this research suggest an outcomes-based approach provides more choice and control for the individual.

Be able to lead practice that promotes social, emotional, cultural, spiritual and intellectual well-being

8.2.1 Explain the psychological basis for well-being

In a government report, Huppert (2008) describes psychological well-being as 'life going well' for someone:

■ A combination of feeling good and functioning effectively.

■ Interests, engagement, confidence and affection.

■ Some control over your life.

■ Life having a sense of purpose.

■ Positive relationships.

Sustaining well-being does not mean that an individual will feel good at all times; experiencing painful emotions such as grief or disappointment is a normal part of life. Indeed, managing these negative or painful emotions is essential for long-term well-being.

We can see from this description of well-being that individuals with health or social needs are likely to face situations where they will not experience life going well. This can be described as 'ill-being'. Many of the individuals that approach health and social care services will have feelings of ill-being. How services respond to the needs of individuals in terms of providing services that lead to positive outcomes will influence feelings of well-being.

Figure 8.1 Managing negative or painful emotions is essential for long-term well-being

Activity

1. Reflect on some of the people you support in your service. Following a dialogue with them to elicit their views about the quality of their lives, would you describe them as exhibiting the characteristics of well-being? If not, what aspects of their lives are compromised and are likely to lead to feelings of ill-being?

8.2.2 Promote a culture among the workforce of considering all aspects of individuals' well-being in day-to-day practice

Changing the **culture** of an organisation can take time, and established patterns of working can hinder the rapid development of new initiatives and innovations. As the leader of the service, what you systematically focus on and communicate to staff sends out powerful signals to the rest of the service about what issues are considered important.

Key Term

Culture refers to the traditions, values, policies, beliefs and attitudes in an organisation. It is easier to recognise as the deeply-held beliefs of staff about the way they work, how work should be organised, and how staff are controlled and rewarded. From these descriptions, it can be seen that culture can be a powerful source of influence and control in organisations.

Therefore engaging with staff, communicating the importance of good practice, and creating a culture of openness and trust among the staff team will send out signals of what is valued, which in time will change the service (Scragg, 2010).

As manager you will have many opportunities to ensure staff are introduced to well-being factors. An appreciation of these factors, and how changes in treatment and care regimes can lead to improved outcomes for individuals, has the potential to change the culture of an organisation. This can occur, for example, where staff are introduced to the concept of well-being at induction and through continuing professional development and in supervision, which can provide a deeper appreciation of the factors that impact on the individual and lead to more sensitive responses on the part of staff. As manager of the service you are in a powerful position to influence how staff respond to the needs of individuals by emphasising the crucial importance of well-being and, through your actions, you can influence the culture of the service.

Activity

1. Explain how your staff development processes ensure the development of a positive culture that has individuals' well-being at its core.

8.2.3 Review the extent to which systems and processes promote individual well-being

Creating a positive culture in a service depends ultimately on the quality of leadership and the commitment of senior staff to influence the culture through training, supervision and acting as role models and by supporting the principles and values of a quality service. A positive culture has the potential to influence all aspects of a service's functioning and enable systems and processes to be evaluated for their contribution to individuals' well-being.

In considering the factors that contribute to well-being, often systems and processes in health and social care services can undermine an individual's potential for well-being. An example of this is where a group-living service is organised so that individuals feel they have very little control over their environment. Another example might be in a health service where their confidence is undermined by decisions which ignore their viewpoint.

Activity

When you are evaluating your service systems and processes consider each one in turn against the well-being factors.

1. Identify which processes a) support and which b) undermine well-being.

2. What evidence would you need to make a judgement about the well-being of individuals?

Remember

As the manager of your service you have an important role in ensuring that individuals using the service, who may experience feelings of ill-being, are supported in a way that increases their feelings of well-being. This approach is further reinforced where the culture of the service ensures that all staff have an awareness of well-being factors and respond sensitively to individuals' needs.

Be able to lead practice that promotes individuals' health 8.3

8.3.1 Demonstrate the effective use of resources to promote good health and healthy choices in all aspects of the provision

As manager you have an important responsibility to ensure that resources in the service are used appropriately to promote good health and healthy choices. It is importance to maintain good health, particularly in later life, where the onset of long-term health conditions make some of the greatest demands on health resources. Actions to prevent the onset of health problems and the deterioration in long-term conditions should be an important element of service provision (Rechel *et al*, 2009).

Activity *explain*

1. Describe how you use resources in your service to ensure that individuals are able to maintain a healthy lifestyle.

2. Briefly describe what benefits these have had on the individuals concerned.

8.3.2 Use appropriate methods to meet the health needs of individuals

Meeting the health needs of individuals requires an understanding of a wide range of methods and interventions, with a systematic

approach encompassing the active promotion of a healthy lifestyle. These interventions include:

- maintaining the activities of daily living
- preventing disease through physical activity and good nutrition and stress management
- maintenance of function, confidence and engagement
- provision of health information on issues such as over-reliance on smoking, alcohol and obesity
- having the support of health professionals
- the use of **assistive technologies** to enable individuals to live safely and maintain independence.

All these activities aim to improve or maintain the individual's physical health as well as their social connectedness contributing to a healthy balanced lifestyle.

Key Term

Assistive technology describes a range of equipment and processes that aim to support independent living, for example environmental sensors that indicate whether an individual is moving within their accommodation and devices that monitor 'vital clinical signs' and transmit data to monitoring services.

Figure 8.2 You can support individuals in using assistive technologies to enable them to live independent lives

8.3.3 Implement practices and protocols for involving appropriate professional health care expertise for individuals

When providing support for individuals your practices and **protocols** should guide you in terms of appropriate actions that need to be undertaken within the service or need referral to health care professionals.

Within your service there are likely to be individuals who require regular or periodic health interventions. Some of these interventions can be safely undertaken by staff, whereas others will need the expertise of a health professional. Policies and procedures drawn up with the guidance of health professionals will enable decisions to be made, for example to refer an individual to a general practitioner or a community psychiatric nurse.

Mark is the manager of a residential home for older people where a significant number of the individuals resident in the service are diabetic. Mark has recently attended a diabetes training programme and is aware of the need to plan for the care of the individuals with diabetes. Older people with diabetes in residential care homes are a highly vulnerable group with greater risk of increased disability, pressure sores and hospital admission. Mark has introduced screening for diabetes on admission and an annual health review. He has arranged for staff to undertake delegated tasks, following training by a diabetes specialist nurse, enabling insulin treatment to be safely administered within the home using a protocol planned with the individuals and staff. Mark has also developed an annual audit tool to assess the performance of the service in relation to diabetes care.

1. What processes do you have in place to monitor the health of individuals in your service?

2. Have you developed a partnership with health care specialists to ensure that you can support individuals who have identified health care needs?

8.3.4 Develop a plan to ensure the workforce has the necessary training to recognise individual health care needs

Workforce planning is a critical aspect of your management responsibility. This means estimating the future demand for staff and ensuring that you have sufficient supply of appropriately qualified staff available to meet demand (Imison *et al*, 2009).

Workforce planning has become more complex due to the developments of personalisation, the growth of assistive technologies and individuals having greater control over those who support them. These changes impact on the workforce in services with implications for staff employed, the appropriate skills on entry and the need for ongoing personal development in response to change and innovation in services.

In planning for workforce development, you need to understand the marketplace and what the changes impacting on the sector will mean for your service in the future. A strategic review of your service in the context of wider changes will enable you to plan more effectively in anticipating future demand and what staffing resources you need.

Activity

1. Explain what workforce planning activity you currently engage in.

2. What are the implications of wider changes in health and social care sectors for your particular service?

3. What will these changes mean in terms of the type of staff you employ and their training needs if they are to work with individuals with health care needs effectively?

To assist you in this activity read the report, *Guidance Note on Workforce Planning for Care Providers* at www.thinklocalactpersonal.org.uk. This has a six-step process for managers engaged in workforce planning.

Be able to lead inclusive provision that gives individuals choice and control over the outcomes they want to achieve

8.4.1 Explain the necessary steps in order for individuals to have choice and control over decisions

For individuals to have choice and control over the services they receive, they need to be placed at the centre of the decision-making process. This shift of power to the individual from professionals is still an emerging movement, but has been strengthened by the government policies on personalisation and personal budgets, which is reinforcing the idea that the individual is best placed to know what they need and how those needs can be most effectively met (Duffy, 2011).

Figure 8.3 Individuals need to be placed at the centre of the decision-making process

Activity   *In Practice*

The 'In Control: self-directed support' project was set up as a partnership between an independent development organisation (In Control) working with disabled people, central and local government and MENCAP. It worked with a small number of local authorities to design a new system of self-directed support for people with learning disabilities to enable them to have greater control over their lives and receive the support they needed.

1. Go to the In Control website (www.in-control.org.uk) and study the information on self-directed support. What ideas does this provide for you to test out in your service which could increase the potential for individuals to have greater control in decision-making?

8.4.2 Manage resources so that individuals can achieve positive outcomes

To achieve positive outcomes for individuals means managing resources to ensure the service systems and processes are geared to this aim. As a consequence, all aspects of the care process need to be considered in relation to outcomes. This in turn means much more clarity in terms of:

- the mission and goals of the service
- the focus on results in individuals' lives
- the definition of outcomes provides focus for the work with individuals
- findings become the basis for professional discussion and public statements.

Activity

1. Reflect on the way you use resources in your service. How much do outcomes for individuals influence the management of resources?

2. Are you able to make the link between the management of resources and the outcomes for individuals?

8.4.3 Monitor and evaluate progress towards the achievement of outcomes

If your service has adopted an outcome-based approach then it is likely that you have a much clearer picture of the relationship between the resources allocated to provide the service and the outcomes for individuals. The evaluation of activities means that you need to ensure that you understand the relationship between the resources used (inputs), the activities (outputs) and impact on the individual (outcomes). It is the relationship between these factors that can help you understand if the resources at your disposal are being deployed effectively to improve outcomes for individuals.

Activity

Go to the Charities Evaluation Services website (www.ces-vol.org.uk) and access the report, *The Case for an Outcomes Focus*, which has a number of ideas on the value to be obtained from an outcome-based approach.

1. Explain how you can use the information on outcomes to introduce positive changes in practice, that in turn ensure improvements in the quality of service provided.

2. What techniques could you use or develop to enable you to ensure you have accurate information on outcomes?

8.4.4 Develop a plan to ensure the workforce has the necessary training to support individuals to achieve outcomes

Developing a plan to ensure that your staff are appropriately trained to use an outcome-based approach in their practice starts from an understanding of the needs of individuals using the service. The findings from 'In Control' and similar projects based on personalisation can provide ideas that inform practice.

Duffy (2011) has described some of the approaches that can improve practice, for example:

- empowerment – enabling people to make decisions for themselves
- partnership – greater partnership between the practitioner and the individual, integrating different skills, expertise and perspectives.

Using ideas of empowerment and partnership can help you plan training for staff if they are to support individuals more effectively.

Activity

1. Draw up a staff training plan that incorporates the latest thinking on personalisation, and focuses on how your service can achieve the desired outcomes of individuals.

   Some useful ideas are contained in the Social Care Institute for Excellence (SCIE) report *Personalisation: a rough guide* (2008). This can be accessed at www.scie.org.uk.

8.4.5 Implement systems and processes for recording the identification, progress and achievement of outcomes

Effectively recording the progress towards the achievement of outcomes for individuals means having a system that is able to track the processes that contribute to that goal. This requires several steps:

- A clear definition of outcomes for individuals, based primarily on their perspective.

- Understanding how to achieve individual outcomes through treatment and care practices.

- Recording outcomes in a manner that enables staff and managers to act on the information.

- Feedback from individuals and how far the service has met their personal outcomes.

- Using the combination of information gained through processes and feedback to provide ideas for further improvement.

Activity

1. Describe your current systems and processes for recording outcome-based information.

2. Does this provide you with sufficient evidence to enable you to make decisions that contribute to the improvement of practices that meet individuals' needs and aspirations?

Be able to manage effective working partnerships with carers, families and significant others to achieve positive outcomes

8.5

8.5.1 Analyse the importance of effective working relationships with carers, families and significant others for the achievement of positive outcomes

Working effectively with carers and others who have a close relationship with the individual is important and can influence the quality of outcomes for that individual. Where **carers** are recognised for their contribution to the support of the individual, this can have beneficial effects. This is recognised in numerous reports on carers' experiences of services. For example, Harris *et al* (2005) in their report highlighted carers feeling that they had a negative experience of services and felt they were not listened to.

> ### Key Term
> **Carer** is someone of any age who provides unpaid support to family or friends who cannot manage without this help.

> ### Activity
> 1. How are carers and others who have a close relationship with individuals viewed by your service?
>
> 2. Is there an appreciation of the impact of caring on the person?
>
> 3. Are there ways that your service can support carers?

Figure 8.4 It is important that staff build relationships with those who have a close relationship with the individuals in their care

8.5.2 Implement systems, procedures and practices that engage carers, families and significant others

With greater awareness of carers' needs, you should be in a position to develop approaches that engage with and support carers and family members more effectively. There are several factors that influence your approach to engaging with carers:

- Carers have their own needs that are often overlooked.

- The caring role can be demanding and result in the carer experiencing ill-health.

- Carers can have limited social networks and this can affect their access to friends and services to meet their own needs.

- The death of a carer can result in a crisis in the life of the cared-for individual.

Activity — In Practice

Mr and Mrs Smith are both in their 80s and live with their son Graham, who is 53 and has a severe physical disability. Graham attends a day service but due to his parents' previous experience of services they have become isolated and make no contact with the service.

1. As the manager of the service what could you do to engage with Graham's parents?

2. What actions would ensure that they feel confident in confiding their concerns about the future?

3. What plans need to be put in place to ensure they are able to face the future with confidence?

This case study describes a situation that is all too common, where parents of a disabled person have become socially isolated and make little contact with services, although they will need to start planning for Graham's future when they are unable to care for him. For more information access the Mencap (www.mencap.org.uk) and Carers' Trust (www.carers.org) websites.

8.5.3 Use appropriate approaches to address conflicts and dilemmas that may arise between individuals, staff and carers, families and significant others

It is important to recognise that carers, families and significant others who support an individual often devote their lives to the 'cared-for person' and often communicate on their behalf when needs are assessed or reviewed. Although the carer and individual may have common concerns and views this is by no means always the case (Connelly and Seden, 2003).

Activity — In Practice

Peter has a severe learning disability and attends a day service where he is taking part in a self-awareness group that is exploring personal behaviour and relationships and participating in social activities for young people in the community. His parents are very concerned that this will mean he is placed at risk and will be introduced to activities that they feel are unsuitable for a disabled person.

1. Explain your approach to addressing potential conflicts and dilemmas between carers and the cared-for person.

2. Go the Department of Health website (www.dh.gov.uk) and research different approaches to dealing with conflicts.

Looking at this case study it is important to distinguish between what the individual wants and what the carer feels is appropriate. Working with carers in dealing with this dilemma is a central part of achieving the best outcomes for all concerned.

8.5.4 Explain how legislation and regulation influence working relationships with carers, families and significant others

In the 1990s there was an increasing realisation that carers' needs were ignored. This led to the Carers (Recognition and Services) Act (1995). There has been a series of initiatives to highlight the central role carers play in the lives of individuals and emphasise their importance. This has now led to the recognition that carers constitute a 'third frontier' in care delivery, whose contribution is estimated at approximately £70 billion (Berry, 2011).

Activity

Go to the Department of Health website (www.dh.gov.uk) and familiarise yourself with the legislation and reports on carers and the contribution they make to supporting individuals. Also access the Carers' Trust website (www.carers.org.uk) and read the *Key Facts about Carers*.

1. With a greater appreciation of carers' needs and their contribution, how could you use this information to improve your service?

8.5.5 Implement safe and confidential recording systems and processes to provide effective information sharing and recording

The Data Protection Act (1998) allows individuals to gain access to their files, and the Act establishes a statutory basis for confidentiality. The Act also affects how information is entered, maintained and stored. Records are now much less likely to contain unsubstantiated opinion, and where opinion is recorded it has to be identified and evidenced.

Activity

Go to the Information Commissioner's Office website (www.ico.gov.uk) and study the principles of data protection.

1. What are the implications of these principles for your service?

2. Do they suggest areas where you could improve the management of recording systems and the maintenance of records, both paper and electronic?

Are you ready for assessment?

☑ Do you know what outcome-based practice is?

☑ Do you know the different approaches to outcome-based practice?

☑ Do you know the effect of legislation and policy on outcome-based practice?

☑ Do you know how outcome-based practice can result in positive changes in individuals' lives?

☑ Do you know the psychological basis for well-being?

☑ Do you know the necessary steps to take to ensure individuals have choice and control over decisions?

☑ Do you know the importance of effective working relationships with carers, families and significant others to achieve positive outcomes?

☑ Do you know how legislation and regulation influence working relationships with carers, families and significant others?

☑ Can you promote a workforce culture that considers all aspects of individuals' well-being in day-to-day practice?

☑ Can you review the extent to which systems and processes promote an individual's well-being?

☑ Can you demonstrate the effective use of resources to promote good health and healthy choices in all aspects of your service?

☑ Can you use appropriate methods to meet the health needs of individuals?

☑ Can you implement practice and protocols for involving appropriate professional health care expertise for individuals?

☑ Can you develop a workforce development plan to ensure staff are trained to recognise individual health care needs?

☑ Can you manage resources to enable individuals to achieve positive outcomes?

☑ Can you monitor and evaluate progress towards the achievement of outcomes?

☑ Can you develop a workforce development plan to ensure staff are trained to support individuals in achieving positive outcomes?

☑ Can you implement systems and processes for recording the identification, progress and achievement of outcomes?

☑ Can you implement systems, procedures and practices that engage carers, families and significant others?

☑ Can you use appropriate approaches to address conflicts and dilemmas that may arise between individuals, staff and carers, families and significant others?

☑ Can you implement safe and confidential recording systems and processes to provide effective information sharing and recording?

References

Berry, C. (2011) *Past Caring? Widening the Debate on Funding Long-Term Care*. London: International Longevity Centre.

Connelly, N. and Seden, J. (2003) 'What Service Users Say about Services: the Implications for Managers', in Henderson, J. and Atkinson, D. (Eds) *Managing Care in Context*. London: The Open University and Routledge.

Department of Health (2011) *The NHS Outcomes Framework 2011/12*. London: The Stationery Office.

Department of Health (2010) *Transparency in Outcomes: a Framework for Quality in Adult Social Care, The 2011/12 Adult Social Care Outcomes Framework*. London: The Stationery Office.

Duffy, S. (2011) 'Personalisation in Social Care – What Does it Really Mean?' *Social Care and Neurodisability*, 2(4),186–194.

Harris, J., Foster, M., Jackson, K. and Morgan, H. (2005) *Outcomes for Disabled Servcie Users*. Social Policy Research Unit, University of York.

Huppert, F.A. (2008) *Mental Capacity and Well-Being, Making the Most of Ourselves in the 21st Century*. London: The Government Office for Science.

Imison, C., Buchan, J. and Xavier, S. (2009) *NHS Workforce Planning: Limitations and Possibilities*. London: The King's Fund.

Rechel, B., Doyle, Y., Grundy, E. and McKee, M. (2009) *How Can Health Systems Respond to Population Ageing?* Copenhagen: World Health Organisation.

Scragg, T. (2010) 'The Power of Culture', in *Managing Change in Health and Social Care Services*. Brighton: OLM-Pavilion.

Acts and Regulations

Carers (Recognition and Services) Act (1995).

Data Protection Act (1998).

Websites

Carers' Trust, www.carers.org, accessed 30 June 2012.

Centre for Workforce Intelligence, www.cfwi.org.uk, accessed 30 June 2012.

Charities Evaluation Services, www.ces-vol.org.uk, accessed 30 June 2012.

Department of Health, www.dh.gov.uk, accessed 30 June 2012.

Diabetes UK, Good clinical practice guidelines for care home residents with diabetes (Jan 2010) www.diabetes.org.uk, accessed 10 July 2012.

IDRIS, www.idris.ac.uk, accessed 3 July 2012.

In Control, www.in-control.org.uk, accessed 30 June 2012.

Information Commissioner's Office, www.ico.gov.uk, accessed 30 June 2012.

Interdisciplinary Disability Research Institute, www.idris.ac.uk, accessed 30 June 2012.

Mencap, www.mencap.org.uk, accessed 30 June 2012.

Social Care Institute for Excellence, www.scie.org.uk, accessed 30 June 2012.

Social Policy Research Unit, www.york.ac.uk/spru/, accessed 30 June 2012.

The King's Fund, www.kingsfund.org.uk, accessed 30 June 2012.

World Health Organisation, www.who.int/, accessed 30 June 2012.

Chapter 9

Safeguarding
and protection
of vulnerable
adults

This chapter will help develop your understanding and practice in relation to safeguarding. In recent years the emphasis has changed from protection to safeguarding and it follows the personalisation agenda in supporting individuals to develop confidence to manage their own risks. The Care Quality Commission (CQC) defines safeguarding as 'protecting people's health, well-being and human rights, and enabling them to live free from harm, abuse and neglect'

By the end of this chapter you will:

1 Understand the legislation, regulations and policies that underpin the protection of vulnerable adults

2 Be able to lead service provision that protects vulnerable adults

3 Be able to manage inter-agency, joint or integrated working in order to protect vulnerable adults

4 Be able to monitor and evaluate the systems, processes and practice that safeguard vulnerable adults

Understand the legislation, regulations and policies that underpin the protection of vulnerable adults

9.1

9.1.1 and 9.1.3 Analyse the differences between the concept of safeguarding and the concept of protection in relation to vulnerable adults and explain the associated legislative framework

In order to explore this area fully, an understanding of the legislative framework and government initiatives is needed:

- Human Rights Act (1998) (adopted by the UK in October 2000): This describes individuals' rights to live free from abuse and violence or torture. It is considered a benchmark against which services can assess how they uphold individual rights.

- Care Standards Act (2000): This led to the National Minimum Standards and means of measuring care service quality.

- 'No Secrets' (2000): This gives guidance created as a result of serious incidents leading to abuse and also the need to ensure compliance with the Human Rights Act. This was a big step forward in relation to adult protection.

- 'Valuing People' (2001): This relates specifically to those with learning disabilities with the key values of civil rights, independence, choice and inclusion. This White Paper is written from a human rights

perspective and started the personalisation agenda.

- 'Safeguarding Adults' (2005): This built on 'No Secrets' and created a change in emphasis with the concept of protection geared towards those who lacked capacity (see also Mental Capacity Act 2005). It resulted in a move towards earlier intervention and prevention. The concept of safeguarding emerged, with individuals taking informed risks and exercising more choices rather than authorities 'stepping in' to take charge.

- Mental Capacity Act (MCA) (2005): This legal framework sets out five key principles to protect vulnerable adults unable to make their own decisions. Prosecutions have been made under Section 44 of this Act for ill-treatment and wilful neglect (Crown Prosecution Service, 2009).

- 'Safeguarding Vulnerable Groups' (2006): This was the creation of a vetting/barring scheme (see page 231 for more information).

- Fraud Act (2006): This created a new offence of 'fraud by abuse of position'. It includes the misuse of money by those appointed to manage it, such as by an Enduring Power of Attorney. Fraud was not well covered by Section 44 of the MCA.

- 'Deprivation of Liberty Safeguards' (2008): This details how those unable to consent to treatment due to a mental impairment should be supported in a way that does not limit their rights. This has led to a major shift in practice and a move away from professionals' apparent arbitrary decision-making.

- Health and Social Care Act (2008) (Regulated Activities) Regulations 2010 and the Care Quality Commission (Registration) Regulations 2009: This led to the creation of the CQC to regulate services using the Essential Standards of Quality and Safety, consisting of 28 regulations and a shift towards outcomes, i.e. what can be expected from the care providers. There are a number of outcomes specific to helping to safeguard individuals.

- Law Commission Review of Adult Social Care (2011): This incorporates safeguarding recommendations and proposes a formal change in terminology from 'vulnerable adult' to 'adult at risk'. **The government will consider the conclusions, with a view to introducing legislation in the second session of Parliament 2012.**

- Statement of Government Principles on Adult Safeguarding (2011): This lists six key principles of Empowerment, Protection, Prevention, Proportionality, Partnership and Accountability. Local multi-agency partnerships should support and encourage communities to find local solutions and further guidance is offered on how these principles could be translated into outcomes.

Activity

evaluate

1. Research the legislation relating to safeguarding.

2. Summarise the aims of each piece of legislation and how it is significant both in terms of its impact on practice and how it reflects changes in the concepts of protection to safeguarding.

A table might be a useful way to record this.

Perceptions of what abuse is have changed as human rights have become more entrenched in our society. Adult protection has been overshadowed by child protection, and as such has received less attention by government.

To conclude, whereas protection implies a domination of others to make decisions for an individual rather than with them, safeguarding accepts that individuals have the right to take risks so long as they have capacity and understand the implications or consequences of any choices. Simply put, the best way to safeguard adults at risk from abuse is to enable them to safeguard themselves. Policy and practice needs to change to reflect this.

9.1.2 Evaluate the impact of policy developments on approaches to safeguarding vulnerable adults in your own service setting

The government's policy objective is to prevent and reduce abuse from occurring while also supporting individuals to have control and make choices. The state aims to provide the vision and direction and for this to then be implemented on a local basis. Key policy developments have been as follows:

- Our Health, Our Care, Our Say (2006) and Putting People First (2007): The **white paper** 'Our Health, Our Care, Our Say' (2006) proposed ways of making adult social care more responsive to people's needs, more cost effective and of a higher quality. This was then developed in the cross-government and social care sector agreement 'Putting People First' (2007), which set out the direction for adult social care planned for at least the next ten years. 'Putting People First – the whole story' (2008) then identified four key areas (universal services, early interventions and prevention, choice and control, social capital) for councils and others to focus on to enable the delivery of personalised care.

■ No Secrets/In Safe Hands (Wales): This guidance gave social services a key role in coordinating local policies and services to protect vulnerable individuals from abuse and led to more collaborative working – a multi-agency approach. This impacted on care services and informed policies and practices, such as the requirement for staff training in this area. Nine years later, the findings of *Safeguarding Adults: Report on the Consultation on the Review of 'No Secrets'* placed a new emphasis on prevention and on the empowerment of individuals to maintain their own safety (Department of Health, 2009). The consultation found that safeguarding can be experienced as 'safety at the expense of other qualities of life, such as self determination and the right to family life'. The report highlighted the importance of achieving a balance between safeguarding and the independence associated with personalisation in adult social care.

■ Vetting and Barring Scheme/ISA: This initially arose from the Soham murders and the subsequent Bichard Inquiry. It was set up to put in additional checks on all those working with vulnerable individuals and supplemented existing schemes. It created additional work and expense for services when employing staff. There has also been a lot of discussion and concern about how this scheme is over-bureaucratic and a deterrent, for example to doing voluntary work with vulnerable groups. The Protection of Freedoms Act 2012 received Royal Assent on 1 May 2012 to re-model this scheme and will be known

as the Disclosure and Barring Service from December 2012. Until then the current barring system continues.

■ Local Safeguarding Adults Boards: These are multi-agency boards led by social services. They ensure local policies comply with national policies and best practice. They encompass social services, health, housing, police and Crown Prosecution Service (CPS), probation, emergency services and the voluntary sector. They aim to provide strategic leadership and promote key principles of prevention and protection. All areas have them but it is not yet a mandatory requirement and their effectiveness is variable. In 2011, however, the Law Commission made a recommendation to put these boards on a statutory footing. Complications can also arise when working across different local authorities with their own policies and practices, for example in reporting protocols.

Activity

1. How has your service changed its policies and approaches to better reflect safeguarding rather than protection?

Consider areas such as risk assessments, choices and autonomy, promoting independence and involvement in services provided.

9.1.4 Evaluate how serious case reviews or inquiries have influenced quality assurance, regulation and inspection relating to the safeguarding of vulnerable adults

A key driver in how policies have developed over the years is the recognition of abuse happening, particularly within institutions, and the need for government to take action to address it.

In recent years there has been an increase in reported failings across different services, such as:

- the Francis Report in 2010 which led to 18 recommendations as a result of exposing the horrific experiences of patients at Mid-Staffordshire NHS Foundation Trust

- BBC Panorama in 2011 exposing Winterbourne View, where the seriousness and level of abuse uncovered led to a **Serious Case Review (SCR)**.

Key Term

Serious Case Reviews (SCRs) are convened when the death or serious injury of an adult at risk has occurred and is related directly or indirectly to adult abuse, and multi-agency learning can be identified from this.

- The Homecare Association has expressed concerns following the Equality and Human Rights Commission (EHRC) report 'Close to Home' which examined the impact of the increase in personalisation on homecare for older people. The report highlights how councils are reducing the time commissioned, pushing down the prices paid to providers which is then having a negative impact on service quality. The EHRC states that 'given the nature and pace of these changes it is important to make sure that the legislative, regulatory and quality control systems we have in place are able to keep up, and the elements in place make sure that human rights are fully protected'. They admit they doubt this is the case.

Sarah Pickup, incoming director of the Association of Directors of Adult Social Services (ADASS) said in *Community Care* on 20 April 2012 that home care providers should not bid for local authority contracts if they cannot provide quality care for the prices offered as the contract 'would not have called for poor care'. However providers do not always feel they have this option when survival of the business is at stake.

Activity

1. Research two or three reports into failings of practice and write down key themes and areas of concern you identify.

2. How can you apply this to your service and what does it mean for your systems?

Key themes emerging from inquiries and reports are:

- a lack of management skills and transparency

- poor induction processes

- inadequate training and supervision with poor practice remaining unchallenged.

In a time of efficiency savings and resource cuts the potential for failings in practice is more acute than ever without a proactive approach to guard against them. As a manager this is a vital part of your role.

Activity

1. How does your service compare to the core tasks below set out for managers by the 'Champion', leader and protector guide (published in the April 2012 edition of Community Care)?

The guide is designed to help raise the status of residential care and managers, by setting out a vision for the role as a champion of social care values, leader of professional practice and protector of residents' safety and rights.

- Workforce planning and development, including undertaking a skills analysis to indentify gaps, and ensuring access to appropriate training and high-quality supervision.

- Ensuring all residents are involved in their person-centre plan, based around outcomes they want to achieve.

- Being open to whistleblowers and ensuring staff attend relevant safeguarding training.

- Ensuring processes are compliant with the Mental Capacity Act (2005) and that clear processes are in place to monitor individuals' decision-making capacity.

- Getting the balance right in risk assessments between enabling residents to make choices and fulfilling the home's duty of care.

9.1.5 Explain the protocols and referral procedures when harm or abuse is alleged or suspected

This section only briefly covers this area as you will have had specific mandatory training already. As a manager you will firstly assess the gravity of an incident. If considered minor, with no apparent harm or potential for significant harm having occurred, then the procedures for incident reporting in line with regulatory requirements should be followed. This would be the case if an incident occurred which could be addressed via internal procedures, for example a one-off incident of poor practice with no significant harm. This should of course all be documented and actioned. However, if you have more serious concerns then an alert should be made and the following protocols followed:

- Ensure the adult at risk is made safe and medical attention sought if needed.

- Consider if the police need to be called if a criminal offence might have occurred (in which case preservation of evidence is paramount).

- Ensure any person who may have caused harm has no contact with the adult at risk.

- Consider issues of consent.

- Raise an alert at the earliest opportunity, which should be no later than the end of the day on which the incident happened.

Details of the appropriate Adult Social Care department to contact to seek advice regarding alerts or to raise an alert must be easily accessible.

It is the manager's responsibility to have clear internal reporting procedures for staff with safeguarding concerns, detailing which staff are responsible for deciding whether or not to alert the local authority. This is particularly important for services where the formal manager may not be available during out-of-office hours. When an alert is raised, the Safeguarding Adult Manager will plan with others a proportionate response based on the available information in line with local procedures.

Be able to lead service provision that protects vulnerable adults

9.2

9.2.1 Promote service provision that supports vulnerable adults to assess risks and make informed choices

The whole agenda surrounding personalisation and safeguarding will impact on how your provision delivers its service. There might be work to change the culture of the service, for example attitudes to risk will vary. Remember, it is the service users who will be doing an activity so it is they who should decide.

The principles of personalisation are admirable, but issues do arise in practice. Skills for Care in 'Learning to Live with Risk' identified some key areas of concern as 'organisational and professional risk-aversion, which can hinder choice, control and independent living.' SCIE's report in 2010 on enabling risk and ensuring safety identifies a barrier as 'practitioners possibly not being confident about sharing responsibility for risk if their organisation does not have a positive risk enablement culture and policies'.

Figure 9.1 Attitudes to risk can vary according to experience, recent events, advice or training and individual differences between workers

Person-centred approaches of individuality, choice, privacy, rights, dignity, respect and independence will all reduce the likelihood of abuse taking place as the individual is empowered and central in all aspects of their life. Active participation gives the individual control. However, processes need to be in place so service users can make their views known and access information to help inform choices.

Appropriate discussions then need to take place with the individual to consider the consequences of any actions. This should always be documented in the form of a person-centred risk assessment, which demonstrates how an individual is supported to manage risks based on what is important to them, with happiness being just as important as safety. It is also about opportunity and inclusion.

Activity   *In Practice*

Download *Safeguarding Adults at Risk of Harm: A Legal Guide for Practitioners* from www.scie.org.uk/publications/reports/report50.pdf. It has a range of case studies, from pp4–43, covering many complex situations relating to safeguarding. Read through a selection of these.

1. Reflect on the range of strategies used to safeguard individuals while maintaining their rights and choices.

2. Analyse how you can use these examples to inform your practice.

Key Term

Indicator can be defined as any sign or symptom that alerts a person to suspect something might be wrong.

9.2.2 Provide information to others on indicators of abuse, measures that can be taken to avoid abuse taking place and steps that need to be taken in the case of suspected or alleged abuse

An **indicator** of abuse does not confirm abuse is happening, but it does warrant further assessment. It is impossible to list all possible indicators, but some to consider might be:

- lack of respect being shown
- unexplained or untreated injuries, or poor physical condition
- significant changes in behaviour, routines or mood.

Any indicator that is considered unusual must be investigated. It is also important to empower all staff, service users and families with the information regarding the potential for abuse and what possible indicators might be.

A comprehensive, person-centred assessment of need is key in helping to prevent abuse. Care/support plans should be 'live' documents that are constantly updated, and reviews should happen on a regular basis. Susceptibility to abuse will always vary according to the individual's unique circumstances and the support mechanisms in place. Having a clear and accessible comments and complaints system in place will help to identify issues or problems.

Within services training in safeguarding is key to good practice so any potential abuse is quickly identified. Also supervision of staff is vital so any issues, for example stress or being overwhelmed by workloads, can be addressed. In these times of efficiency savings and scarce resources this has never been more important.

9.2.3 Identify the policies and procedures in your own work setting that contribute towards safeguarding and the prevention of abuse

Good risk management systems are instrumental to reduce the likelihood of abuse. Risk assessments can cover many different areas, from environmental risks to those posed by individual behaviours. Some organisations undertake comprehensive risk screening at the outset, which can help to ensure person-centred risk assessments. Once risks have been identified, you can then begin to consider how to minimise them.

Every service will also have clear safeguarding policies to follow in the event of possible or actual harm/abuse. An accessible comments and complaints system is vital so that everyone knows how to highlight any issues. Other areas such as robust recruitment with appropriate vetting procedures, references taken up and thorough inductions are vital tools to ensure individuals are safeguarded.

A National Competence Framework for Safeguarding Adults is a useful practice resource to assess services at varying levels within safeguarding systems.

9.2.4 and 9.2.5 Monitor the implementation of policies and procedures that support protection, and provide feedback to others on practice

Audits and spot checks are key tools that help ensure policies and procedures are being followed. Audits can cover questions such as these:

- Are care plans and risk assessments updated/reviewed?
- Are records completed adequately?
- Do regular supervisions occur?
- Is training up to date?
- How accessible is the comments and complaints system?

Once an audit template has been devised, these duties may be delegated to relevant staff with the proviso that if any issues are identified they must be reported back for a manager to address. This involvement has the effect of all staff taking more ownership. Simply knowing audits are happening and practice is being checked helps to ensure policies are adhered to.

Undertaking staff meetings, regular supervisions and appraisals is also vital as a way to monitor how well policies are implemented, and it is good practice to have safeguarding as a routine item on any agenda. Within these forums, feedback can also be given, whether on individual practice or simply to share updated information on good practice.

Activity

1. Create an audit template of areas within your service that you can audit related to safeguarding. Use the questions listed above to get you started.

Be able to manage inter-agency, joint or integrated working in order to protect vulnerable adults

9.3

There are clear links between this learning outcome and Unit 5 on Partnership Working. It is fair to say that what is considered as abuse has changed, and new areas of concern have emerged over the years such as radicalisation, forced marriages, prostitution or domestic violence. In addition, living in a multicultural society and the need to value diversity brings challenges and dilemmas. We cannot be experts in all these areas, so being able to work with others with specialist knowledge is vital.

9.3.1 Follow agreed protocols for partnership working with other organisations

The roots of partnership working came from 'No Secrets' in 2000, when clear protocols were put in place to ensure a multi-agency approach. This has been built on in subsequent years via 'Safeguarding Adults' in 2005, which set out a National Framework, much of which related to how partnerships should be established and how they should operate.

Figure 9.2 In order to safeguard the adults in your care, it is vital to work with others with specialist knowledge

Local authorities are charged with setting up Local Safeguarding Adult Boards and there will be representatives from statutory agencies such as social services, primary care trusts, housing, education, welfare/benefit agencies and CQC, as well as those from the voluntary and independent sector. The purpose is for a multi-agency approach to develop effective safeguarding strategies in each area.

Each area has responded according to local need and produced guidelines that apply locally. You should be familiar with the relevant procedures for your area and the agreed protocols relating to:

- boundaries
- areas of responsibility
- information sharing
- limits of authority
- decision making
- recording information.

9.3.2 Review the effectiveness of systems and procedures for working in partnership with other organisations

The organisations you work with will depend on the nature of your service. As stated there are many statutory agencies and also those from the voluntary sector such as groups specialising in a particular area of social care, for example dementia, mental health, learning disabilities, drug services, domestic abuse and hate crimes. There are also carer groups, service user forums and advocacy groups. The Serious Case Review after the death of Steven Hoskin, a man with learning disabilities, brings into sharp focus what can happen when partnership working is ineffective.

Steven made repeated calls to services asking for help as he was being harassed and bullied yet no action was taken. Safeguarding can only be achieved by joint working and planning and as such effective partnerships are crucial to ensure the safety of adults at risk.

Activity

1. Draw up a list of five other agencies you work with and rate how effective the relationship is, with 1 being non-existent and 10 being highly effective. Then consider any actions you can take to improve relationships. Record your responses in a four-column table headed: Agency/Rating/Why effective/Actions to improve.

Remember

As society has evolved and progressed the issue of safeguarding has become more complex. Working with others who specialise in key areas is the only way to empower vulnerable individuals to safeguard themselves.

Be able to monitor and evaluate the systems, processes and practice that safeguards vulnerable adults

9.4

9.4.1 Support the participation of vulnerable adults in a review of systems and procedures

With the emergence of person-centred care, it follows that service users should be fully involved in reviewing safeguarding procedures. This was initially highlighted in the Health and Social Care Act 2001, then more specifically in 'Safeguarding Adults' in 2005 under Section 11 and again in 'Putting People First' in 2007. We have focused a lot on what services can do in relation to their systems for safeguarding, but an important aspect is actually to inform and train vulnerable adults to recognise abuse too.

SCIE has undertaken significant research into this area and has produced a report called 'User Involvement in Adult Safeguarding' (SCIE 2011). Potential barriers to increased involvement have been fears about the appropriateness of discussing abuse in case this generated difficult feelings for individuals and maybe caused additional harm. Other aspects might be explaining the complexities of safeguarding when looking at individual choice versus duty of care or public safety or even legal requirements.

There are examples of individuals having increased involvement in safeguarding issues. For example within learning disabilities, user groups have been directly involved in staff training or producing a DVD/film for 'Keeping Safe' training. Research does, however, conclude that this training is untested as yet in real life situations. Accessibility is also a key issue for some individuals (SCIE, 2011b). Many services have little in place in this respect; a good starting point is discussing the issues in one-to-one sessions or as part of a service user meeting.

The 'Adult Social Care Outcomes Framework' was published in March 2012 by the Department of Health and details a simple framework for asking service users how 'safe they feel'.

Activity

1. How does your provision involve the service users in contributing to safeguarding procedures?

2. What can you implement to improve this?

9.4.2 and 9.4.4 Evaluate systems and procedures to protect vulnerable adults and recommend improvements

It is useful to have set criteria to evaluate your systems against. While these may vary slightly between different services, the following are areas to consider:

- complaints and comments
- accident/incident reports
- service user involvement in reviews
- whether risk assessments reflect service user needs and choices
- whether all support/care plans are current.

Activity

1. In light of all the work and reflection around safeguarding, identify how effective your systems are. Consider asking staff, service users and families for their views and also auditing areas such as complaints to see how accessible the system is or how many alerts/concerns have been raised. This could form part of a normal quality assurance questionnaire.

2. Make recommendations as a result of your findings.

9.4.3 Challenge ineffective practice in safeguarding

Ineffective practice must be challenged. There may be many different reasons why it happens, but each case must be fully investigated to ascertain what has occurred. This could come in the form of a complaint or a safeguarding alert, or else it might be the result of whistle blowing or even what you observe. Everything must be documented according to your own service's policies. It might also be appropriate to record on a supervision record in a staff file, depending on the nature of the situation. As well as the potential for a safeguarding alert, a situation could also end up as a staff disciplinary action so accurate recording is vital.

Should practice need to be challenged, approach the situation in an assertive manner and consider the following areas in advance:

- Are you clear about the facts of the situation?
- What policies and procedures guide the practice in question?
- Has adequate training been delivered?
- Are there any other factors that led to the poor practice?

Remember to listen to the employee's explanation. While it is good practice to have a 'no blame' culture, it is still your responsibility to address the situation.

Activity

1. Consider why ineffective or poor practice might happen and what you would do in the following examples:

   - Poor support for service users with mobility problems.
   - You hear a staff member discouraging a service user from taking a risk as 'there will be lots of paperwork to complete'.
   - No staff are present in the dining room during residents' meal times.
   - You notice that while you were away the health and safety checks were not completed.

Are you ready for assessment?

- Do you know the differences between the concepts of safeguarding and protection?

- Do you know the impact of policy developments on approaches to safeguarding?

- Do you know the legislative framework for safeguarding?

- Do you know how serious case reviews or inquiries have influenced quality assurance, regulation and inspection relating to safeguarding?

- Do you know the protocols and referral procedures when harm or abuse is alleged or suspected?

- Can you promote service provision that supports vulnerable adults to assess risks and make informed choices?

- Can you provide information to others on indicators of abuse, measures that can be taken to avoid abuse taking place, steps that need to be taken in the case of suspected or alleged abuse?

- Can you identify the policies and procedures in your own work setting that contribute to safeguarding and the prevention of abuse?

- Can you monitor the implementation of policies and procedures that aim to safeguard vulnerable adults and prevent abuse from occurring?

- Can you provide feedback to others on practice that supports the protection of vulnerable adults?

- Can you follow agreed protocols for working in partnership with other organisations?

- Can you review the effectiveness of systems and procedures for working in partnership with other organisations?

- Can you support the participation of vulnerable adults in a review of systems and procedures?

- Can you evaluate the effectiveness of systems and procedures to protect vulnerable adults in your own service setting?

- Can you challenge ineffective practice in the promotion of the safeguarding of vulnerable adults?

- Can you recommend proposals for improvements in systems and procedures in your own service setting?

References

Department of Health (2000) *No Secrets: Guidance on Developing Multi-Agency Policies and Procedures to Protect Vulnerable Adults from Abuse*. London: Department of Health.

Department of Health (2007) *Putting People First: A Shared Vision and Commitment to the Transformation of Adult Social Care*. London: Department of Health.

Websites and Web-based Articles

ADASS (2005) Safeguarding Adults: A National Framework of Standards for Good Practice and Outcomes in Adult Protection Work. London: ADASS, www.adass.org.uk/old/publications/guidance/safeguarding.pdf, accessed 3 July 2012.

Bichard, M. (2005) *The Bichard Inquiry: Final Report*. London: Cabinet Office, www.bichardinquiry.org.uk/10663/report.pdf, accessed 3 July 2012.

Carr, S. (2008) *Personalisation: A Rough Guide*. Social Care Institute for Excellence, www.scie.org.uk/publications/reports/report20.pdf, accessed 3 July 2012.

CPS (2009) *Policy for Prosecuting Crimes Against Older People*. London: HMSO, www.cps.gov.uk/publications/docs/caop_policy_leaflet.pdf, accessed 3 July 2012.

Department of Health (2007) *Independence, Choice and Risk: a Guide to Best Practice in Supported Decision Making*. London: Department of Health, www.dh.gov.uk, accessed 3 July 2012.

Department of Health (2009) *Safeguarding Adults: Report on the Consultation on the Review of 'No Secrets'*. London: Department of Health, http://www.dh.gov.uk/prod_consum_dh/groups/dh_digitalassets/documents/digitalasset/dh_102981.pdf, accessed 4 July 2012.

Department of Health (2011) *Statement of Government Policy on Adult Safeguarding*. London: Department of Health, www.dh.gov.uk/prod_consum_dh/groups/dh_digitalassets/documents/digitalasset/dh_126770.pdf, accessed 3 July 2012.

Galpin, D, and Morrison, L. (2010) *National Competence Framework for Safeguarding Adults*. Bournemouth: Bournemouth University, www.scie-socialcareonline.org.uk/profile.asp?guid=6798bf64-9784-43d8-9fdf-129aea3a912f, accessed 3 July 2012.

Home Office (2011) *Vetting and Barring Scheme Remodelling Review – Report and Recommendations*. London: HMSO, www.homeoffice.gov.uk/publications/crime/vbs-report?view=Binary, accessed 3 July 2012.

Law Commission (2011) *Adult Social Care*. London: HMSO, lawcommission.justice.gov.uk/docs/lc326_adult_social_care.pdf, accessed 3 July 2012.

SCIE (2010) *Enabling Risk, Ensuring Safety: Self-Directed Support and Personal Budgets*. Social Care Institute of Excellence, www.scie.org.uk/publications/ataglance/ataglance31.pdf, accessed 3 July 2012.

SCIE (2011a) *User Involvement in Adult Safeguarding*, www.scie.org.uk/publications/reports/report47/files/report47.pdf, accessed 3 July 2012.

SCIE (2011b) *Prevention in Adult Safeguarding: A Review of the Literature. Social Care Institute of Excellence*, www.scie.org.uk/publications/reports/report41/files/report41.pdf, accessed 3 July 2012.

Serious Case Reviews and Failings in Practice Documents:

Death by Indifference, www.mencap.org.uk/74deaths, accessed 3 July 2012.

Dementia abuse case (Panorama exposé), www.communitycare.co.uk/Articles/18/04/2012/118151/care-worker-jailed-for-abuse-of-vulnerable-dementia-sufferer.htm, accessed 3 July 2012.

Home Care Inquiries, www.equalityhumanrights.com/legal-and-policy/inquiries-and-assessments/inquiry-into-home-care-of-older-people/, accessed 3 July 2012.

Robert Francis QC Report Mid Staff NHS, www.dh.gov.uk/en/Publicationsandstatistics/Publications/PublicationsPolicyAndGuidance/DH_113018, accessed 3 July 2012.

Winterbourne View CQC, www.cqc.org.uk/public/our-action-winterbourne-view#scr, accessed 3 July 2012.

Chapter 10

Lead and
manage group
living
for adults

It is increasingly recognised that the design, management and organisation of a group-living environment plays a significant role in the creation of positive outcomes for individuals. The aim of this chapter is to enable you to lead and manage a group-living service that meets the needs and aspirations of individuals.

Successful completion of this chapter should assist you in meeting more effectively the needs of individuals in a well-designed and managed group-living environment.

By the end of this chapter you will:

1 Be able to develop the physical group-living environment to promote positive outcomes for individuals

2 Be able to lead the planning, implementation and review of daily living activities

3 Be able to promote positive outcomes in a group-living environment

4 Be able to manage a positive group-living environment

Be able to develop the physical group-living environment to promote positive outcomes for individuals

10.1

10.1.1 Review current theoretical approaches to group-living provision for adults

Group living can include facilities for adults with significant personal needs in residential homes, nursing homes or sheltered/extra-care housing. It can also include specialist rehabilitation services for people with neurological problems where the focus is on therapeutic interventions. A further example is rural communities for people with learning disabilities or with mental health needs that provide a shared community life. It is estimated that approximately half a million people use these services, the majority being older people (Bowers, 2009).

Figure 10.1 A group-living environment is designed to meet the specific needs of individuals

Your understanding of effectively managing a group-living facility can be enhanced by an appreciation of some of the theories that have informed debate on these services. Wolfensberger (1975) identified some of the negative features of large-scale institutions, where individuals were segregated from society, often kept in degrading conditions and treated inhumanely. From his knowledge of institutional care, Wolfensberger developed the concept of '**normalisation**', which encouraged the closure of large institutions and their replacement by residential homes and, more recently, supported housing.

> **Key Term**
>
> **Normalisation** means creating group-living environments for people in situations that are as normal as possible rather than institutional care.

10.1.2 Evaluate the impact of legal and regulatory requirements on the physical group-living environment

It is also important that you are familiar with the main legislation that impacts on group-living services and the specific regulations for your service.

Activity

1. Go to the Department of Health website (www.dh.gov.uk) and access the National Minimum Standards for your service, as this will enable you to identify the standards required. Remember that these documents describe 'minimum' level of resources that provide the basis for a quality service.

2. Go to the Care Quality Commision website (www.cqc.org.uk) and read the pages that explain the regulatory requirements for your service and how the standards provide the basis for ensuring that the facilities you offer lead to positive outcomes for individuals.

Activity

1. Describe the risk management processes you use when working with individuals to ensure you are able to explore the levels of risk they want to take.

2. What actions have you taken to ensure that individuals are safe and secure in the group-living environment, but also have the freedom to make choices, which may include some degree of risk?

10.1.3 Review the balance between maintaining an environment that is safe and secure and promoting freedom of choice

A difficult area in group living is creating an environment that ensures individuals are safe, but also have the right to take risks so that their lives are not overly restricted. Risk assessments also help managers and support staff feel reassured they have acted in the best interests of the individual.

Remember that although safety is a good thing, it is only one aspect of life and cannot be absolute or the only goal in life, otherwise life would be meaningless. What good is making someone safe if it merely makes them miserable? (Department of Health, 2007)

10.1.4 Explain how the physical environment can promote well-being

There is a close relationship between the physical environment and the well-being of individuals, although people with different needs will need design features that are related to their particular requirements.

Some useful questions to ask (based on Burton, 1998) are:

■ What is this building for?

■ Which needs are we trying to meet in the way the internal structure and furniture and fittings are arranged?

■ What does the building convey to people who use this service by the way it is designed?

In answering these questions, you should begin to view the group-living environment in a different way. It should enable you to rethink fundamentally how you see buildings by putting yourself in the shoes of the service users and their carers.

Taking these ideas a stage further, a helpful way of exploring how an environment is designed to enhance well-being can be found in the work of Judd *et al* (1997). Although this focused on the needs of individuals with dementia, it nevertheless has important lessons for how a group-living environment caters for the different needs and users of a facility. Judd *et al* (1997) consider the following:

Does the design of the building:

- compensate for disability?

- maximise independence?

- enhance self-esteem and confidence?

- demonstrate care for staff?

- enable service users to negotiate the internal environment easily?

- reinforce personal identity?

- welcome relatives and the local community?

Group-living facilities have to serve a range of purposes, and some of these may conflict and compromises have to be found. You have an important role in ensuring that the different uses of a building are able to meet the varied needs of people living, working and visiting (Peace and Reynolds, 2003).

10.1.5 Justify proposals for providing and maintaining high quality decorations and furnishings for group living

An important aspect of a group-living environment is the interior design decorations and furnishing. It has long been recognised that there is a relationship between the design and quality of the environment and its impact on relationships and social interaction. Good design and the avoidance of an 'institutional' look and feel, common in care homes for older people, should be the first consideration.

Figure 10.2 It is important to think carefully about the interior design of a group-living environment. What do you notice about this environment?

10.1.6 Develop an inclusive approach to decision making about the physical environment

A well-managed group-living service will strive to be as inclusive as possible when it comes to making decisions about the physical environment. In practical terms, this means taking into consideration the views of all those people who live, work and visit there.

Activity

1. Describe what processes you have in place in your service for eliciting the views of people who use that service.

2. Do you understand why some individuals may be reluctant to voice their opinions?

3. What can you do to ensure that service users' voices are heard and their views respected?

Be able to lead the planning, implementation and review of daily living activities

10.2.1 Evaluate the impact of legislation and regulation on daily-living activities

Legislative and regulatory demands on group-living services are intended to ensure that the provision of daily-living activities takes place in an environment where the needs of service users is paramount. As manager, you have to make decisions, which present challenges and dilemmas.

Activity

1. Think of a daily-living activity that your service has a duty to perform. What demands does this place on you if your resources are stretched?

2. Research the range of legislation and regulations that apply to your service, and identify those that are most important in terms of ensuring that individuals can access high quality daily-living activities. An example could be the Human Rights Act (1998, Article 3) which is concerned with degrading treatment or punishment (Cooper, 2006).

10.2.2 Support others to plan and implement daily-living activities that meet individual needs and preferences

As the manager of a group-living service, you are responsible for ensuring that you and your staff plan and implement activities that meet the needs and preferences of service users. Some of the important elements of this work include:

- a clear understanding of the needs of individuals using the service

- supporting individuals to express their views about the service they receive

- ensuring where individuals have complex needs or challenging behaviour for which staff are suitably trained and supported.

10.2.3 Develop systems to ensure individuals are central to decisions about daily-living activities

As part of the personalisation of social care services, increasing emphasis is placed on consulting people who use services to ensure they are central to decisions made about their lives. The origins lie in the wide range of developments that have taken place, particularly in learning disability services, where emphasis is placed on respect for the person's views, their right to self-determination and designing services around their specific needs.

The Department of Health visualises personalisation applying to all individuals who use services in all care settings, and has equal resonance for those living in group settings where personalised approaches may still be less developed. This is particularly important in view of the findings of a study into older people's views about their long-term care, which found that there was a significant gulf between personal aspirations and the services offered in group-living services (Bowers, 2009).

Activity

Go to the SCIE website (www.scie.org.uk) and read the pages on personalisation and on residential and nursing care.

1. Try to identify how some of the developments in personalisation in different services could be adopted by your own service.

2. What difference would some of the initiatives mentioned on this website make to the lives of individuals using your service when it comes to inclusive approaches to decision making?

Activity   *In Practice*

Sarah is newly appointed to manage a residential service for people with dementia, which has used traditional approaches that emphasise safety and containment, with limited focus on personalised approaches. She is committed to the development of a person-centred approach to working with people with dementia (National Institute for Health and Clinical Excellence (NICE/SCIE, 2006)) and wants to introduce a number of innovations, including:

- recognition and respect for the individual (Kitwood, 1997)

- person-centred communication

- life story/memory books

- dementia care mapping, which considers the viewpoint of the person with dementia who is unable to express their own views (Brooker and Surr, 2005).

She believes the introduction of these techniques could transform the quality of life for individuals with dementia, creating a service that will meet the aims of the personalisation agenda. She has to convince her staff that adopting these techniques will improve the lives of individuals, requiring a different approach, with the development of new knowledge, skills and attitudes to supporting individuals.

Put yourself in Sarah's position:

1. What would you need to do to create a climate for innovation in the service?

2. What evidence do you need to convince staff of the value of these techniques?

3. What support would members of staff need to respond positively to these new developments?

10.2.4 Oversee the review of daily-living activities

In managing a group-living service, your goal should be the achievement of a high-quality service. It is important that you understand how to manage the monitoring and evaluation of services provided. Some of the components you could use when reviewing a service include:

■ obtaining feedback from those using the service

■ obtaining feedback from relatives and carers

■ reviewing how effective care plans have been implemented, and whether goals identified have been met

■ obtaining feedback from staff, particularly those frontline workers who have daily contact with service users.

Ultimately the measure of a high-quality service is that experienced by the individuals who use it and the outcomes in terms of the quality of their lives.

Figure 10.3 Getting feedback on daily living activities from service users will help you evaluate the services provided

Be able to promote positive outcomes in a group-living environment

10.3

10.3.1 Evaluate how group living can promote positive outcomes for individuals

A helpful way of exploring how a group-living environment can promote a positive outcome is to consider the kind of lifestyle the service enables individuals to have. Although this idea was originally developed for people with learning disabilities, it can be applied to any group-living service. The elements that can be considered include the following questions:

■ Does the service enable individuals to participate in everyday household and community activities?

■ Does the service enable individuals to continue to develop their skills and experience thereby increasing the extent they can direct their own lives?

■ Does the service enable individuals to increase and maintain their network of supportive friendships and relationships?

Mansel (1986) argues that the key component of the effectiveness of a service is the kind of lifestyle that it enables individuals to have. Lifestyle is a combination of factors, including the needs of the individual , the imagination, skills and commitment of staff who support them, wider factors such as the policies and practices of the service, and the quality of guidance and support available to staff.

Activity

Reflect on the three lifestyle elements described above and the wider organisational factors and how these impact on outcomes for individuals.

1. What support do you need in place to ensure that individuals can achieve a lifestyle that meets their needs and preferences?

10.3.2 Review the ways in which group activities may be used to promote the achievement of individual positive outcomes

One of the risks is the assumption that because individuals live in a group setting, they will want to participate in group activities. This was one of the major criticisms of the institutional model of residential care, where activities were arranged on a group basis that took no account of individual needs and preferences.

Activity

1. In reviewing the activities in your service, were you able to ensure that where group activities are provided, individuals can make an informed choice about whether or not they participate, rather than the activities being arranged as a convenient way of managing groups of individuals?

Figure 10.4 It is important to support the relationships the individuals in your care have with friends and family members

10.3.3 Ensure that individuals are supported to maintain and develop relationships

Bigby (2010) has argued that personal and informal relationships are fundamental to inclusion and citizenship, and that this means connections with others, relationships with family, friends, neighbours and acquaintances. These relationships help foster a sense of community and belonging. What is apparent from many studies of group living is that ageing or loss of function means that social networks can shrink. Thus, lives of people in residential care can mean loneliness, even though they are in a group-living environment.

Individuals who enter group living are often at the point of significant life transition, such as declining function, bereavement or the onset of long-term health problems. This may also be a time when their personal relationships are fractured by losses of different kinds, including close friends, relations and spouses (Scragg, 2012).

Activity

1. Reflect on why it can be difficult for individuals to develop and maintain personal relationships in group-living services.

2. What can you do to enable individuals to maintain personal relationships and avoid the loneliness of group living?

Remember

Group-living environments can inadvertently assume that all individuals have similar needs and interests and organise routines and activities that fail to recognise individuals' preferred choices. Lack of opportunity to express personal choice and participate in chosen activities can quickly lead to institutional practices that undermine individuals' quality of life.

10.3.4 Demonstrate effective approaches to resolving any conflicts and tensions in group living

In situations where people are living and working in close proximity, it is inevitable that at times individual differences of opinion will lead to disagreements. If these escalate into conflict then it is important that they are dealt with promptly before lasting damage is done to relationships.

Where individuals feel they are in conflict with the service, it is important that there are well-established procedures to enable them to voice their concerns.

It is also important to remember that not all conflicts should be viewed negatively, as they can reveal important questions about issues that individuals have found difficult to articulate.

Activity

1. What procedures do you have in place in your service to enable individuals to voice their concerns about their care or other matters that concern them?

Be able to manage a positive group-living environment

10.4

10.4.1 Evaluate the effects of working schedules and patterns on a group living environment

The effective management of a group-living service depends significantly on the way staff ensure that individuals' needs are met. How this is carried out will depend on the specific needs of individuals, the levels of support provided and the resources available to managers. The key question should be whether the working patterns of staff are contributing most effectively to meeting the needs of individuals. Leading good practice plays a significant part in communicating this priority to staff.

Figure 10.5 Supporting individuals to achieve their expectations is a key part of group living

10.4.2 Recommend changes to working schedules and patterns as a result of evaluation

In reviewing staff working patterns regularly, ensures that systems are working effectively.

This process can take place in a number of ways, including reviewing:

■ how individual members of staff are performing during supervision

■ the effectiveness of working patterns in team meetings

■ with individuals the care they are receiving and whether this is meeting their needs

■ with senior managers the level of staffing resources and whether it is adequate to meet the needs of individuals using the service

■ the reports of inspectors following visits to your service

■ the findings of research that discuss the staffing of group-living environments.

Activity

1. Give a recent example of where you introduced a change in the staff work schedule based on an evaluation of feedback from individuals using the service.

10.4.3 Develop a workforce development plan for the group living environment

A major responsibility of a manager is ensuring that a service maintains its effectiveness by successful planning. A workforce plan ensures:

- you have the appropriate number of staff for your service

- staff are provided with training and development opportunities, and you are able to provide a career ladder to maintain the loyalty and commitment of staff

- you are able to anticipate staff changes by having a succession plan.

Activity

1. When discussing staff training and development, are you able to make a link between the physical environment, the structure of daily activities and the way the service is managed and positive outcomes for individuals?

10.4.4 Support staff to recognise professional boundaries while developing and maintaining positive relationships with individuals

As the manager of a group-living service, it is important that you ensure staff are trained and supported through supervision to be aware of the importance of professional boundaries, as there are considerable risks to both individuals using the service and staff where boundaries are threatened or crossed. When support staff break professional boundaries this can cause significant distress to individuals using a service and expose them to abuse or exploitation. The continuing revelations of abuse in group-living services highlights the importance of a thorough understanding of the legal and policy framework of safeguarding adults.

The General Social Care Council (GSCC) have stated that professional boundaries concern what is acceptable and unacceptable for a professional both at work and outside work.

The GSCC suggest some useful questions to ask yourself about the relationship between an individual and a professional:

- Is your relationship focused on promoting the well-being of the service user?

- Are your personal needs being met by your contact with the service user?

- Has the service user ever behaved in a way that suggests they may have misunderstood your professional role?

- Is your relationship with the service user, their friends or family, adversely influencing your professional judgement?

- Is the only relationship you are having with the service user, their friends or family, a professional one? If not have you made your employer aware of this?

Activity   *In Practice*

Simon manages a residential service for severely disabled individuals and is conscious of the need to ensure staff are aware of professional boundaries when carrying out caring tasks. He has based a training session for staff on the General Social Care Council (GSCC) report, 'Professional Boundaries: Guidance for social workers' (www.collegeofsocialwork.org). He wants the training session to focus on ensuring staff recognise the power balance between themselves and those they support, and wants to encourage staff to be open about their practice and to use supervision to discuss any concerns they may have.

1. What professional boundary issues occur in your service?

2. Do you ensure that staff are familiar with the service's policies on professional behaviour and also the guidance from the Regulator?

3. Do you ensure you always model appropriate behaviour in order to influence staff to act professionally?

10.4.5 Use appropriate methods to raise staff awareness of the group dynamics in a group-living environment

Group-living environments are unique settings where there is a complex range of relationships between all those present in the environment. This has implications for the effectiveness of the service. To understand the group dynamics in your service, you need to consider the following three dimensions:

■ the relationships between individuals who are resident in the service

■ the relationship between individuals and staff

■ the relationship between members of staff.

Your role as manager is to ensure that you understand how group living impacts on individuals and the influence of group dynamics on individuals. This will involve creating an environment where individuals feel safe to share their lives with others.

Similarly, with staff, the emphasis will be on:

■ managing the team to enable them to work together

■ building trust between staff members so that they feel positive about collaborating

■ communicating in teams.

Activity

1. Use the internet to research the concept of group dynamics.

2. How do group dynamics influence the way that groups of people relate to each other?

3. What is the value of an understanding of group dynamics for the management of your service?

Activity

1. Thinking about group dynamics, what have you observed about the interaction of members of your staff team?

2. How have the dynamics of the group changed over time?

3. What has been the impact of new members joining the team?

4. Can you identify how each member makes a unique contribution to the team's effectiveness?

10.4.6 Review the effectiveness of approaches to resource management in maintaining a positive group-living environment

An important aspect of your role is the management of all the resources that contribute to the different service requirements. Resources that support group-living environments encompass a wide range of factors that need consideration when reviewing the performance of the service. It is important to recognise that each makes its own contribution to the overall performance of a service. When you are reviewing different resources, consider how each supports positive outcomes for individuals.

Activity

1. Consider how you could deploy the resources under your control more effectively.

2. Review staffing, equipment and finance, and identify whether they are sufficient to meet the aims of the service and what changes would improve the performance of the service.

Are you ready for assessment?

- ✔ Do you know the ways in which the physical environment can promote well-being?

- ✔ Can you review current theoretical approaches to group-living provision for adults?

- ✔ Can you evaluate the impact of legal and regulatory requirements on the physical group-living environment?

- ✔ Can you review the balance between maintaining an environment that is safe and secure and which promotes freedom and choice?

- ✔ Can you justify proposals for providing and maintaining high-quality decorations and furnishings for group living?

- ✔ Can you develop an inclusive approach to decision making about the physical environment?

- ✔ Can you evaluate the impact of legislation and regulation on daily-living activities?

- ✔ Can you support others to plan and implement daily-living activities that meet individual needs and preferences?

- ✔ Can you oversee the review of daily-living activities?

- ✔ Can you evaluate how group living can promote positive outcomes for individuals?

- ✔ Can you review the ways in which group activities may be used to promote the achievement of individuals' positive outcomes?

- ✔ Can you demonstrate effective approaches to resolving any conflicts and tensions in group living?

- ✔ Can you evaluate the effects of the working schedules and patterns on a group-living environment?

- ✔ Can you recommend changes to working schedules and patterns as a result of evaluation?

- ✔ Can you develop a workforce development plan for the group-living environment?

- ✔ Can you support staff to recognise professional boundaries while developing and maintaining positive relationships with individuals?

- ✔ Can you use appropriate methods to raise staff awareness of the group dynamics in a group-living environment?

- ✔ Can you review the effectiveness of approaches to resource management in maintaining a positive group-living environment?

References

Bigby, C. (2010) 'Growing Old: Adapting to Change and Realising a Sense of Belonging, Continuity and Purpose', in Grant, G., Ramacharan, P., Flynn, M. and Richardson, M. (Eds) *Learning Disability, a Life Cycle Approach* (2nd edition). Maidenhead: Open University Press.

Bowers, H. (2009) *Older People's Vision of Long-Term Care*. York: Joseph Rowntree Foundation.

Brooker, D. and Surr, C. (2005) *Demetia Care Mapping: Principles and Practice*. Bradford: Bradford Dementia Group.

Burton, J. (1998) *Managing Residential Care*. London: Routledge.

Cooper, J. (2006) *The Care Homes Legal Handbook*. London and Philadelphia: Jessica Kingsley Publishers.

Department of Health (2003) *Care Homes for Older People, National Minimum Standards and the Care Home Regulations 2000*. London: The Stationery Office.

Department of Health (2007) *Independence, Choice and Risk: a Guide to Best Practice in Supported Decision Making*. London: The Stationery Office.

Judd, S., Marshall, M. and Phippen, P. (1997) *Design for Dementia*. London: Hawker Publications.

Kitwood, T. (1997) *Dementia Reconsidered: The Person Comes First*. Buckingham: Open University Press.

Mansel, J. (1986) 'The Nature of Quality Assurance' in Beswick, J., Zadic, T. and Felce, D. (Eds), *Evaluating Quality of Care*, Kidderminster: BIMH Conference Series.

NICE/SCIE (2006) *Dementia: Supporting People with Dementia and their Carers in Health and Social Care*. London: National Institute for Health and Clinical Excellence.

Peace, S. and Reynolds, J. (2003) *Managing Environments*, in *Managing Care in Context*, Henderson, J. and Atkinson, D. (Eds). London: Routledge.

Scragg, T. (2012) 'Working with Loss and Bereavement in Older People' in Hall, B. and Scragg, T. *Social Work with Older People, Approaches to Person-Centred Practice*. Maidenhead: Open University Press.

Wolfensgberger, W. (1975) *The Origins and Nature of Our Institutional Models*. Syracuse: Human Policy Press.

Websites

Department of Health, www.dh.gov.uk, accessed 3 July 2012.

Care Quality Commission, www.cqc.org.uk, accessed 3 July 2012.

General Social Care Council, www.gscc.org.uk, accessed 3 July 2012.

Chapter 11

Understand
safeguarding of
children and young people
(for those working in the adult sector)

This chapter will help you to understand your responsibilities towards safeguarding children and young people. Professionals who come into contact with children, parents and carers in the course of their work, albeit in the context of adult social care, need to be aware of their safeguarding responsibilities towards children and young people.

While abuse of a child or young person within your setting might seem unlikely, clear policies and procedures should nonetheless be in place should you need to respond and take action. If you are in a service such as mental health, substance abuse or domestic abuse, where contact with parents and carers of children and young people is more frequent, it is likely you will have clear safeguarding policies in place.

This chapter can only offer an overview of safeguarding of children and young people as it is a complex and specialised area.

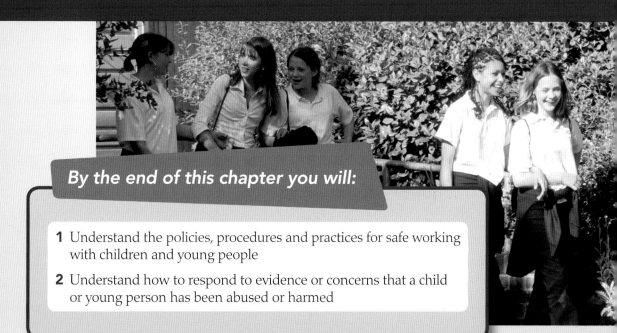

By the end of this chapter you will:

1 Understand the policies, procedures and practices for safe working with children and young people

2 Understand how to respond to evidence or concerns that a child or young person has been abused or harmed

Understand the policies, procedures and practices for safe working with children and young people

11.1.1 Explain the policies, procedures and practices for safe working with children and young people

While there are some similarities between safeguarding adults and children, there is a different approach to mental capacity, with a presumption of capacity in adults and a presumption of incapacity in **children**. Local authorities are the lead agency for both safeguarding of children and young people and safeguarding adults. Services do not always neatly divide into those for adults and those for children; there will be circumstances when adult services and children's services overlap. There is legislation supporting safeguarding of children but nothing comparable for adults.

Figure 11.1 It is important to make time to listen if a young person wants to talk to you about any concerns they have and record facts correctly

Key Term

A child is defined as anyone who has not yet reached the age of 18 years.

Public outcries from serious failings in practice and subsequent reviews have led to a more robust approach to safeguarding of children and young people. The National Society for the Protection of Children (NSPCC) estimate that at least one child is killed every ten days by their parents or carers, and thousands more suffer serious harm at the hands of those who are supposed to be caring for them. Many of these cases of abuse could be prevented if public and professionals worked together.

While the principles of child protection are generally familiar, the principles of safeguarding go one step further and encourage a wider, more preventative approach to meet the needs of children. This involves agencies working more closely together in an attempt to alleviate problems before they occur.

Current principles underpinning the safeguarding of children are based on legislation first established in 1989.

- Children Act (1989): All services, including those specifically for adults, have a duty of care towards children. A general duty was placed on local authorities to safeguard and promote the welfare of children in their area who are suffering or likely to suffer harm (Section 47).

- 'Every Child Matters' (2003): This was published alongside the formal response to the report into the death of Victoria Climbié. It set out five outcomes that are key to children and young people's well-being: be healthy; stay safe; enjoy and achieve; make a positive contribution; achieve economic well-being.

■ It also introduced the concept of the Common Assessment Framework to standardise and improve the consistency of assessments.

■ Children Act (2004): This sets out the five outcomes in statute. Section 11 of this Act outlines a 'duty to cooperate' among key people and bodies to promote the welfare of children. The Act established that although services might be provided to adults, the **paramountcy principle** makes the child's welfare an essential consideration for those working in adult services. The Act also created Local Safeguarding Children Boards.

■ Safeguarding Disabled Children (2009): This highlights that disabled children are more vulnerable to abuse for a variety of reasons such as the fact they are more socially isolated, they depend more on others for their physical personal care, they may be non-verbal with poor communication skills.

■ The Children's Plan (2007): This was developed in line with the principles and articles of the UN Convention on the Rights of the Child (adopted by the UK in 1992). It sets out the role of government and a wide range of agencies and professionals in improving children's lives.

■ 'Working Together to Safeguard Children' (2010): This sets out how organisations and individuals should work together to safeguard and promote the welfare of children and young people in accordance with the Children Acts of 1989 and 2004. All practitioners working to safeguard children and young people must understand fully their responsibilities and duties by law. This latest revision follows the publication of Lord Laming's report, 'The Protection of Children in England: A Progress Report', in March 2009.

■ Munro Report (2011): This might lead to another revision of statutory guidance. It proposes reform to the over-bureaucratised child protection system, which is concerned with compliance, to one that is focused on children, i.e. child centred.

■ Safeguarding Children Across Services (2012): This is an extensive, ongoing government funded research programme to better understand and develop practice relating to safeguarding children.

Activity   In Practice

You are the manager of a dementia unit. Oliver, one of your service users, has his son, daughter-in-law and two grandchildren visiting. You have suggested to the son that it might not always be appropriate to bring his children in due to the decline in Oliver's health; there have been issues with Oliver and his grandchildren before as they do not understand their grandfather's illness. As children, they can become quite loud and boisterous, which then confuses Oliver and can lead to him becoming aggressive towards them. Oliver's son wants to talk to you about his father's care costs, as he is looking after his finances, and he asks if you can spend some time with him and his wife to talk through some figures. He says his children can sit with his father during the discussion as he will not be able to concentrate if the children are in the office.

1. How would you react in this situation?

2. Explain what your responsibilities would be.

3. How can you ensure everyone is clear about the children's safety when on the premises?

Understand how to respond to evidence or concerns that a child or young person has been abused or harmed

11.2.1 Describe the possible signs, symptoms, indicators and behaviours that may cause concern in the context of safeguarding

A person may **abuse** by either inflicting harm or failing to act to prevent harm occurring. Anyone, be this an adult or child, can potentially abuse in any setting. The abuser may or may not be known to the individual. Research from the USA suggests that disabled children are more likely to be abused than those without disabilities.

> ### Key Term
>
> **Abuse** or significant harm is an action that is sufficiently serious to adversely affect progress and impair healthy development.

'Working Together to Safeguard Children' (2010) defines abuse in terms of four categories:

1. Physical abuse: causing physical harm to a child.

2. Emotional abuse: the persistent emotional maltreatment of a child causing severe and persistent adverse effects on the child's emotional development (some level of emotional abuse is involved in all types of maltreatment of a child, though it may occur alone).

3. Sexual abuse: forcing or enticing a child or young person to take part in sexual activities, not necessarily involving a high level of violence, whether or not the child is aware of what is happening.

4. Neglect: the persistent failure to meet a child's basic physical and/or psychological needs, which is likely to result in the serious impairment of the child's health or development.

(See 'Working Together to Safeguard Children' (2010) for comprehensive definitions.)

A more recent concern for authorities has been the possible radicalisation of vulnerable young people, and this now features within the government counter-terrorist strategy under the name of 'Prevent'. Authorities are currently looking to see how Prevent could be synthesised with existing safeguarding mechanisms, such as the Common Assessment Framework, to better identify young people at risk.

While cultural and religious issues must be taken into account when considering possible abuse, these cannot be used to excuse anything of concern. Some 'cultural norms' such as female genital mutilation, 'Beating the Devil Out' practices and arranged/forced marriages need to be handled sensitively but nonetheless addressed. There has also been a growing awareness that 16- and 17-year-olds experience domestic abuse yet currently laws and services are for those aged 18 and over; the Home Office is therefore looking to redefine the domestic abuse laws to include those under 18.

Activity

1. Identify types of possible abuse and actions you would take for each scenario below.

Type of harm/abuse	Sign or symptom	Action I would take
	Child visiting grandma has a small circular burn on hand	
	Child sits quietly rocking and twisting hair and does not want to play or talk	
	A young person says he hates to be left alone with Uncle Fred as he does not like the way he looks at him	
	You hear a young child telling his granny 'Mummy doesn't have any time for me as she is always working and I have to make tea when she is not there'	

This activity is just to get you thinking; there may be very plausible explanations for what you have heard or seen.

11.2.2 Describe the actions to take if a child or young person alleges harm or abuse in line with policies and procedures of your own setting

While it will not be your responsibility to investigate any allegations, it is your responsibility to take appropriate action within the scope of your role and in line with organisational policies. You might be made aware by a full disclosure when you or a colleague are told directly, or it might be a partial disclosure where just hints are made, or else an indirect reference such as 'someone I know...'.

If a disclosure of abuse is made to you it is important to:

■ stay calm

■ reassure the child and show concern

■ believe them

■ listen carefully

■ do not interrupt or ask leading questions

■ do not promise to keep anything a secret.

Do not let a child see if you are shocked, as it might stop them talking and add to any shame they feel. Also do not confront an alleged abuser.

Another scenario might be witnessing something of concern that needs further investigation. When making a professional judgement, you would need to assess areas such as basic care and safety needs, emotional warmth, stimulation, appropriate boundaries and stability.

However you are made aware of potential or actual abuse, report it as soon as you are able and seek expert help at the earliest possible opportunity. This could be via an advice line, such as the NSPCC or a local authority advice line on safeguarding.

Figure 11.2 There are always advice lines to call if you are unsure about what action to take, but do act quickly, as a child might be at risk of harm

Remember that any child protection issue will always take precedence over data protection. You must then record in writing all the relevant information with the level of detail you would for an adult safeguarding issue, which as a minimum should have:

■ date, time and place

■ child/young person's name, date of birth and address if known

■ nature of the disclosure or allegation or a factual account of what you observed

■ a description of any visible injuries if present or seen

■ any immediate actions taken, e.g. police or ambulance requested.

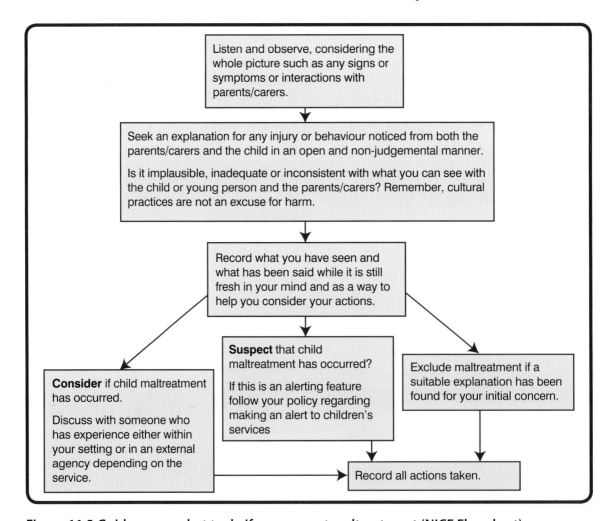

Figure 11.3 Guidance on what to do if you suspect maltreatment (NICE Flowchart)

Yolanda is a 15-year-old girl who does voluntary work at weekends. Her duties consist of helping with teas and supper. One Saturday she lets a senior worker know that she no longer wants to do Sunday shifts, and when the senior asks her why she says she would prefer not to say as she does not want anyone to get into trouble. Following reassurance that this certainly would not happen, she reveals that a male carer has been talking to her inappropriately and this has made her feel very uncomfortable and worried. The senior recognises the urgency of the situation and calls you.

1. Explain what actions need to be taken by both the senior on duty and you as a manager.

2. What lessons can you learn from this case study? What might you implement within your service to reduce the likelihood of something like this happening?

11.2.3 Explain the rights that children, young people and their families have in situations where harm or abuse is suspected or alleged

The UN Convention on the Rights of a Child (1989) states that children's views should be sought in all matters affecting them and given due weight in a sensitive and age-appropriate way. Although the government has made a commitment to this, it is not as yet part of UK law as it is in Wales via the Rights of Children and Young People (Wales) Measure. However the Human Rights Act (1998) incorporates the European Convention on Human Rights into UK law, and children are considered 'persons' in the eyes of the law.

Rights of children include being protected from abuse and being able to express their views and be listened to. However, when a child is at significant risk of harm then the paramount concern is to make them safe and ensure their best interests are met.

Parents and carers have a right to be kept informed of any allegations of abuse. The Data Protection Act (1985) does not apply in cases of child abuse, and information can be shared across relevant agencies if required.

Are you ready for assessment?

✔ **Do you know the policies, procedures and practices for safe working with children and young people?**

✔ **Do you know how to respond to evidence or concerns that a child or young person has been abused or harmed?**

✔ **Do you know the possible signs, symptoms, indicators and behaviours that may cause concern?**

✔ **Do you know the rights of children, young people and their families where harm/abuse is suspected or alleged?**

References

Department for Education (2011) *A Child-Centred System: The Government's Response to the Munro Review of Child Protection. London.* London: Department for Education.

Department for Education (2003) *Every Child Matters.* London: The Stationery Office.

HM Government (2010) *Working Together to Safeguard Children: A Guide to Inter-Agency Working to Safeguard and Promote the Welfare of Children.* London: Department for Children, Schools and Families.

Munro, E. (2011) *The Munro Review of Child Protection: Final Report. A Child-Centred System.* London: Department for Education.

Acts, Regulations and Reports

Children Act (2004).

Data Protection Act (1985).

'Every Child Matters' (2003).

Human Rights Act (1998).

Munro Report (2011.

Safeguarding Children Across Services (2012).

Safeguarding Disabled Children (2009).

Children Act (1989).

The Children's Plan (2007).

The UN Convention on the Rights of a Child (1989).

'Working Together to Safeguard Children' (2010).

Websites and Web-based Reports

Department of Health, www.doh.gov.uk, accessed 30 June 2012.

Every Child Matters: Change for Children, www.education.gov.uk/publications/eOrderingDownload/DfES10812004.pdf, accessed 30 June 2012.

Munro Report (2011), www.education.gov.uk/publications/eOrderingDownload/Munro-Review.pdf, accessed 4 July 2012.

The National Society for the Protection of Children (NSPCC), www.nspcc.org.uk, accessed 30 June 2012.

Safeguarding Across Services, www.education.gov.uk/publications/eOrderingDownload/DFE-RR164.pdf, accessed 30 June 2012.

Safeguarding Children and Young People who may be Affected by Gang Activity, www.education.gov.uk/publications/standard/publicationDetail/Page1/DCSF-00064-2010, accessed 30 June 2012.

Safeguarding Disabled Children, www.education.gov.uk/publications/eOrderingDownload/00374-2009DOM-EN.pdf, accessed 30 June 2012.

Safeguarding Disabled Children – Practice Guidance, www.education.gov.uk/publications/standard/publicationDetail/Page1/DCSF-00374-2009, accessed 4 July 2012.

Working Together to Safeguard Children 2010, www.education.gov.uk/publications/eOrderingDownload/00305-2010DOM-EN.pdf, accessed 30 June 2012.

HM Government (2011) *Prevent Strategy*. The Stationery Office, London, www.homeoffice. gov.uk/publications/counter-terrorism/ prevent/prevent-strategy/prevent-strategy-review?view=Binary, accessed 30 June 2012.

NSPCC (2011) An Introduction to Child Protection Legislation in the UK, www. nspcc.org.uk/inform/research/questions/ child_protection_legislation_in_the_uk_pdf_ wdf48953.pdf, accessed 30 June 2012.

Chapter 12

Lead
person-centred
practice

The aim of this chapter is to help develop your understanding of the theory and principles that underpin person-centred practice. You are given opportunities to enhance the knowledge and skills that will enable you to lead the implementation of person-centred practice. By encouraging active participation, the individual is put at the centre of your care, and others including family members, friends and colleagues are seen as valued contributors to the practice of person-centred care.

This chapter will enable you to review critically approaches to person-centred care and analyse issues that arise in your work setting.

By the end of this chapter you will:

1 Understand the theory and principles that underpin person-centred practice

2 Be able to lead a person-centred practice

3 Be able to lead the implementation of active participation of individuals

Understand the theory and principles that underpin person-centred practice

12.1.1 Explain person-centred practice

Person-centred practice is an approach that puts the individual at the centre of their care and involves them in making decisions about things that affect them (Health Foundation, 2012). Talerico *et al* (2003) identifies several key components of person-centred care. These are:

- knowing the person as an individual and being responsive to their individual and family characteristics

- providing care that is meaningful to the person in ways that respect the individual's values, preferences and needs

- viewing care recipients as **biopsychosocial** human beings

- fostering development of consistent and trusting care-giving relationships

- emphasising freedom of choice and individually defined, reasonable risk-taking.

Key Term

Biopsychosocial is a humanistic approach to care that sees individuals encompassing a biological, psychological and social dimension to their being.

As you can see, using a person-centred approach means engaging with individuals in their care in such a way that they are not seen as a set of problems waiting to be solved, but as a

real person with a right to make decisions about their own needs. Person-centred care should therefore take account of the individual's culture and ethnicity, their wishes and personal choices, be holistic and include others as necessary and as the individual desires.

Figure 12.1 Everyone has a right to make decisions about their own needs

Activity

1. Reflect on your practice and identify an example that demonstrates each component of person-centred care identified by Talerico *et al*.

12.1.2 Critically review approaches to person-centred practice

The individual plays a central role in person-centred approaches, from being consulted about how services are organised to delivery of their own personal care.

Person-centred care should be needs-led and comprehensive so that it covers all aspects of health and social care (Hasan, 2009) and is a core element of all good practice (Nolan *et al*, 2004). Certain **values** that help **empower** individuals are required, such as:

■ respect for the individual as a person

■ ensuring their rights are maintained

■ enabling the person's independence as far as is possible and safe

■ ensuring that the individual has real choices

■ helping the person to maintain their **dignity**.

Key Terms

Values are principles or standards held by people or groups.

Empowerment is about the individual gaining control over aspects of their life, making decisions and overcoming barriers to participation. The person is said to be empowered.

Dignity concerns the person's sense of worth and importance.

Table 12.1 A critical review of approaches to person-centred care

Approach	Explanation	Critical review
Personalisation	The person is an individual with strengths, preferences and aspirations. The individual is at the centre of the process of identifying their needs and making choices about how and when they are supported to live their lives (Carr, 2010).	The individual has information, advocacy and advice so they are able to make informed decisions about their care. However, this can be difficult to achieve if they disagree with assessments made by professionals and do not want to comply with agreed ways of working.
Biographical life-story work	Life-story work is a biographical approach that gives people the opportunity to talk about their life experiences. Their major life events are recorded and used to benefit them in health and social care work (Murphy, 2000).	Individuals are seen as having a past with real-life experiences that can contribute to their assessment and care planning. It helps care workers see the person behind the patient (Clarke *et al*, 2003). However, life-story work can bring back memories of disturbing events, which can cause the individual distress.
Reablement	Reablement is an approach to care that aims to help people do things for themselves rather than others doing things for them. It aims to improve people's confidence and independence (SCIE, 2012).	Reablement focuses on restoring independence rather than resolving health care issues. However, while it focuses on the needs of the individual and regaining skills, it does not seem to aim to develop new or retain existing skills.
Psychosocial interventions	Psychosocial approaches are based on psychological principles that take into account the wider social context of the individual (Hatton, 2002).	They can be used with a range of client groups including older people and individuals with mental health problems. However, Dagnan (2007) identified that they are poorly developed for people with intellectual disabilities. They also do not fully take into account the person's life story.

Activity

1. How do you demonstrate person-centred values with individuals in your care? In what ways can you lead others in demonstrating person-centred values?

12.1.3 Analyse the effect of legislation and policy on person-centred practice

The government continues to drive the policy agenda to modernise public services by promoting, through legislation, person-centred approaches, such as the drive to offer choice (Department of Health, 2005a).

Activity

1. Make a list of the laws that impact on your care setting.

2. When you have completed the list, identify any policies that relate to person-centred care where you work. What legislation are they founded on?

The Health Foundation (2012) reports that implementing 'no decision about me, without me' required a considerable change in culture and practice in care settings. Law and policy have gone hand in hand to achieve this aim.

The NHS Commissioning Board has a critical role to play in making shared decision-making the norm across all health and social care settings (Department of Health, 2009). The more recent proposals to broaden the range of providers and introduce more competition into care services (Department of Health, 2010) is another attempt to underpin person-centredness. The overall

effect of legislation has been to promote person-centred care as the highest standard in health and social care, and an approach that individuals and their families can expect.

12.1.4 Explain how person-centred practice informs the way in which consent is established with individuals

Person-centred practice can inform how **consent** is established with individuals. When individuals are asked to consent to a care activity, care workers act in ways that represent person-centred values. These include ensuring that the individual:

- can express thoughts and ask questions
- has personal values and beliefs
- is treated with respect and has dignity
- has the necessary information to make an informed decision.

Key Term

Consent means informed agreement to an action or decision. The process of establishing consent will vary according to an individual's assessed capacity to consent.

Figure 12.2 Seeking consent to a care activity represents person-centred values

Activity

1. Reflect on ways that you establish consent with individuals. How do you demonstrate person-centred values?

12.1.5 Explain how person-centred practice can result in positive changes in individuals' lives

The overarching aim of person-centred care is to make positive changes to enable individuals to feel more in control of their lives. There are psychological and social benefits: gaining confidence, feeling listened to, raising self-esteem and feeling valued. Positive social changes include:

- developing and maintaining new relationships with care workers and others who take a special interest in the individual as a person

- choosing and doing activities that expand the individual's horizons and integration into community life.

Activity   *In Practice*

Clara asks for a meeting about her mother, Connie, who has dementia, with the manager of Greenfields where she is a new resident. During the meeting she praises one member of the care team in particular. This carer, she says, had gone out of her way to ensure Connie settled in and she had spent longer with her than the family ever expected in making sure she felt at home. The family, Clara says, is pleased and surprised that Connie has renewed her interest in singing songs from musicals.

1. In what ways might the carer be demonstrating a person-centred approach?

2. What social and psychological benefits does Connie experience from the person-centred approach?

Activity

1. Review the example you identified of each component of Talerico *et al*'s person-centred practice above.

2. How can person-centred care lead to a positive change in each component for an individual?

Be able to lead a person-centred practice

Leading a person-centred practice requires skills in supporting others to work with individuals in their care. This includes supporting them:

■ to take individuals' personal histories in order to establish their preferences, wishes and needs

■ to review and adapt approaches in response to individuals' emerging needs or preferences.

12.2.1 Supporting others to work with individuals to establish their history, preferences, wishes and needs

A key element of leadership is the ability to communicate and develop relationships with colleagues in the work setting, with individuals who are in your care and with their family and other supporters. These might include: friends, carers, advocates and other professionals. Leadership in supporting others to work with individuals in establishing their personal history can be demonstrated by:

■ showing how a biography can be established even with individuals who have communication problems

■ explaining the importance of establishing a personal history and how it can influence care

■ providing supervision to reflect on care provided.

Remember that appropriate communication improves the quality of life of people with dementia. (National Care Forum (NCF), 2007)

Figure 12.3 A key element of leadership is the ability to communicate and develop relationships with colleagues

Activity   *In Practice*

Sam is leading the shift at Green Lane House, a residential facility for people with dementia. He asks Mandy, a care worker, to sit with Mrs Owen, a newly arrived resident, to find out about her life history as part of the Home's assessment procedure.

After ten minutes, Sam hears Mandy say, 'No, that isn't the case. It says in your notes from the social worker that you were a school dinner lady after you got married.' Sam notices that Mrs Owen has become tearful. As he approaches, Mandy says to him, 'I told her we don't like tears because it upsets the other residents.'

1. In what ways should Sam support Mandy in developing a more person-centred approach to establishing a personal history from Mrs Owen?

Taking life stories ensures a good understanding of individuals. Recording and using biographical information benefits the person in health and social care work (Murphy, 2000) and it helps care workers see the person behind the patient (Clarke *et al*, 2003).

However, life-story work can bring back memories of disturbing events, which can cause the individual distress.

12.2.2 Support others to implement person-centred practice

Life-story work helps care workers understand the perspective that others bring to the care setting. In the Activity above, Mrs Owen's past experiences were not affirmed by Mandy. Sam has a leading role in supporting Mandy to know about and to understand the value of taking a personal history.

Life-story work enables workers to see the person they are caring for now in relation to the person they were in the past (Clarke *et al*, 2003).

■ The individual's rights and dignity are maintained. This is fundamental to good and safe practice. Listen to what people say and show an interest in what they are saying. Life-story work with an individual with dementia enables their family and carers to connect with them as a person and maintain a positive relationship as well as stimulate conversation and meaningful interaction.

■ It enables the person's independence and identity as far as is possible and safe. The individual continues to be a person in their own right even though they have social or health needs.

■ It ensures that the individual has real choices. This may not be possible in all areas of life, but in dress and other personal activities there is a great deal of scope to personalise care.

You can read more about life-story work at www.lifestorynetwork.org.uk.

Activity — In Practice

Sam realises that he should have explained to Mandy what taking a personal history entails and its importance in person-centred care. He asks her to accompany him to see Mrs Owen who at this time is resting in the lounge.

Sam: 'How are you settling in?'

Mrs Owen: 'It won't be long before father comes to take me home, but I'm OK at the moment.'

Sam: 'Would you like to talk about your life and family, what you have done and so forth?'

Mrs Owen: 'There isn't much to say, but I remember coming home from school – it must have been a few weeks ago I suppose – during the war. Nan lived with us then – she'll be wanting her tea!'

Sam: 'Where did you live? Was it a nice house?'

Mrs Owen: 'It was small but we called it home. I always like a good chat in the evenings and a hot drink before bed.'

Mandy listens as Sam gradually finds out more about Mrs Owen's personal history. It becomes apparent that this biographical approach has its advantages but is limited by Mrs Owen's memory lapses.

1. How might Sam respect Mrs Owen's rights and dignity?

2. How might Sam enable Mrs Owen's sense of her own identity?

3. What sort of real choices can Mrs Owen now be offered?

12.2.3 and 12.2.4 Support others to work with individuals to review and adapt approaches in response to individuals' needs or preferences

One way of reviewing and adapting approaches is by **supervision**, a process that supports the development of knowledge, skills and values to improve the quality of work. Constructive feedback during supervision should be part of the learning process for workers (Skills for Care, 2007).

Key Term

Supervision is a process to support the development of knowledge, skills and values as part of the learning process for workers.

During supervision, care workers can reflect with their line managers and discuss what was effective and what they found more challenging. It is an opportunity that also allows alternative approaches to be assessed before they are tried in practice.

Activity

1. Reflect on an occasion when you have received feedback on your performance from your line manager or another senior practitioner.

2. To what extent did it influence your subsequent practice?

Sometimes a need emerges during care delivery that was not previously apparent. For example, an individual suffering a cerebrovascular accident (stroke) or a young woman with learning disabilities might need protection from exploitation from an acquaintance. While a biographical approach is appropriate in the early stages of getting to know an individual, it may not be suitable as care progresses. Leadership of others entails guiding and, when necessary, prescribing a particular approach depending on the current and emergent needs, wishes and preferences of the individual.

12.3.1 Evaluate how active participation enhances the well-being and quality of life of individuals

While a good understanding of leading person-centred practice is essential, it is also vital to include individuals as **active participants** in their care. This is a central component of person-centredness (Talerico *et al*, 2003). Without active participation, there is no person-centred practice, because individuals are not being fully included in their own care.

Key Term

Active participation is a way of working that recognises an individual's right to participate in the activities and relationships of everyday life as independently as possible; the individual is regarded as an active partner in their own care, rather than a passive recipient.

Activity

1. Think about how you lead in ensuring active participation by individuals in your care setting.

2. What leadership characteristics do you demonstrate?

It is easy to assume that active participation enhances the well-being and quality of life of individuals, but you should evaluate your practice to find out if this is actually the case. When evaluating care delivery it is usual to use a systematic method to ensure consistency. One such method is to apply SMART criteria in collaboration with the individual and others. Take the example of an individual who has regained the ability to walk to the shops alone. You can, for instance, ask the individual the questions in Table 12.2:

Table 12.2 Using SMART criteria to evaluate care

	Criteria	Example
S	Specific	'How has that made you feel in yourself?
M	Measurable	'You walked the first hundred metres without a stick. Can you go further next time?
A	Achievable	'You said you could do it. I bet you're pleased?'
R	Relevant	'Was it something you wanted to do?'
T	Timely	'Would you have preferred to try next week, or was this the right time to have a go?'

12.3.2 and 12.3.3 Implement systems, processes that promote active participation and support the use of risk assessments

An important criterion for leadership is about path making. Cook (2004) sees this as different from management: leaders do what is required in the circumstances. When implementing active participation, leaders therefore need to do what is necessary and **contingent** (meaning depending on the circumstances). Implementing systems and processes might be required, as well as supporting the use of risk assessment in all aspects of individuals' lives to achieve the goal of implementing active participation.

Key Term

Contingency theory is leadership by doing what is required to achieve change depending on the circumstances at the time.

Activity

Imagine you are leading a care team and trying to implement a person-centred approach to meal planning where one member of staff makes it very clear that the staff should select meals for residents. This member of your team constantly undermines your authority by telling residents what meals to choose.

1. What systems and processes might you develop to deal with conflict within the team that also promote a person-centred approach to care?

Ellins and Coulter (2005) found that certain groups need to be supported if they are to become active participants in their health care. These include: older people, the less educated and the chronically ill. From these findings it can be suggested that person-centredness is a valuable and effective approach, but there are limitations to people's ability to make unsupported decisions about their care. Indeed, for long-term conditions, which many older people experience, there is a need for high-quality personalised care to meet their needs (Department of Health, 2005b).

Activity

1. How can you facilitate a person-centred approach to care where the individual has limited understanding and impaired ability to make decisions?

Systems and processes to promote active participation include ensuring that there are agreed ways of working that encompass policies and procedures, for example:

- a personal history for each individual in your care (if this is not possible from the individual, then others who know the person well can be asked)

- a full assessment on each individual for their potential and current abilities, needs, wishes and preferences on a regular basis, remembering that emergent needs and preferences can alter the care that is appropriate

- asking each individual what they want from services

- respecting cultural and other personal characteristics, whether due to ethnicity, age, gender or other criteria

- evaluating risk assessments against the extent to which they enable the individual to participate actively in their own care (remember, it should never be assumed a person is unable to carry out an activity of daily living without good evidence that this is the case)

- establishing regular supervision sessions.

Are you ready for assessment?

- ☑ Do you know the meaning of person-centred practice?

- ☑ Do you know the approaches to person-centred practice?

- ☑ Do you know the effect of legislation and policy on person-centred practice?

- ☑ Do you know how person-centred practice informs the way in which consent is established with individuals?

- ☑ Do you know how person-centred practice can result in positive changes in individuals' lives?

- ☑ Can you support others to work with individuals to establish their history, preferences, wishes and needs?

- ☑ Can you support others to implement person-centred practice?

- ☑ Can you support others to work with individuals to review approaches to meet individuals' needs and preferences?

- ☑ Can you support others to work with individuals to adapt approaches in response to individuals' emerging needs or preferences?

- ☑ Can you evaluate how active participation enhances the well-being and quality of life of individuals?

- ☑ Can you implement systems and processes that promote active participation?

- ☑ Can you support the use of risk assessments to promote active participation in all aspects of the lives of individuals?

References

Batson, P., Thorne, K. and Peak, J. (2002) 'Life Story Work sees the Person beyond the Dementia', *Journal of Dementia Care*, 10(3), pp15–17.

Carr, S. (2010) *Personalisation: A Rough Guide (Revised Edition)*. London: Social Care Institute for Excellence.

Clarke, A., Hanson, E.J. and Ross, H. (2003) 'Seeing the Person Behind the Patient: Enhancing the Care of Older People Using a Biographical Approach'. *Journal of Clinical Nursing*, 12(5), pp697–706.

Cook, M.J. (2004) *Six Steps to Effective Management* in *Managing and Supporting People in Health Care.* (Eds. Hyde, J. and Cook, M. J.), Oxford: (Bailliere Tindall) Elsevier.

Dagnan, D. (2007) 'Psychosocial interventions', in *Psychiatric and Behavioural Disorders in Intellectual and Developmental Disabilities* (Eds. Bouras, N, Holt, G.), Cambridge: Cambridge University Press.

Department of Health (2005a) *Independence, Well-Being and Choice: Our Vision for the Future of Social Care for Adults in England*. London: Department of Health.

Department of Health (2005b) *Supporting People with Long-Term Conditions*. London: Crown Copyright.

Department of Health (2010) *Equity and Excellence: Liberating the NHS*. London: Crown Copyright.

Ellins, J. A. and Coulter (2005) *How Engaged are People in their Health Care?* London: The Health Foundation.

Hasan, T. (2009) *Person-Centred Care, Age and Ageing* 38(1), p133. British Geriatrics Society, Oxford Journals.

Hatton, C. (2002) 'Psychosocial Interventions for Adults with Intellectual Disabilities and Mental Health Problems: A Review'. *Journal of Mental Health*, 11, pp357–73.

Hewitt, H. (2000) 'A Life Story Approach for People with Profound Learning Disabilities'. *British Journal of Nursing*, 9(2), 90–5.

Murphy, C. (2000) 'Cracking Lives: An Evaluation of a Life Story Book Project to Assist Patients from a Long Stay Psychiatric Hospital in Their Move to Community Care Situations', in McKeown, J., Clark, A. and Repper, J. (2006) Life Story Work in Health and Social Care: Systematic Literature Review. *Journal of Advanced Nursing*, 55(2), pp237–47.

National Care Forum (2007) *Statement of Best Practice. Key Principles of Person-Centred Dementia Care*. Coventry: National Care Forum.

Nola, M. R., Davies, S., Brown, J., Keady, J. and Nolan, J. (2004) 'Beyond 'Person-Centred Care': a New Vision for Gerontological Nursing'. *Journal of Clinical Nursing*, 13 (Supp. S1), pp45–53.

Skills for Care (2007) *Providing Effective Supervision*. Leeds: Skills for Care and the Children's Workforce Development Council.

Talerico, K. A., O'Brien, J. A. and Swafford, K. L. (2003) 'Person-Centred Care: An Important Approach for 21st century Health Care', *Journal of Psychosocial Nursing and Mental Health Services*, 41(11), pp12–16.

Websites

Department of Health, www.dh.gov.uk, accessed 30 June 2012.

Department of Health (2009) *Supporting People with Long-Term Conditions: Commissioning Personalised Care Planning*. London: Department of Health, www.dh.gov.uk, accessed 30 June 2012.

Health Foundation (2012) www.health.org. uk/areas-of-work/topics/person-centred-care, accessed 30 June 2012.

Life Story Network, www.lifestorynetwork. org.uk, accessed 30 June 2012.

Social Care Institute for Excellence (SCIE) (2012) *Reablement: Implications for GPs and Primary Care*, www.scie.org.uk, accessed 30 June 2012.

The National Care Forum, www.nationalcareforum.org.uk, accessed 30 June 2012.

Chapter 13

Assess the
individual in
a health
and social care setting

In this chapter you will explore the use of assessment and develop the knowledge and skills needed to understand and implement assessment. You are introduced to different forms of assessment processes and how partnership working can provide a positive contribution to this process. You are then guided into how to contribute to, and lead, assessments, and how to manage their outcomes. In doing so you are encouraged to promote others' understanding of the role of assessment, including families and other key individuals.

By the end of this chapter you will:

1 Understand assessment processes

2 Be able to lead and contribute to assessments

3 Be able to manage the outcomes of assessments

4 Be able to promote others' understanding of the role of assessment

5 Review and evaluate the effectiveness of assessment

Understand assessment processes

13.1

For this learning outome you are required to compare and contrast the range and purpose of different forms of **assessment** and be able to explain how partnership working can positively support assessment processes. Assessment can be defined as involving the collection and analysis of information about people with the aim of understanding their situation and determining recommendations for any further professional intervention (Crisp *et al*, 2003). As such it is an essential component of any care setting; without an assessment, care is unlikely to meet individuals' needs.

13.1.1 Compare and contrast the range and purpose of different forms of assessment

There is not only one single purpose to assessment; the purpose depends on the individual's circumstances. However, according to Whittington (2007), assessment should reflect the match between need and availability of resources that takes into account an evaluation of the risks posed and the urgency of the situation.

> ### Key Term
>
> **Assessment** is the collection and analysis of information about people with the aim of understanding their situation and determining recommendations for any further professional intervention.

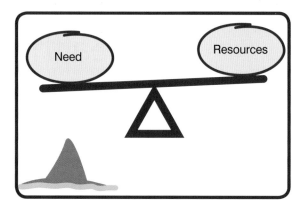

Figure 13.1 Assessment should reflect the match between need and resources, bearing in mind risks

Whittington (2007) identified five purposes to assessment:

1. To protect the individual and the public.

2. To identify service user and carer needs.

3. To represent or advocate for the service user or carer.

4. To act on an agency's policies or priorities.

5. To inform other agencies or professionals.

Assessment might be in response to a particular policy initiative. Policies might, for example, aim to protect vulnerable children and adults; to integrate socially excluded people back into mainstream society; to prolong or improve independence; or to encourage people back to work. Each of these policies requires an assessment of the need, which is reflected in the resources made available to meet the need. Assessment also takes place within a legal context. Protection of service users is a common feature of assessment systems, as is the application of human rights legislation.

Specific laws in England (for example the National Service Framework for Older People) led to work on a Single Assessment Process (Department of Health, 2001).

Activity *evaluate*

1. Think about different forms of assessments where you work.

2. How do they compare in respect of their purposes?

You might think of assessment as something you do to gain a picture of how an individual is, and the ways you can help that individual, while considering the aims and limitations of the care setting where you work. Assessment, however, can be seen as a range of activities that have specific forms.

There are several different forms of assessment, as shown in Figure 13.2.

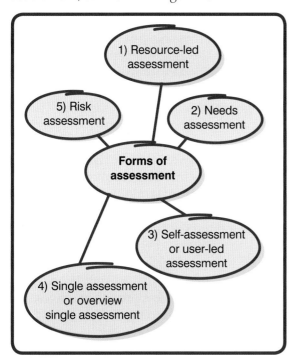

Figure 13.2 Forms of assessment

- Resource-led assessment: This is a means by which care is provided. It uses the assessment process to ration resources or disguise their absence. A service will offer a particular intervention or range of care interventions, and individuals accept the care even if it does not meet their needs.

- Needs-led assessment: This is based on a diagnosis of the situation that individuals might find themselves in. It is not determined by what is available, but by what the person requires in terms of support and care. Needs-led assessment does not have to focus on an individual's deficits or what they cannot do, but can pay attention to the individual's strengths and what they can do.

- User-led assessment (person-centred approach): This requires that the individual's views are given paramount importance in the assessment, and responsibility for decisions made are a shared responsibility with the individual. This has been encapsulated in the phrase 'No decisions about me, without me' (Coulter and Collins, 2011). The individual should take the lead in assessing their needs and how they can be met. This can include arranging care meetings, deciding who should be involved and organising the recording and reporting on the assessment outcomes.

- Single assessment process (SAP): This is an assessment tool that aims to ensure that older people are treated as individuals and they receive care that meets their needs. It was intended to make sure that professionals worked together instead of carrying out their own individual assessments without discussion with other interested parties (Department of Health, 2001). As such it takes away from individuals the ability to lead on their own assessment, but transfers the responsibility back to professional care workers. Individual need can still be assessed, though, but the process can be time consuming and has the potential to overwhelm people in need and discourage their full participation in the process. All older people who need access to social services must have an overview single assessment. This is carried out in accordance with a government table of risk and need, the Fair Access to Care Services (FACS) framework, which has four eligibility levels: Low, Moderate, Substantial and Critical. Local councils are obliged to provide service for any person whose needs or risks to health and safety are assessed as Substantial or Critical. Individuals whose needs are assessed as Low or Moderate are monitored by means of an annual review (Social Care Services, 2008a).

- **Risk assessment**: This takes into account an evaluation of the risks posed and the urgency of the situation (Whittington, 2007). It determines the possibility of accident or danger in relation to a given situation or any existing recognised threat (Social Care Services, 2008b). However, if the sole focus was to keep individuals safe then it would not be possible to carry out person-centred care work. The Key Lines of Regulatory Assessment (KLORA) stipulate that risk assessments should not be focused simply on keeping people safe at all costs, but that they should be person-centred and promote independence, choice and autonomy.

Key Term

Risk assessment is establishing the possibility of accident or danger in relation to a given situation or any existing recognised threat.

Remember

Assessment has different purposes, but can also have different forms. It should, however, always be a match between the individual's need or needs, and the resources that are available to meet the need or needs.

13.1.2 Explain how partnership work can positively support assessment processes

In the document *A Vision for Adult Social Care* (Department of Health, 2010), the government set out how they wished to see services delivered for people. One of the seven principles underpinning their vision is partnership. Care and support should be delivered in partnership between individuals, communities, private and third sector agencies as well as statutory organisations.

Activity

1. Think about all the different people and agencies you work with.

2. What do they contribute to individuals' assessment?

Working in partnership can have a positive influence on the assessment process. Care workers should work in partnership with the individuals in their care and, when appropriate, with their family and other informal carers. The benefit of working in partnership with these central characters in the care setting (which can be the individual's home as well) is that they can make an effective and personal contribution to the care process. The individual at the centre of the care is often the person who knows best how their condition affects them. Partnership working reduces duplication and overlap of assessment and service delivery, but also brings a range of professional perspectives, knowledge and skills to the assessment process.

Be able to lead and contribute to assessments

13.2

In order to lead in assessments within your care setting it is first essential to show that you can contribute to assessments yourself. Working towards meeting this learning outcome provides the opportunity to demonstrate your skill in assessment; first by initiating the early assessment of the individual, then by supporting the individual's active participation, while working within the boundaries of your role and making recommendations for referral when necessary.

Certain characteristics are required in order to lead assessment:

- The ability to take the initiative.
- The ability to support others in the assessment process.
- Awareness of the boundaries of your own role.
- Clarity on what you are expected to do and what you are not expected to do.

13.2.1 Initiate early assessment of the individual

One of the benefits of self-assessment is being alerted to need early (Whittington, 2007). The earlier a need is known the sooner it can be addressed, whether it is a potential risk or an everyday personal care preference. However, early assessment runs the risk of not fully identifying the ways that issues affect the individual.

Activity

1. Think about what you need to do as a leader in your care setting to make early assessment possible.

You might have thought about the following for early assessment to be initiated:

- Individuals in your care setting to feel able to discuss their needs and preferences.
- Access for family and other carers and supporters.
- Preparation of others in the care setting to participate in assessment.
- The availability of assessment documentation and means to record and report on the assessment.

Remember

The earlier a need is known, the sooner it can be addressed, whether it is a potential risk or an everyday personal care preference. For early assessment to be effective individuals must feel able to discuss their needs and preferences.

13.2.2 Support the active participation of the individual in shaping the assessment process

Individuals value services that are offered by those who work within a collaborative philosophy and that are user focused (Innes *et al*, 2006). Quality is thereby measured partly by the extent to which individuals are supported in shaping the assessment process.

Activity

1. What do the terms 'experts by experience' and the 'Expert Patient Programme' mean to you?

The term 'experts by experience' has been coined to describe someone who has used social care services, and refers to the direct involvement of individuals in the development, delivery and evaluation of services (Commission for Social Care Inspectorate (CSCI), 2007). The **Expert Patient Programme** aims to support people living with a chronic condition by increasing their confidence, improving their quality of life and helping them manage their condition more effectively (NHS Choices, 2010).

Key Terms

Experts by experience are those who have used social care services, and refers to the direct involvement of individuals in the development, delivery and evaluation of services (CSCI, 2007).

Expert Patient Programme is a self-management programme for people living with a chronic (long-term) condition.

Enabling the individual to lead and take an active role in the assessment process involves the individual identifying their own social care needs, expressing these needs and planning how to meet them. However, due to their situation this might not always be possible; they might for instance have a severe learning disability or be recovering from a stroke. In these situations the individual might need support during the assessment process.

Activity

1. Think about how you support active participation of individuals in the assessment process.

2. What examples can you think of from your practice?

Figure 13.3 Experts by experience have direct involvement in the development, delivery and evaluation of services

Support can be offered by considering:

- the place where the assessment is to be carried out
- questions that are going to be asked
- offering choice and information.

13.2.3 Undertake assessments within the boundaries of your own role

According to Banton (1965), roles comprise sets of rights and obligations. It is helpful therefore to think of your role as a care worker as not only comprising your job description (which can be interpreted as your obligations) but also allowing you certain rights.

1. Think about your rights in respect of assessing others. To what extent are your rights upheld by the policies and ways of working in your care setting?

When working in health and social care we often think about the rights of the individuals in our care, their right to a decent standard of living perhaps, or their right to be treated with respect and consideration. However, care workers also have rights which help enable them to carry out their job properly and safely. In respect of assessments this includes the right to know what an assessment is, the right to training in order to carry out assessments, and the right to seek assistance if required. To carry out an effective assessment, therefore, you need to be able to assess while also having your rights to proper training and preparation to assess upheld.

Read the In Practice Activity about Dan, who has been asked to carry out an assessment.

13.2.4 Make recommendations to support the referral processes

Working within the boundaries of your role also means that you have the right and the obligation to seek assistance when necessary. The primary reason for this is to protect the individual by ensuring that proper care is sought.

Dan has worked within the boundaries of his role by carrying out the assessment and arranging an appropriate assessment environment. He has made sure that his rights to proper training and preparation to assess have been fulfilled. However, he should not act outside the limitations of his competence, and ought to refer Lucy to another professional to assess the cause of the deterioration in her hearing.

Activity   In Practice

As the person in charge at Addison House, a supported-living resource centre, Dan is responsible for ensuring all new referrals are properly assessed according to local policies. Lucy has recently been referred to Addison House in order to support her in attaining new skills in shopping and meal preparation. Dan is confident of his ability to carry out the assessment because he has been trained and feels well prepared to take on this role. As the person in charge he has also arranged for other members of the care team to work with designated clients visiting Addison House.

Dan ensures that the room where the assessment is to take place is suitable and, aware that Lucy has difficulty hearing, makes sure that the hearing loop system is working properly. Lucy is accompanied by her mother, who sits quietly as Dan assesses Lucy's current ability and asks what her goals are.

During the assessment, Dan discovers Lucy is able to choose her own meals if presented with a number of choices, but has not yet prepared a simple meal for herself, even with support. Towards the end of the interview, Lucy's mother adds that Lucy's hearing has deteriorated recently, saying that she mishears what people say to her, and that there is a red swelling behind her left ear. Dan, with Lucy's permission, confirms this by looking.

1. In what ways has Dan worked within the boundaries of his own role?

2. What recommendation should Dan make in respect of Lucy's hearing?

3. Why should Dan refer Lucy to another professional?

Be able to manage the outcomes of assessments

13.3

Care plans acknowledge that there are issues in addition to medical needs that can impact on a person's total health and well-being (Department of Health, 2009). Personalised care planning is about addressing an individual's full range of needs. The outcome of assessment may therefore depend on a range of factors.

Remember

Individuals in care have the same needs as everyone else, but they also have particular needs based on their health and their condition or other factors.

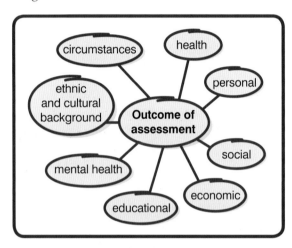

Figure 13.4 Managing outcome of assessments depends on a range of factors

Care plans sometimes reflect an approach in which needs are identified in terms of the care that can be provided by the service. A more person-centred approach would base care and support plans on the needs of the individuals. You might have to show leadership in adapting what the service offers in order to meet individuals' assessed needs.

Activity

1. Make a list of things you need to think about when developing a care plan.

13.3.1 Develop a care or support plan in collaboration with the individual that meets their needs

Care plans are documents that record details about an individual's care and support needs, wishes and preferences (and how these can be met), the desired outcomes, and who will be involved in meeting the identified needs. They represent an opportunity to demonstrate a person-centred approach by involving the individual in a way that reflects their individuality as a person and their particular needs.

When developing a care plan you should ensure that it is based on:

■ the assessed needs of the individual

■ their current circumstances

■ the individual's views and priorities

■ their strengths, interests and preferences

■ their desired outcomes

■ their safety.

13.3.2 Implement interventions that contribute to positive outcomes for the individual

The well-being of individuals can be promoted by those around them. Attitudes and actions that encourage the use and development of individuals' knowledge and skills, and that help maintain their interests and sense of purpose, are fundamental to an environment that leads to positive outcomes.

Figure 13.5 The well-being of individuals can be promoted by those around them

Activity

1. How can you implement interventions that promote well-being?

Care workers implement interventions that lead to positive outcomes based on:

- the individual's assessed needs
- the individual's strengths and aspirations
- the availability of resources for the individual.

Activity

1. Think about ways that an individual's well-being can be undermined. As a leader in your practice setting, make a list of ways that you can prevent this happening.

It is also important to understand that care workers, if they are not careful, have the potential to undermine the individual's well-being.

Careful and open reflection on practice and discussion between team members might identify a number of ways that individuals' well-being can be undermined. For example, ignoring individuals and not responding to their communication can be overcome by ensuring that individuals are given proper attention. For instance, in a residential setting, as a leader you might negotiate a policy in which all team members are expected to talk to each individual when they come on duty.

Most individuals receiving social care support are likely to be assessed as having a substantial or critical level of need. Achieving positive outcomes, therefore, might not be straightforward. The benefits of a healthy diet and choice of nutritional food and drink are well established, but there may be complications such as the individual's cognitive ability or cultural preferences that make healthy choices more difficult.

Martha (87) is unable to eat or drink without assistance. She is supported at her home by a social care agency. Around mealtimes Martha needs help washing her hands and face, ensuring her dentures are worn properly, wearing a protective apron and eating. This causes significant embarrassment to Martha and a consequential loss of dignity.

1. What can you do to ease Martha's embarrassment and uphold her dignity?

2. How can you promote her dignity?

3. What positive outcomes for Martha are there?

Read the practice study on the left about Martha who has been assessed as having substantial needs.

In this situation positive outcomes rely not only on Martha receiving sufficient nutrition, but that interventions promote her dignity. Interventions that are sensitive and confirm the individual's identity are required. For Martha her self-image and self-esteem are intertwined. Working to get to know Martha and her values, beliefs and preferences can all reinforce her sense of identity, and at the same time show that you respect and value her.

Be able to promote others' understanding of the role of assessment

13.4

It is one thing to understand assessment yourself, and quite another thing to be able to promote an understanding of assessment in others. For this learning outcome you are required to develop others' understanding of assessment and how it can have a positive or negative impact, and the contribution others can make. By 'others' is meant: colleagues, informal carers such as family members or friends and supporters, professional workers or **advocates**.

> ### Key Term
>
> **Advocate** is someone who can listen to you and speak for you in times of need.

13.4.1 Develop others' understanding of the functions of a range of assessment tools

Assessment of older people requires a comprehensive collection of information about the physical, biological, psychosocial, psychological and functional aspects of the older person. It will enquire into physiological functioning, growth and development, family relationships, social networks, religious and occupational pursuits (Department of Health, 2002). While this has been said about older people's assessment, it also applies to other client groups as well. Individuals in mental distress, with learning disabilities or sensory impairment each need a comprehensive collection of information as part of their assessment.

There is a wide range of assessment tools available, depending on where you work and the type of care setting it is.

Below is a list of some of the tools available. An internet search will provide information on a lot more.

- Index of independence for activities of daily living.
- The Waterlow score which gives an estimated risk of an individual developing pressure sores.
- Pain scales to measure the intensity of pain.
- The general health questionnaire.
- The Beck Inventory for depression and anxiety.

Figure 13.6: The Waterlow score card is an easy-to-complete assessment of pressure sores. One side shows the risk assessment scoring system and the other provides nursing care guidance for the levels.

13.4.2 Develop others' understanding that assessment may have a positive and/or negative impact on an individual and their families

You might recall that Whittington (2007) identified five purposes to assessment:

- Protection
- Identification of need
- Advocacy
- Policy action
- Informing professionals and agencies.

Achieving these purposes or aims has the potential to impact both positively and negatively on the individual and their families.

Table 13.1 below illustrates some of the potential positive and negative impacts following assessment.

13.4.3 Develop others' understanding of their contribution to the assessment process

Assessment is not the responsibility of one person only; it is a shared activity in which others have a role. As a leader in your care setting you are not solely responsible for all the different forms of assessment carried out with individuals. The legal and policy context supports contributions from a range of individuals and agencies. For example, the Single Assessment Process for Older People (Department of Health, 2001) emphasises the need for agencies to work together.

The contribution by others to assessment should not be underestimated. Table 13.2 summarises particular contributions other people can bring.

Table 13.1 Positive and negative impacts of assessment

Impact	Positive	Negative
Financial	Financial support or assistance through state benefits	Cost of buying expensive equipment Loss of income due to inability to sustain employment
Psychological	Reassurance of knowing what is responsible for a health or social condition	Fear and guilt about being a burden to others
Physical	Qualifying for assistance from services such as a personal assistant	Needing assistance with mobility
Practical	Gaining information about how to adapt the home or living environment	Adaptations making the home less homely and more like a formal care setting

Remember

Assessment can lead to both positive and negative outcomes which individuals and their families should be prepared for.

Table 13.2 Other people's contributions to assessment

Other people	Contribution	Specific examples	Benefits and challenges
Professional (doctor, nurse, social worker)	Specialist knowledge and skills		
Relatives and friends	An understanding of the individual as a person, their relevant history, likes, wishes and preferences		
Advocate	Knowledge about what the individual can expect of services and information on local provision		
Colleague	Knowledge about how the care setting can support the meeting of the individual's needs		

Activity

1. Add to Table 13.2 by providing your own specific examples of:

   ■ who contributes and what their contribution is

   ■ the benefits and challenges of their contribution.

Whatever the contribution, there are benefits if others engage in the assessment process. These include:

■ the provision of early interventions to arrest the deterioration in the condition

■ easier and quicker access to services

■ improved quality of service

■ clarity between roles and responsibilities.

Activity

Think about your care setting.

1. Who would you seek assistance from if you thought an individual's condition was deteriorating?

2. Who can help you gain easier and quicker access to a service?

3. In what ways can others improve the quality of service individuals experience?

4. How is your role different from the others you describe above?

As a leader you are sometimes called upon to make judgements. However, any judgements you make should be based on evidence. It is therefore essential that you are clear about the evidence you present to another person about an individual so that they can understand what their contribution to the assessment process is based on accurate information.

Review and evaluate the effectiveness of assessment

13.5

The effectiveness of any assessment should be reviewed and evaluated to determine:

- if it is suitable
- whether appropriate tools are used
- whether it meets the needs of the individual.

Evaluation is about using a standard or yardstick to measure assessment to see if it is working. To do this the assessment process should be reviewed based on feedback from the individual and others involved, or from those who have been affected by the assessment process.

13.5.1 Review the assessment process based on feedback from the individual and/or others

On completing an assessment, you should review the process to make sure that you assessed what you intended to assess in a way that is acceptable to the individual and others.

Activity

1. After completing an assessment, reflect on and review the process you followed in consultation with the individual and others. You might like to use one of the models of reflection identified on p31.

2. When reviewing the assessment process, you need to consider what important aspects of the process you are going to evaluate. Use a table like the one below to organise your review:

Aspect of the process	Reflection and review
Was the purpose of the assessment clear to the individual and others?	
Was the form of assessment appropriate?	
In what ways was partnership working evident?	
How was active participation promoted?	
How did care workers work within their role?	
Were referrals made to other agencies or professionals and, if so, why?	

13.5.2 Evaluate the outcomes of assessment based on feedback from the individual and/or others

Care workers implement interventions that aim to lead to positive outcomes based on the individual's assessed needs, their strengths and aspirations and the availability of resources. However, not all outcomes are positive or intended. When evaluating outcomes for assessment, it is therefore necessary to gain a balanced view that acknowledges that outcomes can be both positive for the individual but may also have a detrimental effect.

The way you gather feedback is therefore crucial to gaining a balanced evaluation of the outcomes of assessment. In order to do this the evaluation needs to permit both positive and negative outcomes.

Activity In Practice

Patrick Jarman (82) was referred to social care following a stroke and hospitalisation. The care plan identified he needed support in getting out of bed in the morning, washing, dressing and preparing breakfast. After a month the outcomes of his care package were evaluated. Table 13.3 summarises the criteria by which the outcomes were evaluated, who provided the feedback and the outcome of the evaluation.

1. Why is evaluating Patrick's care essential?

2. What are the potential consequences of not evaluating his care?

3. In your care setting who takes responsibility for evaluating individuals' care?

Table 13.3: Using SMART criteria to evaluate outcomes

SMART Criteria	Type of feedback	Outcome
Specific	From the social worker/ care manager	A referral to a care agency was made and Patrick was funded for a care visit lasting 20 minutes each morning
Measurable	From Patrick	The care workers have not missed a day and he has been pleased with the light breakfast they have prepared
Achievable	From the care agency manager	20 minutes is just enough to carry out the interventions agreed
Realistic	From Patrick's daughter	Thinks her father manages at the moment but is worried that if he has another stroke the care plan would have to be amended
Timely	From Patrick's daughter	On several occasions the agency carer arrived too late and Patrick had to get himself out of bed to use the toilet

13.5.3 Develop an action plan to address the findings

The In Practice study above illustrates the necessity to reassess individuals should their circumstances change, with any adverse outcomes being investigated further. Remember, assessment may have a positive or negative impact on an individual and their families; everyone should be prepared for both. The causes of negative outcomes have to be examined. Could they have been prevented?

Activity

1. What would you do if adverse outcomes were identified during an evaluation of the assessment process?

2. Examples are given in the table below. Add more examples from your own practice experience.

Table 13.4 Potential action plans to address findings of an assessment

Outcome	Example	Action
Financial loss	Cost of buying equipment	Refer for financial assessment
Psychological distress	Realising that a condition is long-term or terminal	Refer for counselling
Physical impairment	Finding out the individual needs a mobility aid	Investigate potential aids with the individual
Practical difficulties	Requiring adaptations to the individual's home	To ensure the individual has access to proper advice

Are you ready for assessment?

✔ Do you know the range and purpose of different forms of assessment?

✔ Do you know how partnership work can positively support assessment processes?

✔ Can you initiate early assessment of the individual?

✔ Can you support the active participation of the individual in shaping the assessment process?

✔ Can you undertake assessments within the boundaries of your own role?

✔ Can you make recomendations to support referral processes?

✔ Can you develop a care or support plan in collaboration with the individual that meets their needs?

✔ Can you implement interventions that contribute to positive outcomes for the individual?

✔ Can you develop others' understanding of the functions of a range of assessment tools?

✔ Can you develop others' understanding that assessment may have a positive and/or negative impact on an individual and their families?

✔ Can you develop others' understanding of their contribution to the assessment process?

✔ Can you review the assessment process based on feedback from the individual and/or others?

✔ Can you evaluate the outcomes of assessment based on feedback from the individual and/or others?

✔ Can you develop an action plan to address the findings?

References

Banton, M. (1965) *Roles: An Introduction to the Study of Social Relations*. London: Tavistock Publications Ltd.

Coulter, A. and Collins, A. (2011) *Making Shared Decision Making a Reality. 'No decision about me, without me'*. London: The King's Fund.

Crisp, B. R., Anderson, M. T., Orme, J. and Lister, P. G. (2003) *Knowledge Review 01: Learning and Teaching in Social Work Education – assessment*. London: Social Care Institute for Excellence.

Crisp, B. R., Anderson, M. T., Orme, J. and Lister, P. G. (2005) *Learning and Teaching in Social Work Education: textbooks and frameworks on assessment*. London: Social Care Institute for Excellence.

CSCI (2007) *People Who Use Services and Experts by Experience*. London: Commission for Social Care Inspectorate.

CWDC (2009a) *The Team Around the Child (TAC) and the Lead Professional: A Guide for Managers*. Leeds: Children's Workforce Development Council.

CWDC (2009b) *The Common Assessment Framework: A Guide for Managers*. Leeds: Children's Workforce Development Council.

Department of Health (2001) *The National Service Framework for Older People*. London: Department of Health.

Department of Health (2002) *Guidance on the Single Assessment Process for Older People*. London: HMSO.

Department of Health (2010) *A Vision for Adult Social Care: Capable Communities and Active Citizens*. London: Central Office of Information.

Innes, A., MacPherson, S. and McCabe, L. (2006) *Promoting Person-Centred Care at the Front Line*. York: Joseph Rowntree Foundation/SCIE.

Whittington, C. (2007) *Assessment in Social Work: a Guide for Teaching and Learning*. London: Social Care Institute for Excellence.

Websites

Department of Health (2006) *Single assessment process*, www.dh.gov.uk/PolicyAndGuidance/HealthAndSocialCareTopics/SocialCare/SingleAssesmentProcess/fs/en, accessed 12 April 2012

Department of Health (2009) *Care Planning*, http://webarchive.nationalarchives.gov.uk/+/www.dh.gov.uk/en/Healthcare/Longtermconditions/DH_093359, accessed 3 July 2012.

NHS Choices (2010) *The Expert Patient Programme*, www.nhs.uk/conditions/Expert-patients-programme-/Pages/Introduction.aspx, accessed 3 July 2012.

Social Care Services (2008a) *The Overview Single Assessment*, www.socialcareservices.co.uk/overview-single-assessment, accessed 3 July 2012.

Social Care Services (2008b) *Risk Assessment*, www.socialcareservices.co.uk/risk-assessment, accessed 3 July 2012.

Key legislation

This section covers some relevant laws (Acts of Parliament) and published governmental guidance on various aspects of the care provision sector. Government guidance documents are based on best practice or evidence-based practice and are used to inform the sector on how policies and procedures are to be written and what they should contain. Guidance will usually set out what organisations should do, and can link to specific legislation. Guidance provides more detail than laws so can help organisations and individuals to understand how specific legislation will impact on their lives.

Care Standards Act (2000)

This is legislation which led to the National Minimum Standards and is a means of measuring care service quality.

Control of Substances Hazardous to Health (COSHH) (2002)

COSHH regulations are an extension of the Health and Safety at Work Act (1974) and apply to every workplace. They control people's exposure to hazardous substances arising from workplace activities. Hazardous substances must be labelled corrosive, irritant, harmful or toxic and may also carry warning diagrams. It is illegal to carry out work involving any substance hazardous to health without an assessment of the risk.

Corporate Manslaughter and Homicide Act (2007)

If a fatality were to occur as a result of a breach of health and safety regulations, legislation or possible negligence then this Act could be used in a prosecution. This was introduced to hold individuals, generally at a senior level, accountable in the event of a death occurring.

Data Protection Act (1998)

The Data Protection Act covers the confidential storage, retrieval and handling of verbal, written and electronic information to protect the rights of the individual. It sets out guidelines and describes what is considered to be good practice in relation to disclosing information and breaches of confidentiality where this serves to protect the individual or others from harm.

The eight principles of the Act are that information must:

1. be secure

2. be accurate

3. be adequate

4. be relevant and not excessive to requirements

5. not be kept longer than necessary

6. be processed for limited purposes (i.e. only those agreed with the person)

7. be processed in line with people's rights

8. not be transferred to others without adequate protection and must be fairly and lawfully processed.

Deprivation of Liberty Safeguards (2008)

The Mental Health Act (2007) amended the Mental Health Act (1983) and was used to introduce the deprivation of liberty safeguards into the Mental Capacity Act (2005). The key points are that people who have a disorder or disability of the mind, for example, dementia or a profound learning disability, which results in a lack of capacity to consent to the care or treatment they need, should be cared for in a way that does not limit their rights or freedom of action.

Some vulnerable people do, however, need to be deprived of their liberty for treatment or care which is in their best interests or to protect them from harm. The deprivation of liberty safeguards strengthen the rights of hospital patients and people in care homes, provides legal protection and complies with the European Convention on Human Rights. It is designed to avoid arbitrary decisions (i.e. those that are based on personal wishes or perceptions and are random and inconsistent) to deprive a person of their liberty and to give rights to challenge deprivation of liberty authorisations.

Disability Discrimination Act (DDA) (2005)

The DDA protects disabled people against widespread discrimination and aims to ensure that they are treated in a fair and equal way. It also gives them rights and recognises disability as an equalities issue in the same way as ethnicity and gender. The Act places duties on providers of goods, facilities and services and makes it unlawful for a service provider to discriminate against a disabled person by:

- refusing to provide (or deliberately not providing) any service which it provides to other members of the public
- providing a lesser standard of service for disabled people.

Equality Act (2010)

This Act brings together a number of previous existing pieces of legislation, including race and disability. One of the key changes is that it extends the protected characteristics to encompass:

- age
- disability
- gender reassignment

- marriage and civil partnership
- pregnancy and maternity
- race
- religion or belief
- sex and sexual orientation.

The Act also makes explicit the concept of 'dual discrimination', where someone may be discriminated against or treated unfairly on the basis of a combination of two of the protected characteristics.

Food Hygiene Regulations (2006)

These regulations require all businesses providing food to ensure they identify all food safety hazards and risks and have control measures in place to prevent problems. They must document their arrangements for ensuring the safety of their food and take into account the 'four Cs' of cooking: Cooling, Cross-Contamination, and Cleaning.

Food Safety Act (1990)

Health and social care providers must ensure they do not include anything in food, remove anything from food or treat food in any way which means it would be damaging to the health of people eating it and to ensure that the food they serve is of the nature, substance or quality which consumers would expect.

Freedom of Information Act (2000)

This Act gives you the right to ask any public body for all the information they have on any subject you choose. Unless there's a good reason, the organisation must provide the information within 20 working days. You can also ask for all the personal information they hold on you. If you ask for information about yourself, then your request will be handled under the Data Protection Act.

Health and Safety at Work Act (1974)

Every workplace is covered by this law. Everyone has a responsibility to ensure their own health, safety and welfare, as well as that of their colleagues and others. Employers have an additional responsibility to ensure that employees have the correct training and safety clothing and equipment appropriate for the job they are doing.

Health and Social Care Act (Regulated Activities) Regulations (2010) and the Care Quality Commission (Registration) Regulations (2009)

These led to the creation of the Care Quality Commission (CQC) to regulate services using the Essential Standards of Quality and Safety, consisting of 28 regulations and a shift towards outcomes, i.e. what can be expected from care providers.

Human Rights Act (1998)

This Act clearly describes individuals' rights to live free from abuse, violence or torture and is considered a benchmark against which services can assess how they uphold individual rights.

Article 8 states the right to respect for private and family life:

1. Everyone has the right to respect for his private and family life, his home and his correspondence.

2. There shall be no interference by a public authority with the exercise of this right except such as is in accordance with the law and is necessary in a democratic society in the interests of national security, public safety or the economic well-being of the country; for the prevention of disorder or crime; for the protection of health or morals; or for the protection of the rights and freedoms of others.

Law Commission Review of Adult Social Care (2011)

This incorporates safeguarding recommendations and proposes a formal change in terminology from 'vulnerable adult' to 'adult at risk'. The government will consider the conclusions, with a view to introducing legislation in the second session of the 2012 Parliament.

Manual Handling Regulations Operations (1992)

Introduced to enforce safer moving and handling at work, these regulations enhance the Health and Safety at Work Act and the main provision is that employees should be trained in safe techniques of moving and handling loads. They require an employer to carry out risk assessments that take into account whether it is reasonable to automate or mechanise lifting in the workplace. The employer must provide equipment to avoid the hazardous manual handling of loads. The regulations apply wherever things or people are moved by hand or bodily force.

Mental Capacity Act (2005)

This provides a legal framework to empower and protect vulnerable people who are unable to make their own decisions. It sets out who, how and when decisions can be made. The Act is underpinned by five key principles:

1. A presumption of capacity: every adult is considered capable unless it is proved otherwise.

2. The right for the individual to be supported to make their own decisions: ensuring that people are given appropriate help to do this.

3. Adults retain the right to make what may appear to others as unwise or eccentric decisions.

4. Best interests: everything done on behalf of someone who lacks capacity must be in their best interests.

5. Whatever is done must have the least restrictive impact on their basic rights and freedoms.

The Act also replaces current legal schemes for enduring power of attorney and Court of Protection receivers with reformed and updated schemes.

It includes provisions for vulnerable adults such as being able to appoint an Independent Mental Capacity Advocate, making advanced decisions regarding the refusal of treatment and making it a criminal offence to ill-treat or neglect someone who lacks mental capacity.

'No Secrets' (2000)

This provides guidance created as a result of serious incidents leading to abuse and also the need to ensure compliance with the Human Rights Act. This was a big step forward in relation to adult protection.

Personal Protective Equipment (PPE) at Work Regulations (1992)

The main requirement of the PPE at Work Regulations (1992) is that personal protective equipment is to be supplied and used at work wherever there are risks to health and safety that cannot be adequately controlled in other ways. The regulations also require that PPE is properly assessed before use to ensure it is suitable, maintained and stored properly, provided with instructions on how to use it safely, and used correctly by employees.

Public Interest Disclosure Act (1999)

This provides the means by which individuals can raise genuine concerns about negligence; dangers to health and safety; crime; and miscarriages of justice, regardless of the confidential nature of the information. The Act therefore protects people who have raised these concerns from losing their job, or from being victimised because they have effectively 'blown the whistle'. It is why this is often referred to as the 'Whistle Blowing Act'.

Reporting of Injuries, Diseases and Dangerous Occurrences Regulations (RIDDOR) (1995)

This requires employers and anyone with responsibility for health and safety within the workplace to report and keep records of work-related deaths; serious injuries; cases of diagnosed industrial diseases; and certain 'dangerous occurrences' (near misses). The law changed on 6 April 2012; now if a worker sustains an occupational injury resulting from an accident, their injury should be reported if they are incapacitated for more than seven days (previously it was three days, but records must still be kept).

'Safeguarding Adults' (2005)

This builds on 'No Secrets' and created a change in emphasis with the concept of protection geared towards those who lacked capacity (see also Mental Capacity Act 2005), resulting in a move towards earlier intervention and prevention. The concept of safeguarding emerged with individuals taking informed risks and exercising more choices rather than authorities 'stepping in' to take charge.

'Safeguarding Vulnerable Groups' (2006)

The vetting/barring scheme created a new offence of 'fraud by abuse of position' and includes the misuse of money by those being appointed to manage it such as by an enduring power of attorney. Fraud was not well covered by Section 44 of the Mental Capacity Act.

Statement of Government Principles (2011) on Adult Safeguarding

This listed six key principles of Empowerment, Protection, Prevention, Proportionality, Partnership and Accountability. Local multi-agency partnerships should support and encourage communities to find local solutions, and further guidance is offered on how these principles could be translated into outcomes.

'Valuing People Now' (2009)

This relates specifically to those with learning disabilities. With the key values of civil rights, independence, choice and inclusion, this White Paper is written from a human rights perspective and started the personalisation agenda.

Glossary

360 degree feedback is a process in which people who know and understand the work of the team rate the team member's performance. The feedback can include reports by peers, line managers, service users or carers.

Abbreviations are shortened words and are very common in social care such as 'meds' for medication.

Abuse or significant harm is an action that is sufficiently serious to adversely affect progress and impair healthy development.

Accountability refers to being answerable for something, or having responsibility for it.

Acronyms are words formed from the initial letters of other words, and used for quick reference.

Active listening is a method of listening which involves understanding the content of a message as well as the intent of the sender and the circumstances under which the message is given.

Active participation is a way of working that recognises an individual's right to participate in the activities and relationships of everyday life as independently as possible; the individual is regarded as an active partner in their own care, rather than a passive recipient.

Advocate is someone who can listen to you and speak for you in times of need.

Assessment is the collection and analysis of information about people with the aim of understanding their situation and determining recommendations for any further professional intervention.

Assistive technology describes a range of equipment and processes that aim to support independent living, for example environmental sensors that indicate whether an individual is moving within their accommodation and devices that monitor 'vital clinical signs' and transmit data to monitoring services.

Benchmark is a standard used as a basis against which something can be assessed or measured.

Biopsychosocial is a humanistic approach to care that sees individuals encompassing a biological, psychological and social dimension to their being.

Blissymbol is a series of meaning-based symbols and pictures used by people who are unable to communicate verbally. Other sign and pictorial communication methods can be found on the internet.

Carer is someone of any age who provides unpaid support to family or friends who cannot manage without this help.

A **child** is defined as anyone who has not yet reached the age of 18 years.

Consent means informed agreement to an action or decision. The process of establishing consent will vary according to an individual's assessed capacity to consent.

Contingency theory is leadership by doing what is required to achieve change depending on the circumstances at the time.

Culture is described by Mead (2000) as a complex pattern of shared behaviours that distinguishes people from each other and is transmitted over time it refers to the traditions, values, policies, beliefs and attitudes in an organisation. It is easier to recognise as the deeply-held beliefs of staff about the way they work, how work should be organised, and how staff are controlled and rewarded. It can be a powerful source of influence and control in organisations.

Devolve means to transfer or delegate power to a lower level.

Dignity concerns the person's sense of worth and importance.

Empowerment means to give (someone) more power, usually making them more confident in controlling their own life, claiming rights and overcoming barriers to participation.

Evaluation is examining something in order to reach a conclusion about its value, quality or worth.

Expert Patient Programme is a self-management programme for people living with a chronic (long-term) condition.

Experts by experience are those who have used social care services, and refers to the direct involvement of individuals in the development, delivery and evaluation of services (CSCI, 2007).

Facilitators encourage and support individuals to take control of their own assessment and support plan, so that it is tailored to their particular needs and circumstances. They support and empower the individual by providing ideas and information on service options.

Hazard is anything that may cause harm, such as chemicals, electricity, working from ladders, an open drawer, etc.

Indicator can be defined as any sign or symptom that alerts a person to suspect something might be wrong.

Jargon refers to terminology used in a particular profession that may not mean anything to someone outside of that profession.

Learned helplessness means the act of giving up trying as a result of consistent failure to be rewarded.

Normalisation means creating group-living environments for people in situations that are as normal as possible rather than institutional care.

Outcome-based practice is an activity or process that has a beneficial impact on the individual's life. It can be an action taken or a service delivered. Another way to describe it is to say that the 'output' is the *effort* made and the 'outcome' is the *effect* on the individual.

Paralanguage communicates non-verbal elements of speech, for example intonation, pitch and speed, hesitation noises, facial expression and gesture.

Personalisation is the process by which state-provided services are adapted to suit the needs and preferences of the service user; in social care this means everyone having choice and control over the services they receive along with greater emphasis on prevention and early intervention.

Positive risk taking is part of the process of measuring risk and involves balancing the positive benefits that are likely to follow from taking risks against the negative effects of attempting to avoid risk altogether.

Protocols are codes of behaviour and give detailed instructions for the care of an individual. They provide a standardised approach that reduces the risk of variation in the quality of treatment and the best outcomes.

Qualitative means relating to quality, using words and descriptions.

Quantitative means relating to quantity, using measurable numerical data.

Regulations are the law, and prescribe a specific course of action, which must be complied with.

Risk is the uncertainty of outcome, whether positive opportunity or negative threat, of actions and events. The risk has to be assessed by combining the likelihood of something happening and the impact that arises if it does actually happen.

Risk assessment is establishing the possibility of accident or danger in relation to a given situation or any existing recognised threat.

Serious Case Reviews (SCRs) are convened when the death or serious injury of an adult at risk has occurred and is related directly or indirectly to adult abuse, and multi-agency learning can be identified from this.

Slang refers to informal words, such as 'grub' instead of 'food'.

Social model of disability means that some people with disabilities believe they are disabled by society and are proactive in fighting for equality and inclusion. They reject the notion that disabled people should be segregated and treated as incapable of making decisions.

Supervision is a process to support the development of knowledge, skills and values as part of the learning process for workers.

SWOT stands for:

Strengths

Weaknesses

Opportunities

Threats.

The Mental Capacity Act 2005 (MCA 2005) see page 230.

The paramountcy principle means that a child's welfare is the paramount consideration when making any decisions about a child's upbringing.

The personlisation agenda is the building of a system of care and support in which individuals define their own requirements.

Values are principles or standards held by people or groups.

White papers are also known as command papers; they signal intention by government for something to be adopted as law.

Work design means to improve both job satisfaction and quality, and to reduce employee problems such as absenteeism or grievances.

Index